VIRGINIA
◆ S·E·A·S·O·N·S ◆

New
Recipes
from the
Old
Dominion

Proceeds from the sale of **Virginia Seasons** will be used to support the projects of the Junior League of Richmond which focus on children and education.

For additional copies, use the order forms at the back of the book or write:

Virginia Seasons

205 W. Franklin St.
Richmond, VA 23220
(804) 782-1022

Price $16.95 plus $3.00 postage and handling.

Virginia residents add $.76 sales tax.

Add $1.00 per gift wrapped copy.

Published by the Junior League of Richmond

Copyright 1984 Junior League of Richmond,
Richmond, Virginia. All rights reserved.
First Edition
First Printing   November 1984   10,000 copies
Second Printing   March 1985   10,000 copies
Third Printing   September 1986   10,000 copies
Fourth Printing   October 1989   10,000 copies
Fifth Printing   May 1991   10,000 copies
Sixth Printing   February 1993   10,000 copies
ISBN 0-9614056-0-0

Printed in the USA by
WIMMER BROTHERS
A Wimmer Company
Memphis • Dallas

Original Cookbook Committee

Chairman
Kathy Degenhardt Adair

Assistant Chairmen
Mary Candler Powell, recipe editing and computer programming
Sue Hawkins Reynolds, recipe testing

Production Chairmen
Trygve Lee Garter, printing
Bernice Chase Pittman, proofing
Missy Jenkins Ryan, recipe testing
Cabell Goolsby West, title and theme

Editor
Robin Traywick Williams

Sustainer Advisors
Joyce Davern Farrell
Martha Luck Robertson
Trudie Gerbis Steel

Liaison to Executive Committee
Deborah Andrews Dunlap
Judy Simpson Brown

Committee Members

Len Dixon Archer
Lea Camp Ayers
Kitty Moss Bayliss
Mary Conner Bland
Mary Anna Toms Broadbent
Judy Donaldson Brooks
Suzanne Jones Brown
Missy Mallonee Buckingham
Lynn Davis Congdon
Rosemary Martin Davenport
Martha Reynolds Davidson
Linda Fischer Desvernine
Anne Kinnier Driscoll
Debbie Andrews Dunlap
Karen Holden Feigley
Lou McKenzie Gambill
Carolyn Walke Gard
Margaret Conner Gentil
Julie Rehrig Goodell
Anne Maslin Grier
Ann Hedges Haskell
M. Jane Johnson

Sandy Davis King
Lynne Marie Kreger
Nel Laughon
Gerry Brieff Lewis
Patti Smith Loughridge
Charmian Turney Matheson
Pat Taylor Morrison
Sally Bushnell Moxley
Becky Major Newman
Katrina McGurn Parkinson
Michael Nexsen Robertson
Joanie Woltz Robins
Susanna Fowlkes Sauvain
Pat Clary Short
Louisa Wilson Sirles
Joanne Eisenhooth Smith
Nancy Cox Vaughan
Jean Aitcheson Vertner
Etta Nachman Wallace
Robin Wilson Ware
Bettie Dade Wood
Betsy Bearden Worthington

Maureen O'Gara Hackett

Illustrations by Jane Johnson
The Junior League of Richmond would like to express sincere appreciation to all those who submitted and tested recipes.

3

Who We Are:

The Junior League of Richmond, Va., is an organization of women trained for effective participation in community activities and dedicated to the belief that volunteer service is an essential part of responsible citizenship. Founded as a non-profit group in 1926 by 59 young women, the Junior League of Richmond was affiliated in 1927 with the Association of Junior Leagues (AJL), which serves in a resource and advisory capacity.

The Junior League of Richmond has more than 1400 active and sustainer members. Regular volunteer service is required of active members, who give approximately 30,000 volunteer hours annually.

What We Do:

The League educates and trains its members to provide effective volunteer service, to research changing community needs and to initiate pilot projects or expand services to meet those needs. It provides administrative, financial and volunteer support for projects and facilitates the permanent sponsorship of programs by appropriate community organizations. Programs are evaluated yearly. The League also contributes to the metropolitan area through monetary grants and board representation. Since its founding, the Junior League of Richmond has donated more than $1,500,000 to the community.

How We Do It:

Membership dues finance all the administrative expenses. The funds which support community programs that focus on children and education are generated by the Clothes Rack, our thrift shop at 2618 W. Cary St., the Annual Book and Author Dinner, co-sponsored for many years by Miller & Rhoads department store and proceeds from the sale of our cookbook, Virginia Seasons.

Contents

A Word about Virginia Seasons

Americans are becoming more and more conscious of what they eat and how it affects their health. These new recipes from the Old Dominion reflect the growing interest in meals that are lighter and have fewer calories. In contrast to many general cookbooks with their huge sections on sweets, Virginia Seasons has larger-than-usual sections on vegetables, salads, poultry and seafood, the sine qua non of light eating.

In addition, there is an emphasis on using the fresh local produce and commodities readily available in Virginia during the four seasons. Most of the recipes call for imaginative combinations of foods and flavors rather than depending on the can-of-soup-of-your-choice.

Seasonings give health-conscious people a tasty alternative to salt and cholesterol-rich butter and other fats, but the use of herbs and spices is a mystery to many. So we've added an herb primer with a chart full of suggestions to get you started.

Besides the cream of old family recipes made modern, Virginia Seasons has more than 40 recipes from renowned resorts, inns and restaurants of the Old Dominion. These recipes show how professional chefs—several of international reputation—take advantage of Virginia's richly stocked pantry.

Food has figured prominently in the history and traditions of the Old Dominion ever since Captain John Smith landed here in 1607. In those early years, the natural bounty of the land often meant the difference between survival and death.

The colonists found the forests of their new land teemed with wildlife: quail, pheasant, deer, rabbit, duck and more. They found the prolific waterways full of succulent oysters, crabs, fish and other seafood to tempt their appetites with new tastes.

The settlers learned about maize, or corn, from the Indians and went on to develop their own recipes for fritters, muffins, chowders and souffles. And that most Virginian of dishes, Smithfield ham, grew out of old Indian methods of salting, smoking and aging meat for preservation.

The colonists soon found that the variety of soils and the mild, seasonal climate provided a nearly year-round harvest of foodstuffs.

Thomas Jefferson was convinced that the soil and climate of Virginia, so similar to Europe's, would produce fine table wines, and he imported several varieties of vines to test his theory. Jefferson's theory was borne out in the late 1800's when Virginia claret won medals in international competition.

Today, after a lull in production, Virginia viticulture is enjoying a dynamic renaissance. Virginia wines are again winning medals here and abroad and attracting critical acclaim from wine authorities.

There are more than two dozen wineries in the state, all opened in the last 10 years. They are located in almost every part of the state, although most are clustered around Charlottesville, Winchester and Middleburg. Most are open for tours and tastings.

At the end of the beverage chapter, we've put some information on cooking with and serving Virginia wines. Comparable wines from other regions can be substituted if Virginia wines are not available.

In Virginia, food is part of every season, and Virginians have made food part of every celebration, from the first Thanksgiving, held at Berkeley Plantation on the James River in 1619, to a tailgate picnic at the Strawberry Hill Races. Each of the seasons brings another round of harvest festivals: Highland County's Maple Festival, Chincoteague's Seafood Festival, Ashland's Strawberry Faire, Surry County's Pork, Peanut and Pine Festival, Richmond's Historic Farmers' Market Festival, the Albemarle Harvest Wine Festival and Criglersville's Apple Harvest Festival, to name just a few.

If you can't join us at our festivals, join us at our table.

17th STREET MARKET

JANIE
JOHNSON

Spring

STRAWBERRY HILL

JANET JOHNSON

Tailgating at the Strawberry Hill Races

Mint Tea (p. 41) or Orange Julius (p. 44)
Caviar Casserole (p. 23)
Pasta Salad Milanese (p. 82)
Strawberry Pretzel Salad (p. 87)
Molly Peckham's Crab Mold (p. 22)
Miniature Quiches (p. 34)
Authentic French Bread (p. 104)
Martha's Pie (p. 268)

Blue Ridge Brunch

Mimosas (p. 43)
Breakfast Casserole (p. 127)
Italian Asparagus (p. 145)
Cheesy Garlic Grits (p. 131)
Fruit Salad with Poppy Seed Dressing (p. 91)
Mousse de Kiwi Napoleon (p. 274)

Garden Week Luncheon

Grandmother's Fruit Tea (p. 41) or Sherry Cobbler (p. 43)
Broccoli Bisque (p. 55)
Long Run Quiche (p. 124)
Two Layer Tomato Aspic (p. 84)
Buttermilk Biscuits (p. 107)
Black Bottoms (p. 294)

Summer

A Chesapeake Seafood Feast

Williamsburg Bisque of Hampton Crab (p. 66)
Hot and Spicy Baked Shrimp (p. 246)
Fishing Bay Bluefish (p. 254)
Fresh Broccoli Salad (p. 71)
Creamy Mushroom Bake (p. 157)
Anadama Bread (p. 100)
Angel Lime Pie (p. 263)

A Fourth of July Picnic

Super Fantastic Gazpacho (p. 50)
Chicken Fishing Bay (p. 209)
Potato Salad (p. 76)
Marinated Vidalia Onions (p. 28)
Spinach Casserole (p. 161)
Sweet Pickles (p. 92) or Cold Tomato Relish (p. 95)
Cheese Bread by Betty T. (p. 103)
Homemade Ice Cream (p. 282)
Cattle Range Cookies (p. 303)

A Virginia Summer's Harvest Supper

Watermelon Rind Pickles (p. 92)
Pork Tenderloin with Cinnamon (p. 190)
Corn Timbale (p. 152)
Eggplant Casserole (p. 153)
Fire and Ice Tomatoes (p. 72)
Crumbsnatchin' Apple Bread (p. 109)
Ellie's Grandma's Zucchini Cookies (p. 305)

Fall

MONTICELLO

JAMES JOHNSON

Cocktails on the Terrace

Cheddar Smithfield Spread (p. 25)
Spinach-Artichoke Dip (p. 40)
Hot Crab Dip (p. 39)
Filet of Beef, Served with Party Rye (p. 172)
Dill Weed Dip with Raw Vegetables (p. 39)
Pickled Okra (p. 93)
Double-Daters (p. 302)
Russian Tea Cakes (p. 302)

Fall Football Buffet

Beer Cheese (p. 35)
Down South Barbecue (p. 192)
Good and Easy Coleslaw (p. 71)
Gorgeous Fries (p. 155)
Calico Baked Beans (p. 147)
Dad's Favorite Coffee Pecan Chews (p. 309)

Thanksgiving Dinner, Virginia-Style

Rosy Relish on Cream Cheese (p. 95)
Chilled Consomme (p. 53)
Breasts of Wild Duck in Gravy (p. 231)
Cranberry-Orange Chutney (p. 96)
Mrs. Strupe's Sweet Potatoes (p. 159)
Green Beans Vinaigrette (p. 146)
Wild Rice and Oyster Casserole (p. 243)
Christmas Wine Jelly (p. 271)

Winter

JANE
JOHNSON

A Williamsburg Candlelight Dinner

Scallops in Bacon with Sweet and Sour Sauce (p. 21)
Avocado Salad with Grandmother's Dressing (p. 90)
Braised Lamb Rosemary (p. 197)
Mushroom Florentine (p. 157)
Mashed Potato Casserole (p. 158)
Traditional Sally Lunn (p. 100)
Chocolate Mousse Pie (p. 269)

Apres Ski

Hot Buttered Rum (p. 46)
Cheese Biscuits (p. 31)
Marinated Rare Beef (p. 173)
Savannah Rice (p. 133)
Bourbon Apples (p. 167)
Rolls (p. 107)
Hummers (p. 45)

George Washington's Birthday Do

Chilled English Stilton Soup (p. 64)
Christian's Parmesan Chicken (p. 221)
Bing Cherry Salad (p. 86)
Baked Limas with Sour Cream (p. 147)
Popovers (p. 108)
Elegant Bread Custard (p. 275)

An Herb and Spice Primer

It's hard to imagine how monotonous food in other times must have tasted. Today's American has vast choices in food brought by prosperity and the mixture of cultures in the United States.

Nearly all Roman food, for instance, tasted similar because of the use of liquamen, a salty sauce made from rotting fish, similar to the sauce common in Southeast Asian cooking today.

Fifteen hundred years later, Virginia colonists had far greater variety in their cooking because of the discovery of herbs and spices. Herb gardens came to the Commonwealth by way of the European monastic herb gardens. Spices came to Virginia from the East and West Indies, but then, as now, herbs were used more frequently than spices for flavoring food.

Spices

In centuries past, spices were often used as currency. The Arabs, the Venetians, the Portugese and the Dutch held various monopolies causing certain spices to soar in price. Present society's desire to expose spices in a spice rack probably comes from the prestige which came to the fortunate wealthy who could afford spices in earlier times.

In Medieval times and during the Renaissance, Europe shipped huge quantities of gold and silver through Venetian banks to the Arab world in exchange for spices. The Portugese ended the golden age of Venice when Vasco da Gama found the sea route to the Spice Islands.

ALLSPICE is the dried fruit of the allspice tree which grows in the West Indies. Allspice resembles the combined flavors of cinnamon, nutmeg and clove. It was discovered by Columbus, who did not consider it valuable because it was not one of the spices Europeans knew. It is excellent for making mulled wine or hot cider.

CINNAMON is a spice bark which came to the Europeans from Arabian merchants who told cunning and fanciful tales of gathering cinnamon from the nest of the giant phoenix. By hiding the true source of the bark, they inflated its value.

CLOVES are the dried, unopened flower buds of the evergreen clove tree, which grows in the Spice Islands (East Indies). In the 1800's, the Dutch kept the price of cloves high by burning several hundred thousand pounds from the overstocked warehouses of the Dutch East India Company. Clove oil has long been used for pain relief, and early Virginians used cloves and oranges as pomanders.

MOCHA (coffee) began to be used as a flavoring relatively recently. Coffee originated in Ethiopia. The first coffee house opened in Constantinople in the 1500's. At first, all coffee came from Mocha, a port in Yemen. Then the Dutch found they could grow it in Java and ended the Arabian monopoly. Coffee became the national beverage after the Boston Tea Party, when patriotic colonists repudiated the heavily taxed tea from England.

NUTMEG is principally exported to the United States from Grenada. It is the seed inside the fruit of the nutmeg tree. MACE is the ground outer covering of the nutmeg seed. First found by the Portugese in the East Indies, the tree was soon propagated by the Spanish and English in their colonies.

PEPPER, both black and white, comes from the berries of the same plant. Black pepper is made from the whole underripe berry which is dried before use. White pepper is made from the ripe berry after the black outer shell is polished off. In Classical Greece, pepper was used as medicine. However, by the fall of the Roman Empire, pepper had become so popular as an additive and preservative that invading barbarians demanded 3,000 pounds of pepper in war reparations. In Medieval times, a field worker had to spend three weeks' wages for one pound of pepper.

Herbs

The use of herbs as seasoning for sauces dates back to Paris in the 1300's. Parisian housewives could buy ready-made sauces from professional sauce makers on the streets. Monastic orders began the tradition of shaping herb gardens in decorative motifs. From these gardens came flavoring for food and remedies for illness.

SWEET BASIL was brought to its present popularity by Italian immigrants. Basil was said by the Greeks to have been the herb of royalty. However, in Puritan Massachusetts, growing the herb was one of many signs attributed to witches. Basil has a strong, clove-like taste.

BAY LEAVES are commonly found in recipes where the ingredients simmer. The bay leaf wreath or laurel wreath was symbolic of victory in ancient Greece. Sweet bay has a highly aromatic leaf which is said to repel all kinds of bugs.

CHERVIL is one of the "fines herbes" and was used as salad in the Middle Ages. Chervil has a delicate parsley flavor and may be substituted for parsley in many recipes. It should be added to dishes just before serving.

MARJORAM is very like OREGANO, but it is a more delicate plant and has a sweet flavor, as opposed to the stronger flavor of oregano. Marjoram was grown in ancient Egypt and the early Greeks attributed the qualities of joy and honor to it. Most of the dried oregano on the American market is actually a form of wild marjoram.

ROSEMARY is a strong and pungent herb that must be used in small quantities. Rosemary symbolized remembrance in the Middle Ages and figured prominently in funerals and weddings. It was burned to stop the plague and came to be strongly associated with the Virgin Mary. Many magical properties were attributed to it.

During the Middle Ages, SAGE was thought to have medicinal properties, but inspection in 20th century laboratories has not borne this out. In earlier ages, sage was thought to impart wisdom. Its slightly bitter taste finds its best use in fatty meats. It is the most popular herb in the United States and large quantities are imported from Yugoslavia.

TARRAGON, when fresh, has a flavor much like licorice, which is lost when it is dried. French tarragon is the preferred variety. Oddly, the name comes from early Arab and French words for dragon. It is the mainstay of bearnaise sauce and tartar sauce.

THYME is a slightly pungent herb that came to the new world from England. There are more than 400 varieties but lemon thyme and French thyme are the most common. Thyme comes from the Greek word for courage (thumas) and in Medieval Europe it was closely associated with chivalry in knights. Thyme was also used for its fumigation properties and was planted on graves.

A Fresh Herb Cooking Table

	Basil	Oregano and Marjoram	Rosemary	Sage	Tarragon	Thyme
Beef	Add basil to meatball recipes.	Marjoram may replace thyme in beef bourguignonne.	Add to butter, salt and pepper and brush on steaks.	Add a pinch to steaks on grill.	Use fresh tarragon and chervil for bearnaise sauce.	Sprinkle lightly over a veal shoulder before roasting.
Pork	Sprinkle lightly over pan-browned pork chops.	Add 2 tsp. oregano to pork goulash.	Rub on pork roast with garlic and sage.	Grind raw smoked ham, sage and favorite ingredients for ham loaf.	Mix small amount with gravy for sliced pork.	Rub leaves on ham before baking.
Lamb	Rub on leg of lamb.	Marinate lamb chops in white wine, onion, bayleaf, pepper and marjoram.	Add to marinade for shish kebob.	Rub over stuffed shoulder of lamb.	Add a pinch to shepherd's pie made with leftover lamb.	Good with leftover lamb in scotch broth.
Poultry	Add with marjoram and thyme to chicken cacciatore.	Add small amount of marjoram to poultry stuffing.	Add some sprigs to pan after frying chicken. Good gravy.	Rub on chicken before baking.	Add to cold chicken salad.	Add to a wine-and-honey-based marinade for chicken.
Fish	Puree 1 cup fresh leaves, cube butter, 3T clam juice. Use basil butter on salmon.	Add small amount of marjoram to buttered bread crumbs for stuffed flounder.	Brush trout fillets with parsley and rosemary butter.	Sprinkle small amount over scallop and shrimp shish kebob.	Cold poached fish with green mayonnaise. Blend spinach, chives and tarragon with mayonnaise.	Marinate left-over broiled fish fillets 24 hrs. with thyme, onion, sliced lemon, olive oil. Serve cold.
Vegetables	Add to ratatouille a few minutes before serving.	Mix either herb with butter and use sparingly with most vegetables.	Sprinkle on peas with butter.	Add a pinch to cold string bean salad with vinaigrette dressing.	Add a small amount to stuffed baked potatoes.	Add 2 tsp. to a pound of mixed vegetables with parsley, lemon, oregano, shallots, butter. Simmer.

Substitute dried herbs at rate of ⅓ to ½ amount of fresh herbs.

Appetizers & Beverages

Appetizers

Cheese

Dips

Meat

Nuts

Seafood

Vegetable

Beverages

Non-Alcoholic

Alcoholic

Wine

outhern hospitality means party food, from ham biscuits
made with country ham to oysters Rockefeller made
with plump oysters dredged from our own Chesapeake Bay.
Party food means bay scallops wrapped in bacon or shrimp
in a mold. It means a cheese platter with slices of crisp, red
Winesap apples from the Shenandoah Valley.

And to complement these home-grown hors d'oeuvres, we
serve award-winning wines from Virginia vineyards.

The Hotel Roanoke built its long-held reputation for culinary
excellence on imaginative use of the stock in Virginia's
extensive pantry—uses like oysters Rockefeller with
bearnaise sauce.

Oysters Rockefeller

½ onion	4 dozen fresh oysters
3 shallots	Worcestershire sauce
3 pounds frozen spinach	Bread crumbs or flour
½ pound butter	Rock salt
½ pound bacon, crisp and chopped fine	

Bearnaise Sauce:

1 pound butter	Juice of two lemons
12 egg yolks	Salt and white pepper
4 tablespoons tarragon leaves	

Wash onions, shallots, and spinach well and grind fine. Melt butter and add vegetables and bacon. Add Worcestershire sauce and season to taste. Thicken with bread crumbs or flour and simmer 10 minutes.

To make sauce, melt butter; keep warm. Beat egg yolks and lemon juice until thick in top of double boiler. Over low heat, beating yolks, add butter by droplets. Add tarragon, salt, and pepper to taste.

Open fresh oysters. Arrange 6 oysters in each of 8 individual serving piepans half filled with rock salt. Cover each oyster with vegetable mixture and top with Bearnaise sauce. Bake at 400° about 6 to 8 minutes or until golden brown. Serves 8.

The Hotel Roanoke
Roanoke, Virginia

Deviled Oysters

3 dozen oysters
1 cup minced onion
½ cup minced celery
4 tablespoons butter
¼ cup chow chow pickle relish
½ cup minced parsley
1 egg, beaten
1 tablespoon Worcestershire sauce
1 tablespoon catsup
1 cup bread crumbs
Clam shells for serving

Grind oysters in blender. Saute onions and celery in 2 tablespoons butter. Add remaining ingredients except bread crumbs and heat. Place mixture in serving shells. Top with bread crumbs and drizzle with remaining butter. Preparation: 25 minutes. Yield: 60 stuffed shells.

An easy yet elegant hors d'oeuvre.

Hermine Nichols

Shrimp Rockefeller

2 8-ounce packages frozen, cleaned, and cooked shrimp or 1½ pounds fresh shrimp, cleaned and cooked
2 packages frozen chopped spinach
½ cup chopped onion
¼ cup water
¾ teaspoon salt
3 slices white bread, without crusts, cubed
½ cup butter
1½ teaspoons Worcestershire sauce
½ teaspoon garlic powder
¼ teaspoon hot pepper sauce
1 teaspoon celery salt
2 tablespoons melted butter
¼ cup grated Parmesan cheese
½ cup dry bread crumbs

Defrost shrimp if needed. Place frozen spinach in large saucepan with onion, water and salt. Cook until spinach is separated and tear apart with fork. Do not drain, but add to spinach the bread cubes, butter, and seasonings. Simmer 10 minutes. Reserve 8 to 10 shrimp for topping each serving. Divide rest of shrimp among 8 to 10 scallop shells or place in shallow greased casserole. Cover shrimp with spinach mixture. Sprinkle with mixture of melted butter, Parmesan, and bread crumbs. Top with reserved shrimp and bake at 400° for 15 minutes. Preparation: 30 minutes. Serves 8 to 10.

Priscilla Alexander

Cocktail Crabmeat

1 pound backfin
  crabmeat
1 tablespoon horseradish
1 teaspoon lemon juice
1 cup mayonnaise
  Dash of Tabasco

Dash of Worcestershire
  sauce
Dash of salt
Shredded Cheddar
  cheese

Mix together all ingredients except cheese and put in greased quiche pan or pie plate. Sprinkle shredded cheese on top. Broil in oven until cheese melts and crabmeat is hot. Serve with Triscuits. Preparation: 15 minutes. Serves 6 to 8.

Mary Meade Davenport

Scallops in Bacon

1 pound scallops, rinsed
  or soaked in milk

1 pound bacon
Soy sauce

Cut large scallops in half. Wrap each scallop in ½ strip of bacon. Secure with toothpick. Sprinkle soy sauce over all. Place in baking dish and bake at 425°, turning once, for 20 to 30 minutes. Dip in Sweet & Sour Sauce.

Sweet & Sour Sauce:

5 tablespoons sugar
⅓ cup cider vinegar
¼ cup red currant jelly
2 tablespoons catsup

1 tablespoon soy sauce
1 tablespoon cornstarch
¼ cup cold water

In a medium saucepan, heat sugar, vinegar, currant jelly, catsup, and soy sauce until jelly is melted. Dissolve cornstarch in cold water. Slowly stir cornstarch into sauce and cook for 5 minutes. Preparation: 25 minutes. Serve 4 to 6.

Jana Thomas

Molly Peckham's Crab Mold

2 tablespoons plain
gelatin (1 tablespoon
more if serving in hot
weather)
½ cup cold water
¼ cup boiling water
2 cups mayonnaise
1 cup Heinz chili sauce
¾ pound crabmeat

1 cup celery, finely
chopped
½ cup green olives with
pimento, chopped
½ cup mild sweet onion
or spring onions, finely
chopped
Pam vegetable spray

Sprinkle gelatin over cold water. Add boiling water; stir well to dissolve gelatin. Combine with mayonnaise and chili sauce. Add other ingredients. Pour into mold sprayed with Pam. Chill until set. Unmold on bed of lettuce. Garnish with olive slices, lemon slices or wedges, or parsley. Serve with Ritz, saltines, or other crackers.

May prepare a day ahead.

Laurie Dudley

Shrimp Mold

1 can tomato soup
2 small packages cream
cheese
2 tablespoons gelatin,
dissolved in ½ cup
cold water
1 cup mayonnaise

1 teaspoon mayonnaise
for greasing mold
1½ cups onion and celery
mixed, finely chopped
2 4½-ounce cans
medium-size shrimp,
rinsed and drained

Bring soup to a boil. Remove from heat and add cheese. Beat until very smooth. Add gelatin and cool. Add celery, onion, and mayonnaise and let it begin to thicken. Grease mold lightly with 1 teaspoon mayonnaise and pour in gelatin mixture. Stir in shrimp. Refrigerate. Unmold and serve with crackers. Preparation: 20 minutes. Serves 20 to 25.

Take out ½ hour before serving to help in unmolding. This is pretty prepared in a fish mold and garnished with parsley and lemon slices.

Jane Cowles

Caviar Pie

9 eggs, hard-boiled
2 tablespoons onion, minced
4 tablespoons melted butter

4 tablespoons mayonnaise
1 cup sour cream
Red caviar
Black caviar

Set aside 3 cooked yolks. Place remaining eggs in a processor. Add butter and mayonnaise and process until smooth. Add onion. Place this mixture evenly in a pie-shaped dish. Mask this with sour cream. Dice the 3 yolks which have been set aside. Spread a ring of red caviar around edge of plate. Then spread a ring of black, then a ring with the diced yolks. Serve with crackers or cut into wedges as a first course. Preparation: 20 minutes. Serves 15.

Katrina Parkinson

Caviar Casserole

6 hard-boiled eggs
1 stick butter, softened
1 large bunch of scallions, chopped
2 small jars black lump-fish caviar

2 cups sour cream
Lemon wedges (optional)
Fresh parsley (optional)

Chop eggs and butter. Press into bottom of quiche dish or pie pan. Sprinkle scallions on top. Cover with caviar. Spread sour cream over top, being careful not to mix it with the caviar. Garnish with lemon and parsley if desired. Refrigerate until ready to serve. Serve cold with crackers. Preparation: 20 minutes. Serves 14 to 16.

This is absolutely, positively, unquestionably simple, yet GLAMOROUS.

Franny Powell

Country Club Pate

1¼ pounds veal (trimmed)
5 ounces veal liver
6 ounces fat back
   (trimmed)
4 ounces onions
1 sprig parsley
2 cloves garlic
1½ tablespoons salt
1½ teaspoons ground
   pepper

2 ounces flour
1 egg
2 ounces Courvoisier
1 ounce Grand Marnier
1 ounce Port
½ teaspoon nutmeg
4 ounces heavy cream

Finely grind 6 ounces veal, 2 ounces liver, 2 ounces fat back, garlic, onion, and parsley. Coarsely grind remaining veal and liver. Reserve remaining fat back. Place meat in mixing bowl and on low speed, mix in egg, flour, heavy cream, spices and liquor. Line loaf pan with thin slices of fat back, covering sides completely with enough over-hang to cover top of pate. Place mixture in pans, pack firmly, and place over-hanging pieces to cover top of pate. Place loaf pan in pan of water high enough to cover sides of loaf pan. Cook in 350° oven until pate reaches internal temperature of 160°. Cool in refrigerator overnight. Unmold in hot water like Jello mold; slice and eat. Preparation: Overnight. Yield: 1 loaf.

Make sure all ingredients are cold.

The Country Club of Virginia
Richmond, Virginia

Apple Slices with Pate

Fresh red apples   Pate

Slice fresh red apples with skins and spread with pate. Arrange on tray.

A delicious flavor combination. Arrange on a platter with "Stuffed Pea Pods" (page 28).

Gayle Summa

Salmon Log

1 1-pound can salmon	1 teaspoon horseradish
1 large package cream cheese, softened	¼ teaspoon salt
	1 teaspoon liquid smoke
1 tablespoon lemon juice	½ cup chopped walnuts
2 tablespoons grated onion	3 tablespoons fresh chopped parsley

Drain and flake salmon, removing skin and bones. Combine salmon with next 6 ingredients. Mix well. Chill several hours. Combine walnuts and parsley and set aside. Shape salmon into a log and roll in the walnuts and parsley mixture. Chill well and serve with crackers. Preparation: 30 minutes. Serves 10.

Wonderful for cocktail parties. May be doubled for a larger log.

Michael Roberston

Cheddar Smithfield Spread

½ cup Cheddar cheese, shredded	½ teaspoon Worcestershire sauce
1 jar Smithfield ham, finely chopped	½ cup mayonnaise

Mix well and serve with assorted crackers.

A great recipe for using up your holiday Smithfield ham! Use ¼ to ½ pound of ham pieces.

Micki Stout

Cocktail Meatballs

Meatballs:

2 pounds ground chuck
⅓ cup onion, chopped
2 eggs
1 cup Progresso Italian
  Bread Crumbs
⅓ cup Romano cheese

¼ cup parsley flakes
½ cup milk
2 dashes of pepper
  Olive oil

Combine all ingredients except olive oil and mix well. Roll into bite-sized meatballs. Brown in a little olive oil over medium heat, until all sides are completely browned. Drain.

Sauce:

1 12-ounce jar chili sauce
1 10-ounce jar grape
  jelly

Juice of 1 lemon

Combine all ingredients in a large skillet; add meatballs and simmer for 1 hour. Preparation: 2 hours. Yield: 60.

May be made ahead and frozen.

JoAnne Klamut

Mini Reubens

½ pound sliced deli
  corned beef
1 small can of
  sauerkraut, drained
¼ to ½ cup Thousand
  Island dressing

1 6-ounce package Swiss
  cheese, sliced
  Party rye bread

Spread rye bread with Thousand Island dressing. Cut beef to fit bread and place 2 pieces of beef on each slice of bread. Place 1 to 2 teaspoons of sauerkraut on beef. Cover with square of Swiss cheese. Bake on cookie sheet at 350° for 10 minutes or until cheese melts. Preparation: 30 minutes. Serves 10 to 15 as appetizers.

May assemble ahead of time and refrigerate. Bake just before serving.

Kelly Painter

Sixty of the Finest Hors d'Oeuvres

1 pound sliced bacon (quality brand)

2 to 3 cans whole water chestnuts (cut in half if they are too large)

Sauce:

1 12-ounce bottle chili sauce

1 pound dark brown sugar

Combine chili sauce and sugar and cook over low heat for about 1 hour. Reserve. Cut bacon slices into thirds; wrap each piece around a water chestnut. Secure with toothpicks. Bake roll-ups on broiling pan at 350° until crisp (about 45 minutes).

To serve, place roll-ups in heated sauce. Stir to coat well. Remove roll-ups to a serving tray (without extra sauce).

May be made ahead and reheated just before serving.

Michele Seass

Spinach Balls

2 10-ounce packages frozen chopped spinach, cooked and drained

2 cups Pepperidge Farm seasoned stuffing

1 large onion, chopped

6 eggs, beaten

¾ cup butter, melted

½ cup Parmesan cheese, grated

1 teaspoon garlic salt

1 teaspoon pepper

1 teaspoon Accent

Cook spinach according to directions on package and drain well. Combine spinach with remaining ingredients and shape into small bite-sized balls. Bake at 350° for 20 minutes. Preparation: 1 hour. Yield: 120 balls.

May also be made into casserole and baked for 30 minutes. May be made ahead of time and frozen. Thaw 1 hour before baking.

Anne Booker

Stuffed Pea Pods

Fresh snow peas   **Boursin cheese**

String snow peas. Blanch quickly in hot water and rinse immediately with cold water. Slit open and stuff with Boursin cheese (recipe on page 35). Chill.

Looks pretty served on same tray with "Apple Slices with Pate" (page 24). Easy and a welcome change.

Gayle Summa

Stuffed Cucumbers

1 cucumber
1 3-ounce package cream cheese, softened
1 small package bleu cheese

¼ cup scallions, minced
Garlic powder to taste
Pimento for garnish

Cut cucumber in half, remove seeds, and run paring knife along skin for decoration. Combine cream cheese and bleu cheese and add scallions and garlic powder to taste. Mix well. Stuff cucumber with cheese mixture and chill. Before serving, slice cucumber and garnish each with pimento strip. Preparation: 10 minutes. Serves 4.

Gayle Summa

Marinated Vidalia Onions

4 large Vidalia onions (Vidalias only available in May, June, July)
2 cups water

¼ cup vinegar
1 cup sugar
1 tablespoon celery seed
½ cup mayonnaise

Slice onions as thinly as possible and reserve. Combine water, vinegar, sugar, and celery seed and boil for 1 minute. Remove from heat. Add thinly sliced onions to boiled mixture and let sit for 20 minutes. Drain. Mix onions with mayonnaise. Chill. Serve with plenty of saltines. Preparation: 15 minutes. Serves 8.

Fabulous! Vidalia onions are a must!

Margaret Bargatze

Mushroom Turnovers

3 3-ounce packages cream cheese
½ cup butter or margarine
1½ cups sifted flour
3 tablespoons butter or margarine
½ pound minced mushrooms
1 large onion, minced
1 teaspoon salt
¼ teaspoon thyme
2 tablespoons flour
¼ cup sour cream
1 egg, beaten

In large bowl with electric mixer at medium speed, beat cream cheese, ½ cup butter or margarine, and 1½ cups flour until soft dough forms. Wrap dough in waxed paper; refrigerate at least 1 hour. Melt 3 tablespoons butter in frying pan and saute mushrooms and onion until tender. Stir in salt, thyme, and 2 tablespoons flour. Stir in sour cream. On floured board, thinly roll out ½ of dough and cut circles with 2¾-inch cookie cutter or glass. On ½ of each circle, place a teaspoon of mushroom mixture. Brush edges with egg; fold over filling and press edges together with fork. Prick tops and place on ungreased cookie sheets. Repeat with remaining ingredients. Brush with egg. Bake 12 to 15 minutes at 450° or until golden. Yield: About 50 appetizers.

May make ahead and freeze before cooking. Well worth the effort.

Sally Ayers

Cheese Stuffed Mushrooms

1½ pounds small fresh mushrooms
1 8-ounce package cream cheese, softened
1 cup freshly grated Parmesan cheese
Dash of salt
Dash of Worcestershire sauce
Dash of ground nutmeg
Dash of freshly ground pepper

Rinse mushrooms and pat dry. Remove stems. Place caps on greased baking sheet. Combine remaining ingredients except 2 tablespoons Parmesan cheese. Mix well. Spoon mixture into mushroom caps. Sprinkle with remaining cheese. Bake at 350° for 15 to 20 minutes. Preparation: 25 minutes. Yield: Approximately 4 dozen.

Carpie Coulbourn

Ham and Cheese Rolls

1 stick butter, softened
2 teaspoons prepared
  mustard
2 tablespoons poppy
  seeds
2 teaspoons Worcester-
  shire sauce
1 small onion, grated

1 package (20) Pep-
  peridge Farm Party
  Rolls
¼ pound thinly sliced
  boiled ham
1 4-ounce package sliced
  Swiss cheese

Mix together butter, mustard, poppy seeds, Worcestershire sauce and onion. Open rolls and spread mixture on both sides of roll. Put in ham and cheese. Wrap in foil and heat at 350° until cheese melts. Preparation: 15 minutes. Yield: 20 rolls.

May make ahead and freeze before baking. These will disappear quickly!

Peggy Crowley

Sausage, Cheese and Bacon Rolls

1 8-ounce package cream
  cheese, softened
½ pound hot sausage,
  cooked and crumbled

15 slices day-old white
  bread
15 slices bacon

Cook sausage until completely browned; drain by blotting with paper towels to absorb all grease and crumble. Mix with cream cheese. Remove crust from bread and spread each slice with cream cheese-sausage mixture. Cut each slice into 4 strips. Cut each bacon slice in half lengthwise and again crosswise. Place bread strip on top of each bacon slice; roll and secure with toothpick. (May be frozen at this point.) Bake on pan with a rack at 400° for 15 to 20 minutes or until bacon is done. Preparation: 35 minutes. Yield: 60 rolls.

Betty Williams

Parmesan Onion Canapes

1 cup mayonnaise
1 cup grated Parmesan
   cheese (fresh if
   available)
½ cup finely chopped
   onion

1 tablespoon milk
1 loaf sliced cocktail rye
   bread

Mix ingredients and spread on bread. Place on baking sheet and broil about 2 to 3 minutes or until slightly bubbly and brown. Preparation: 20 minutes. Yield: 36 plus.

Mixture will keep well in refrigerator in a tightly covered jar for about 2 weeks.

Trygve Garter

Cheese Biscuits

¼ pound sharp cheese,
   grated
¼ pound butter
1 cup flour

Pinch of salt
Dash of red pepper
Pecan halves

Cream together cheese and butter; add flour and salt. Work well until blended; add pepper and mix thoroughly. Shape into log rolls and refrigerate overnight. Cut slices into 1/8-inch pieces and place pecan half in center of each. Bake on ungreased cookie sheet at 325° for 10 minutes. Do not brown. Serves 6 to 8.

May be stored for weeks in refrigerator in a tightly sealed container. For a glazed look, beat 1 egg white and brush on biscuits.

Carole Taylor

Bea's Cheese Wafers

1 small package onion
   soup mix
2 cups flour
1 teaspoon salt
2 sticks butter, softened

1 pound sharp cheese,
   grated
½ cup bacon bits
   (optional)
Dash of garlic powder

Combine soup mix, flour, salt, garlic powder, and bacon bits (optional) and mix well. Work butter in by hand. Add cheese and form into a roll. Chill. Cut in ¼-inch slices. Bake at 350° until golden. Preparation: 25 minutes. Serves 6 to 8.

Robin Traywick Williams

31

Brie in Pastry

1 4½-ounce package Brie
   cheese

1 individual Pepperidge
   Farm frozen patty shell

Preheat oven to 450°. Thaw patty shell. Do not remove center. With a rolling pin, roll out large enough to cover cheese. Carefully pull dough over top and sides, tucking the pastry under the bottom. Put on a cookie sheet and bake until brown, about 15 minutes. Serve with crackers. Preparation: 20 minutes. Serves 6.

Judy Brown

Cheese Puffs

1 1-pound loaf of un-
   sliced sandwich bread
2 3-ounce packages
   cream cheese
1 8-ounce package sharp
   Cheddar cheese, cut into chunks

1 cup margarine or butter
4 egg whites, stiffly
   beaten

Trim crust from all sides of bread. Discard crust. Cut bread into 1-inch cubes and set aside. Combine cheeses and margarine in the top of a double boiler. Cook over boiling water until cheese is melted and mixture is smooth, stirring constantly. Remove from heat. Fold a small amount of the hot cheese mixture into egg whites; fold whites into remaining cheese mixture. Use a fork to dip each bread cube into cheese mixture, coating the bread on all sides. Place bread cubes 1 inch apart on a lightly greased baking sheet. Cover and refrigerate overnight. Remove from refrigerator, uncover, and bake at 400° for 10 to 12 minutes or until golden brown. Serve immediately. Preparation: 45 minutes. Yield: 8 dozen.

Coated cubes may be frozen (unbaked) for up to 2 months. Remove from freezer and bake, while still frozen, at 400° for 12 to 15 minutes. Fabulous!

Peggy Wright

Hot Cheese Croustades

1 pound New York sharp Cheddar cheese, grated	2 boxes Rahms mini croustades
½ pound Parmesan cheese, grated	Pinch of pepper
1 teaspoon concentrated lemon juice	Enough mayonnaise to hold cheeses together

Combine cheeses with lemon juice and pepper and add enough mayonnaise to hold cheeses together. Fill each mini croustade half full with cheese mixture. Place croustades on baking sheet and bake at 350° for 5 minutes or until cheese melts. Preparation: 10 minutes. Yield: 48 mini croustades.

Cheese mixture may be made in advance and refrigerated. Simply delicious!

Susan Hobbs

Fried Cheese

8 ounces whole-milk Mozzarella (Double H brand)	¼ teaspoon oregano
	¼ teaspoon basil
1 egg, beaten with 1 tablespoon water	Flour
	Peanut oil
½ cup cracker crumbs or toasted bread crumbs	Tomato sauce

Cut cheese into 1-inch cubes; toss in flour. Dip in egg; roll in crumbs seasoned with oregano and basil. Refrigerate at least 30 minutes. Heat 1-inch peanut oil in heavy skillet to 375°. Fry quickly (about 30 seconds) and serve with a good tomato sauce. Preparation: 45 minutes. Serves 4.

May simmer canned or bottled pasta sauce with garlic, wine, and seasonings for about an hour to make tomato sauce. Can be served with toothpicks as hors d'oeuvres or in larger squares as a first course or side dish.

Jana Thomas

Appetizers

Miniature Quiches

Pastry:

1 cup butter or margarine, softened	2 cups flour
1 8-ounce package cream cheese, softened	½ teaspoon salt

Combine butter, cream cheese, flour and salt in mixing bowl until well blended. Roll into balls and press into mini muffin pans. Bake at 350° for 3 to 5 minutes.

Filling:

2 tablespoons butter	1½ cups half-and-half
1 medium onion, chopped	½ teaspoon salt
2½ cups Swiss cheese, finely grated	Dash of pepper
3 eggs	Dash of nutmeg

Saute onion in butter until transparent; set aside. Place a teaspoon of Swiss cheese in each tart. Beat eggs, half-and-half, salt, pepper, and nutmeg until well blended. Add onions and pour about 1 teaspoon egg mixture over cheese. Fill ⅔ full. Bake at 350° for 20 to 25 minutes. Preparation: 1 hour. Yield: 60.

May be made ahead and frozen. To serve, thaw and heat uncovered at 300° until hot. Variations: Add crisp bacon, cooked and crumbled, or finely chopped mushrooms.

Beth Witt

Boursin Cheese

2 tablespoons butter, softened
½ teaspoon pressed garlic or garlic powder
¼ teaspoon dried dill
1/8 teaspoon thyme

2 tablespoons parsley
1 tablespoon freeze-dried chives
1 8-ounce cream cheese, softened
Coarse ground pepper

In a small bowl, using a wooden spoon, blend butter with garlic, dill, thyme, parsley, and chives. When well blended, work into cream cheese and blend until smooth. Mold into a ball or other desired shape. Sprinkle with ground pepper until all sides are covered. Cover with Saran Wrap and chill until ready to serve. The longer chilled, the better the flavor. Preparation: 15 minutes. Serves 6 to 8.

Make a few to keep on hand. Flavor definitely improves with age! Serve in "Stuffed Pea Pods" (page 28).

Karen Feigley

Beer Cheese

1 pound Cheddar cheese, shredded
1 pound Swiss cheese, shredded
1/8 teaspoon garlic powder

1 tablespoon dry mustard
2 teaspoons Worcestershire sauce
1 cup beer

Mix all ingredients in blender until smooth. Refrigerate in a covered container for several days. Serve in a cheese crock with assorted crackers. Preparation: 15 minutes. Yield: 2 pounds.

Makes great gifts for friends at Christmas.

Melinda Shepardson

Chutnut Cheeseball

1 6-ounce jar Raffetto Chut-Nut	2 8-ounce packages cream cheese, softened
½ teaspoon curry	Blanched almonds,
½ teaspoon dry mustard	sliced and toasted

Drain Chut-Nut and add curry and dry mustard. Mix into softened cream cheese and shape into ball. Roll in toasted almonds. Preparation: 10 minutes. Serves 8 to 10.

Lynn Congdon

Pineapple Cheese Ball

2 8-ounce packages cream cheese, softened	1/8 teaspoon salt
½ cup green pepper, finely chopped	2 cups chopped pecans (divided)
1 small can crushed pineapple, well drained	Fresh parsley for garnish (optional)

Mix together all ingredients except one cup of nuts. Roll into a ball and coat with remaining nuts. Wrap in plastic wrap and chill well. May be garnished with parsley. Serve with your favorite cracker. Preparation: 15 minutes. Yield: 1 medium cheese ball.

Always a hit! Freezes beautifully.

Margaret Bargatze

Spiced Nuts

2 tablespoons cold water	¼ teaspoon ground cloves
1 slightly beaten egg white	¼ teaspoon ground allspice
½ cup sugar	2 cups pecans
½ teaspoon salt	Butter
¼ teaspoon ground cinnamon	

Add water to the slightly beaten egg white. Dissolve sugar in egg white mixture. Add salt and spices. Mix well. Dip nuts in mixture. Grease cookie sheet with butter. Place nuts flat side down on cookie sheet. Bake at 250° until golden brown, about 45 minutes. Preparation: 45 minutes. Yield: 2 cups.

Great for gift giving!

Carolyn Gard

Cream Cheese with Jezebel Sauce

1 package cream cheese
(any size)

Sauce:

1 18-ounce jar pineapple
preserves
1 18-ounce jar apple
jelly
1 5-ounce jar prepared
horseradish

1 1-ounce can dry
mustard
1 tablespoon cracked
peppercorns

In a bowl, combine the sauce ingredients, mixing well. Pour into airtight containers. Cover and store in refrigerator. Serve over cream cheese as a spread accompanied with crackers. Preparation: 5 minutes. Yield: Approximately 4 cups of sauce.

Great replacement for pepper jelly. Also a wonderful gift idea! May also be served with roast beef or pork.

Dorothea Robertson

Toasted Almond Camembert

1 4½-ounce round of
Camembert cheese
1 tablespoon butter

¼ cup sliced almonds,
toasted

Preheat oven to 325⁰. Place cheese in a small oven-proof serving dish. Place butter on top of cheese and sprinkle almonds on top. Heat for 5 minutes. Serve with assorted crackers. Preparation: 15 minutes. Serves 6.

Cabell West

Appetizers

Mexican Relish Appetizer

1 4-ounce can chopped
  black olives
1 3-ounce can El Paso
  chopped green chilies
1 scallion, thinly sliced
  with top

1 tomato, diced
1 tablespoon garlic salt
1 teaspoon vinegar
1 teaspoon oil
  Tostito chips

Combine ingredients and chill well. Serve with Tostito chips.

Good flavor and not so many calories!

Missy Buckingham

Tex-Mex Layered Dip

1 15-ounce can refried
  beans
2 cups sour cream
1 1¼-ounce package taco
  seasoning
1 8-ounce jar picante
  sauce (or taco sauce)
4 ripe avocados, mashed
2 teaspoons lemon juice

2 medium tomatoes,
  chopped
1 bunch green onions,
  with tops, thinly sliced
1 8-ounce Cheddar
  cheese, grated
1 4-ounce can sliced ripe
  olives
  Tostitos or tortilla chips

On bottom of a 2-quart glass casserole (not too deep) spread refried beans. Mix sour cream with taco seasoning and spread on top of bean layer. Next, layer picante sauce. Mix avocados with lemon juice; layer on top of picante sauce. Continue layering each of the remaining ingredients. Cover. Refrigerate and serve chilled with Tostitos. Preparation: 20 minutes. Serves 25.

May halve recipe but still use all of beans. If avocados aren't ripe, substitute Marie's avocado dressing. This recipe is always requested.

Gay Jewett

Hot Crab Dip

1 8-ounce package cream
  cheese, softened
½ cup sour cream
2 tablespoons mayonnaise
1 tablespoon lemon juice
1 teaspoon Worcester-
  shire sauce

½ teaspoon dry mustard
1 tablespoon milk
½ cup Cheddar cheese,
  grated
1 pound lump crabmeat
Pinch of garlic powder

Combine cream cheese, sour cream, mayonnaise, lemon juice, Worcestershire sauce, dry mustard, and garlic powder in a large bowl and mix until smooth. Add enough milk to make mixture creamy. Stir in half of cheese and fold in crabmeat. Pour into a 1-quart casserole and top with remaining cheese. Bake at 325° until mixture is bubbly and browned for about 25 to 30 minutes. Serve with Sociables or favorite crackers. Preparation: 30 minutes. Serves 6 to 8.

Mimi Kline

Dill Weed Dip

1½ cups mayonnaise
1 cup sour cream
1 teaspoon garlic salt
1 teaspoon Maggi (liquid)
1 teaspoon Accent
1 teaspoon dry mustard

1 tablespoon dill weed
¼ cup parsley, chopped
2 tablespoons olive oil
2 dashes Tabasco
Juice of 1 lemon

Combine all ingredients and blend well. Serve with raw vegetables or as sauce for cooked vegetables. Preparation: 6 minutes. Yield: 1 pint.

Keeps 1 month in refrigerator.

Margaret Bargatze

Spinach-Artichoke Dip

1 can artichoke hearts
1 stick butter
2 packages frozen
chopped spinach
1 8-ounce package cream
cheese
¼ cup bread crumbs
(coarse)

Juice of 1 lemon
Salt, pepper, sweet
basil, dill weed to taste
Parmesan cheese
Chopped parsley
(optional)

Drain and chop artichoke hearts somewhat finely. Melt ⅓ stick butter and pour over hearts with lemon juice. Season with salt, pepper, and sweet basil. Cook spinach and drain. Melt remaining ⅔ stick butter and cream cheese. Blend into spinach. Season with salt and pepper and dill weed. Combine spinach and artichoke hearts with ¼ cup bread crumbs and chopped fresh parsley if desired. Place in baking dish and cover with Parmesan cheese. Bake at 325° for 20 minutes. Serve as a dip with crackers. Preparation: 15 minutes. Serves 6 to 8.

Your guests will rave over this one! Truly foolproof and delicious.

Anne Grier

Spinach Dip

1 cup mayonnaise
1 pint sour cream
2½ teaspoons Salad Supreme
(or salad herbs)
½ teaspoon dill weed
1 package original Hidden
Valley Ranch salad
dressing

½ cup chopped onion (or
1 tablespoon instant
onion)
1 package frozen chopped
spinach, cooked and
drained well
Salt and pepper to taste

Combine ingredients and chill overnight. Serve with raw vegetables. Preparation: 15 minutes. Serves 12.

There have been many requests for this recipe.

Mary Jo Kearfott

Banana Slush

4 cups sugar
6 cups water
1 48-ounce can pineapple
  juice
3 bananas (ripe), mashed

1 cup fresh lemon juice
1 16-ounce can frozen
  orange juice, thawed
4 to 5 quarts ginger ale

Boil sugar and water 5 minutes, or until crystals are completely dissolved. Pour into 5-quart freezer container, and stir in bananas and juices. Cover and freeze overnight. On serving day, remove from freezer about 3 hours before serving (should be slushy). To serve, pour in large punch bowl and add 4 to 5 quarts of ginger ale. Yield: 2½ gallons.

The frozen part can be kept in covered freezer container for about a week. Recipe can be halved successfully. Bernice Pittman

Mint Tea

3 family size Lipton tea
  bags
4 6-inch pieces mint
1 cup sugar

⅓ to ½ cup lemon juice,
fresh or bottled
Boiling water

Boil 2 cups water. Pour over tea bags and mint and steep, covered, for 20 minutes or until cool. Dissolve sugar in 1 cup boiling water and add lemon juice. Remove tea bags and mint from water and combine tea with sugar and lemon mixture. Add 4 cups cold water and refrigerate. Preparation: 30 minutes. Serves 8.

The tea concentrate mixture can be stored in refrigerator and water added when served.

Sally Flinn

Grandmother's Fruit Tea

2 packages Lipton iced
  tea mix with lemon and
  sugar
1 medium can frozen
  orange juice (to make
  ½ gallon)

1 medium can frozen
  lemonade (to make ½
  gallon)
2 medium cans (or 1
  large can) pineapple
  juice
1 quart ginger ale

Prepare tea mix and juices according to package directions. Mix all ingredients together. Before serving, add ginger ale. Preparation: 10 minutes. Serves 20.

Larkin Bynum

Fruit Punch

1 gallon orange juice	4 12-ounce cans apricot
½ gallon lemonade	juice
½ gallon pineapple juice	2 quarts soda water,
1 pound sugar, or to taste	chilled

Combine first 5 ingredients, stirring well to dissolve sugar. Freeze half of this mixture and chill other half. When ready to serve, place frozen juice in a large punch bowl. Pour in chilled juice and soda to taste. Yield: 3 gallons.

A delightful punch for meetings or children's parties. Recipe may be halved easily.

Becky Symons

Hot Vienna Chocolate

3 quarts milk	1 cup sugar
3 ounces baking	2 teaspoons vanilla
chocolate, melted	Whipping cream
8 eggs	(optional)

Place milk in double boiler. When milk is hot, moisten melted chocolate with some of milk. Gradually add remaining milk to chocolate. Beat eggs and sugar together in washed double boiler. Stir milk and chocolate into eggs and sugar and add vanilla. Heat and serve as is or garnish with whipped cream. Preparation: 30 minutes. Yield: 20 5-ounce servings.

Nancy Thomas

Mocha Punch

7 cups chilled coffee	¼ teaspoon salt
2 quarts chocolate ice	2 cups heavy cream,
cream, divided	whipped
1 teaspoon almond	Nutmeg
extract	

Pour chilled coffee into bowl and add 1 quart ice cream. Beat until ice cream melts. Add almond extract and salt. Fold in remaining ice cream and ½ of the whipped cream. Fold in remaining whipped cream and garnish with a dash of nutmeg.

Michael Robertson

Mimosa

2 quarts fresh orange
  juice

2 bottles dry champagne

Stir champagne into orange juice and serve over ice. Preparation: 5 minutes.

Excellent for brunch.

Cabell West

Sangria

½ gallon red wine
1 pint orange juice
½ cup lemon juice
¼ cup sugar
¼ cup brandy

1 quart soda water
2 oranges, sliced
2 lemons, sliced
2 peaches, sliced

Mix and chill first 5 ingredients. Add soda and sliced fruit just before serving. Preparation: 10 minutes. Serves 20.

Michael Robertson

Sherry Cobbler

4 ounces sherry
1 ounce orange juice
2 ounces pineapple juice,
  unsweetened

½ teaspoon sugar
Orange slice
Maraschino cherry

Mix ingredients together and pour into an 8-ounce glass that has been filled with crushed ice. Garnish with an orange slice and a cherry. Yield: one 8-ounce drink.

Great for luncheons. May be multiplied for a batch.

Charlotte Churchill

Bloody Marys

9 ounces vodka
24 ounces V-8 juice
2 tablespoons lemon juice
2 tablespoons sugar

1 tablespoon celery salt
1 tablespoon Worcester-
    shire sauce
1½ teaspoons soy sauce

Mix all ingredients thoroughly. Serves 8.

Melinda Shepardson

Frozen Whiskey Sours

1 6-ounce can frozen
    orange juice
1 6-ounce can frozen
    limeade
1 6-ounce can frozen
    lemonade

4 6-ounce cans water
3 6-ounce cans bourbon
    Club soda or water

Mix first 5 ingredients in blender and pour into a half-gallon container and freeze. To serve, scoop frozen mixture into glasses; add a splash of soda or water. Drinks may need straws. Serves 10 to 12.

First mixture freezes indefinitely. This may also be served, without freezing, as a punch. Can be doubled.

Susan Claytor

Orange Julius

⅓ cup frozen orange juice
    concentrate
½ cup milk
½ cup water

¼ cup sugar
1 teaspoon vanilla
6 ice cubes
2 ounces vodka (optional)

Combine all ingredients in blender until ice is completely crushed. Preparation: 5 minutes. Serves 2.

Nice drink for children without the spirits.

Becky Newman

Kahlua

2½ cups sugar
  4 tablespoons freeze-
    dried coffee

1 quart water
1 teaspoon vanilla
1 fifth vodka

Blend sugar, coffee, and water in saucepan. Simmer 1½ to 2 hours. Cool. Add vanilla and vodka. Bottle in clean jars with tops. Preparation: 2 hours. Yield: 3 bottles.

Annette Chapman

Mocha Coffee

1 ounce Kahlua
½ ounce Creme de Cacao
  Hot coffee

Whipped cream (garnish)
Cocoa (garnish)

In a mug, pour liqueurs, then hot coffee. Top with cream and sprinkle cocoa over all.

Terry Long

Hummers

1 quart coffee ice cream
6 ounces Kahlua or Tia
  Maria

6 ounces Creme de Cacao
4 ounces light cream

Combine all ingredients in blender and blend until smooth. Pour into wine or champagne glasses and serve immediately. Serves 6.

A delicious dessert drink. Sprinkle with shaved chocolate for an extra touch.

Mary Powell

45

Beverages

Hot Buttered Rum

1 pound butter
1 teaspoon cinnamon
1 teaspoon ground cloves
1 teaspoon allspice
3 eggs, beaten

2 pounds dark brown
   sugar
1 to 2 jiggers of rum for
   each mug made

Melt butter, add spices and pour over brown sugar. Blend and cool. Add eggs, beating with mixer 5 minutes after first egg and 15 minutes more after remaining eggs.

For each serving, use 2 heaping tablespoons of batter, 1 to 2 jiggers of rum, and boiling water to fill each mug. Preparation: 25 minutes.

Batter will keep indefinitely in refrigerator. Makes several gifts for friends. Can be halved sucessfully.

Susan Overton

Athole Brose

2 cups whipping cream
1 cup honey

½ cup scotch

Whip cream until stiff. Fold in honey and scotch. Serve in sherbet glasses with a little bitter chocolate shaved on top. Preparation: 5 minutes. Serves 6.

A favorite with men.

Gretchen Gieg

Mother's Christmas Eggnog

12 large eggs, separated
2 cups sugar, divided

2¼ cups bourbon
3 cups whipping cream

The night before, beat egg yolks until very thick and light-colored (about 5 minutes with the electric beater). Add bourbon only and mix well. Refrigerate overnight, covered.

The next day, beat egg whites until stiff and slowly add 1¼ cups sugar. Whip cream until stiff (holds shape), then add remaining ¾ cup sugar. Gently fold whites and cream into yolk mixture with spatula. Yield: 3 quarts.

This takes a large bowl for mixing. Good topped with freshly grated nutmeg.

Bernice Pittman

Dining with Wine

One of the happiest marriages of Virginia wine and food is white Riesling and Smithfield ham. This is a good example of creatively ignoring the white-wine-with-white-meat axiom. The delicate sweetness of the Riesling offsets the characteristic saltiness of the Smithfield ham. Other good choices with country ham are Gerwurztraminer, Champagne or a rosé.

Pastries, plain cookies: Riesling, Aurora, Semillon.

Cold buffet foods: a rosé, Pinot Noir.

Shrimp, crab, fish: Chardonnay, Seyval Blanc.

Poultry: Vidal Blanc, Sauvignon Blanc, Chardonnay, Seyval Blanc.

Pork chops and roasts: Gerwurztraminer, Cabernet Sauvignon, de Chaunac, Foch Nouveau.

Lamb: Cabernet Sauvignon, Foch, Merlot.

Beef: Cabernet Sauvignon, Pinot Noir, Merlot Chancellor, de Chaunac, Foch, Villard Noir, Chambourcin, Chelois.

Cooking with Wine

As a rule of thumb, you should cook with the kind of wine you will serve with your dish. Dry white wine goes best with delicately flavored foods such as poultry, fish or seafood. Dry red wines complement more robust foods such as beef, lamb or game. Rosé wines go well with ham and veal. Semi-dry or slightly sweet wines go well with fruits, desserts and rich sauces. But remember, your own sense of taste is your best guide.

Some foods are not compatible with wine at all. The chief enemy is vinegar. Other flavors which should be toned down when wine is a key element of a meal are curry, horseradish, hot peppers, citrus rinds, excessive fat and oils, and, unfortunately, heavy chocolate.

Most recipes call for a relatively small amount of wine so that its flavor will blend with and not overpower the flavors of the other ingredients. You usually add the wine toward the end of a recipe so that its flavor is not boiled out. During the cooking process, the alcohol (and its calories) will evaporate.

To sweeten coffee maker or thermos bottle, fill it with warm water, add 1 teaspoon soda and let it stand. Store container with a stick of gum inside.

Forming meatballs is easier if hands are first chilled with an ice cube.

Store mushrooms in paper bag to absorb moisture and keep fresh.

Try putting vegetable dips in hollowed-out red cabbage for a pretty platter.

To freeze appetizers for easy separation, put on cookie sheet until frozen, then pack in Ziploc bags.

Use leftover turkey dressing to stuff mushrooms, cherry tomatoes and pieces of zucchini. Makes a quick appetizer.

Make memorable ham biscuits by blending some brown sugar with butter and spreading a little on each biscuit before heating.

One gallon of punch makes 32 servings.

Dress up your punch by floating some of the following on it: lemon slices, grapes, maraschino cherries, strawberries, lime slices.

Soups, Sandwiches & Salads

The versatile goober pea shows up in various Old Dominion dishes from soup to dessert. Peanut soup is a standard item on the menus of many Virginia inns and restaurants.

Peanuts, which came to America in slave ships, first became popular with Union soldiers during the War Between the States. After the war, P. T. Barnum offered hot roasted peanuts to circus audiences, and the popularity of peanuts spread with the circus.

Every Southern school child learns about Dr. George Washington Carver's contributions to Southern agriculture: discovery of the many uses of peanuts and soybeans. After boll weevils destroyed the cotton crop early in this century, Southerners took Dr. Carver's advice and made peanuts their money crop.

Today, peanuts are associated primarily with Southside Virginia, where the bushes thrive in the sandy soil, producing fruit for Virginia kitchens and fodder for the hogs that become smoked hams.

Boar's Head Peanut Soup

7 tablespoons butter
2 tablespoons chopped onions
3 tablespoons chopped celery

6 tablespoons flour
1 quart chicken broth
3 cups finely chopped peanuts

In heavy saucepan or soup kettle, melt butter and stir in onions and celery. Cook until vegetables are soft. Sprinkle with flour. Cook 3 minutes and remove from heat. In separate saucepan, bring broth to a simmer. Stir broth into vegetables; add peanuts. Simmer all for 30 minutes. Add salt and pepper to taste. May garnish with extra chopped peanuts if desired. Serves 8 to 10.

The Boar's Head Inn
Charlottesville, Virginia

Super Fantastic Gazpacho

2 teaspoons chopped chives
1 tablespoon chopped parsley
½ teaspoon Worcestershire sauce
1 teaspoon freshly ground pepper
1 clove garlic, pressed
2 teaspoons salt
½ cup tarragon vinegar
3 cups tomato juice
⅓ cup chopped mushrooms
3 tablespoons olive or vegetable oil
1 cup chopped onion
2 cups chopped fresh tomatoes
1¼ cups chopped green pepper
1 cup chopped celery
1 cup chopped cucumber

Mix all ingredients and serve at once. Preparation: 30 minutes. Serves 10.

May also use food processor for a creamier consistency. Option: 1 jigger of tequila poured on top before serving!

Franny Powell

Cold Tomato Bouillon

1 12-ounce can V-8 juice
1 10½-ounce can bouillon
1 teaspoon sugar
2 tablespoons lemon juice
1 teaspoon Worcestershire sauce
Salt and pepper to taste

Heat V-8 and bouillon up to boiling point. Add other ingredients and taste to correct seasonings. Serve hot or cold. Serves 4.

Kay Williams

Tomato-Orange Soup

2 cups tomato juice
2 cups orange juice
2 tablespoons lemon juice

Tabasco to taste
Lemon slices

Combine ingredients and heat. Serve hot or cold with lemon slice. Preparation: 15 minutes. Serves 4.

Serve with cheese straws.

Priscilla Alexander

Cold Avocado Soup

1 ripe avocado
1 can chilled chicken broth
2 tablespoons rum

½ teaspoon curry powder
½ teaspoon salt
1 cup light cream

Blend all ingredients in blender until frothy. Serve at once in chilled bowls garnished with a lime or avocado slice. Season with freshly ground pepper if desired. Preparation: 10 minutes. Serves 4.

Buy the dark pebbly avocados in summer and let ripen on your windowsill. The big smooth ones are watery and have little taste.

Jana Thomas

Chilled Cucumber Soup

2 medium cucumbers
2 tablespoons butter
1 tablespoon finely
chopped onion
2 tablespoons flour
3 cups strong chicken
stock or broth

2 egg yolks
¼ cup heavy cream
Salt and pepper to taste
Chives

Peel and thinly slice cucumbers. Melt butter in saucepan. Add cucumber and onion and saute until soft, but do not brown. Stir in flour; cook two minutes. Heat stock and add to pan. Season, cover, and simmer 20 minutes. Run mixture through blender and return to pan. Beat egg yolks and cream together and stir into soup. Heat but do not boil. Chill. To serve, garnish with chives. Preparation: 30 minutes. Serves 8.

Martha Davidson

Cold Spinach Soup

1 onion, chopped
3 tablespoons butter
2 10-ounce packages
frozen chopped spinach
3 cans chicken broth

1 tablespoon paprika
2 8-ounce packages
cream cheese, softened
Salt and pepper to taste

Brown onion in butter. Set aside. Thaw spinach, drain, and add to chicken broth with salt, pepper, and onion. Bring to a boil. Place mixture in blender and add cream cheese. Blend and chill. Serves 6 to 8 as first course.

Can use low calorie cream cheese.

Mims Powell

Chilled Consomme

1 can consomme	Celery seed
⅓ soup can water	Slivered almonds
Chopped chives	Sour cream
Chopped parsley	Curry

Combine consomme, water, chives, parsley, and celery seed. Chill until jelled. When ready to serve, place slivered almonds in bottom of each cup. Gently stir consomme to mix herbs and spoon into cups. Top each serving with sour cream seasoned to taste with curry. Preparation: 10 minutes. Serves 6.

Frances N. Barnes

Senegalese Soup

2 cans cream of chicken soup, undiluted	1 cup light cream
1 soup can sour cream (10½ ounces)	1 dash each Tabasco, celery salt, salt and pepper
1 cup chicken bouillon	1 green apple, peeled and minced
2 ounces dry sherry	
1½ teaspoons curry powder	

Place all ingredients, except apple, in blender and blend well. Chill at least 6 to 8 hours. Prepare and stir in apple just before serving. Preparation: 10 minutes. Serves 8.

Connie Garrett

Cream of Acorn Squash Soup

2 tablespoons butter
½ leek, diced
2 medium potatoes, diced
6 squash, diced
1 medium onion, diced

8 to 10 mint leaves
1 cup heavy cream
3 quarts chicken stock
Salt and pepper

Melt butter in a large saucepan; add leek, potatoes, onion, squash, and mint leaves. Stir for 5 minutes. Add chicken stock and bring mixture to a boil; then reduce heat to simmer until vegetables are cooked. Place in food processor, blend and gradually add cream. Add salt and pepper to taste. Serve chilled. Serves 6.

La Petite France
Richmond, Virginia

Cream of Artichoke Soup

2 tablespoons butter
½ cup chopped carrot
½ cup chopped onion
½ cup chopped celery
½ cup chopped mushrooms
½ cup butter
¼ cup flour
1 quart chicken broth
1 dozen raw oysters, undrained (optional)

1 package frozen artichoke hearts, cooked and drained
1 bay leaf
¾ teaspoon salt
½ teaspoon cayenne
¼ teaspoon thyme
¼ teaspoon oregano
¼ teaspoon sage
1 cup whipping cream

Saute chopped vegetables in 2 tablespoons butter for 15 minutes. Melt ½ cup butter in a large pot. Add flour and cook for 5 minutes. Add vegetables, broth, artichoke hearts, and seasonings. Simmer 30 minutes. Whisk in cream and add oysters, if desired. Heat thoroughly. Preparation: 30 minutes. Serves 6 to 8.

An elegant soup with or without the oysters. Try it with some sherry.

Jana Thomas

Broccoli Bisque

1 large bunch broccoli
¼ cup chopped onion
2 cups chicken broth
2 tablespoons butter
1 tablespoon flour
2 teaspoons salt
¼ teaspoon pepper
2 cups half-and-half

Steam broccoli until tender and chop. In a saucepan, combine broccoli, onion, and chicken broth. Bring to a boil, reduce heat, and simmer for 10 minutes. Melt butter in saucepan. Add flour, salt, and pepper and stir until smooth. Stir in half-and-half. Combine sauce and broccoli and cook over medium heat until soup bubbles. Serve hot or cold. Preparation: 30 minutes. Serves 6 to 8.

Corinne Davis

Cauliflower Soup

4 tablespoons chopped onion
¼ cup butter
2 tablespoons all-purpose flour
4 cups milk
1 teaspoon seasoning salt
1 medium head cauliflower, cooked and chopped, or 2 10-ounce boxes frozen cauliflower
1½ cups shredded sharp Cheddar cheese

Saute onion in butter until tender. Blend in flour. Add milk, seasonings, and cauliflower. Cook until smooth and slightly thick. Cool and blend in blender or food processor. Return to pan. Add cheese and stir until melted. Preparation: 20 minutes. Serves 4.

For thinner soup, use only 1 tablespoon of flour.

Nancy Leary

Hearty Corn Chowder

1 pound bacon, fried
   crisp and crumbled
3 tablespoons bacon fat,
   reserved
2 medium onions,
   chopped
½ cup celery, chopped
2 carrots, diced
3 large potatoes, peeled
   and diced

1 bay leaf
1 17-ounce can cream-
   style corn
2 cups evaporated milk
½ teaspoon thyme
½ teaspoon basil
1 tablespoon lemon juice
   Salt and pepper to taste
   Parsley and paprika

In a large saucepan or Dutch oven, saute onions and celery in reserved bacon fat. Add carrots, potatoes and bay leaf with just enough water to cover. Simmer for 15 to 20 minutes or until potatoes are tender. Add corn, milk, thyme, basil, lemon juice, salt, and pepper. Heat well. Stir in bacon and serve chowder garnished with parsley and paprika. Preparation: 40 minutes. Serves 6 to 8.

This chowder tastes best prepared several hours ahead of time to allow the seasonings to blend. Very hearty! Serve with rolls and a tossed salad.

                                        Pamela Wiseman

Cream of Mushroom Soup

6 tablespoons butter
½ cup finely chopped
   onion
2 cups finely chopped
   mushrooms

3 tablespoons flour
3 cups chicken stock
¾ cup light cream
   Freshly ground black
   pepper

In a heavy pan, melt butter and cook onion over medium heat until transparent. Add mushrooms and cook 5 minutes, stirring occasionally. Remove from heat and stir in flour. Add stock, stirring constantly. Place the pan back on the stove and bring stock to a boil. Stir again, reduce heat, and simmer 5 to 10 minutes. Add pepper to taste. Stir in cream before serving. Do not allow to boil once cream has been added. Preparation: 20 minutes. Serves 4.

                                        Almeda Peyton

Curried Apple and Onion Soup

1 bunch celery, chopped
½ medium onion, chopped
2 leeks, white part only, chopped
1 ounce cooking oil
4 ounces butter
½ cup flour
1 to 2 tablespoons curry powder
½ gallon chicken stock, hot

5 large onions, sliced
1 tablespoon butter
1 gallon chicken stock
3 Granny Smith apples, cored, quartered, and sliced
1 cup heavy cream
Salt to taste
Pepper to taste

Saute celery, onion, and leeks for 8 to 10 minutes in cooking oil. In a separate pot, make a roux by melting butter, then adding flour and curry powder, mixing thoroughly. Heat roux over medium heat for 10 to 15 minutes. Add ½ gallon boiling chicken stock to roux. Stir until smooth. Add sauteed vegetables and allow to simmer over medium heat for 45 minutes. Puree mixture in food processor. Keep hot.

In another heavy duty pot, saute sliced onions in butter until transparent. Add hot chicken stock and allow to simmer until liquid is reduced by ½ of original volume.

Combine puree of celery mixture and onion mixture. Add sliced apples and heavy cream. Adjust seasoning with salt and pepper. Serve piping hot.

The Trellis
Williamsburg, Virginia

Potato Soup

6 potatoes, peeled and
   diced
2 onions, chopped
1 carrot, peeled and
   sliced
1 stalk celery, sliced
4 chicken bouillon cubes
1 tablespoon parsley
   flakes

5 cups water
⅓ cup butter
1 tablespoon salt
½ teaspoon pepper
1 13-ounce can
   evaporated milk
Chopped chives

Put all ingredients except evaporated milk and chives in crock pot. Cover and cook on low 10 to 12 hours. (High for 3 to 4 hours). Stir in evaporated milk during last hour of cooking. Serve topped with chives. Preparation: 35 minutes. Serves 6 to 8.

Pat Morrison

Fresh Canadian Split Pea Soup

1 pound dry green split
   peas
1 meaty ham bone
1 cup chopped onion
1 cube chicken bouillon
1 cup sliced carrots
1 cup chopped celery
1 cup grated ham
   (optional)
2 slices bacon

½ cup cream
2 tablespoons butter
Sour cream
Sherry

In large pot, mix peas, ham bone, onion and bouillon with 8½ cups of water. Season with salt and pepper and bring to a boil. Cover, reduce heat, and simmer for 1½ hours, stirring often. Remove ham bone and dice meat. Return meat to soup. Add carrots, celery, and ham, and simmer for 30 minutes. Cook, drain, and crumble bacon. Add bacon, cream, and butter to soup. Garnish with sour cream, sherry, or both. Serves 8 to 10.

Flavor improves with age.

Gwen Weeks

Hearty Lentil Soup

2 tablespoons butter
1 cup cooked ham, cubed
1 cup onion, chopped
1 cup each, celery, carrots, cabbage, sliced
½ clove garlic, minced
½ cup lentils, rinsed
1 cup potatoes, peeled and cubed
1 bay leaf, broken in half
1 whole allspice

½ teaspoon sugar
1 teaspoon Worcestershire sauce
2½ cups water
1 10½-ounce can beef broth
1 cup V-8 juice
1 beef bouillon cube
Ground pepper
Chopped parsley

In a 4-quart heavy pot, lightly saute ham, onion, celery, carrots, cabbage, and garlic in butter for five minutes, stirring often. Cover and simmer five more minutes. Add remaining ingredients except parsley. Simmer covered for 1½ hours. Adjust seasonings. Remove bay leaf and allspice. Garnish with parsley. Preparation: 30 minutes. Serves 8 to 10.

A hearty and flavorful soup. Nutritious, too!

Ruth Hill

Spinach Soup

2 10-ounce packages frozen chopped spinach
1½ cups chopped onions
½ cup butter
6 tablespoons flour
6 cups chicken stock

¼ teaspoon nutmeg
¼ teaspoon dried parsley flakes
¼ teaspoon white pepper
½ cup sour cream

Thaw and drain spinach. Saute onions in butter until transparent. Add flour and mix well. Slowly add chicken stock to flour mixture. Add drained spinach and seasonings. Simmer ½ hour. Slowly blend in sour cream, a little at time. Cook 5 minutes. Garnish with fresh parsley. Preparation: 20 minutes. Serves 8.

Excellent for freezing.

Genya Glass

Peanut Soup

½ pound butter
1 onion, chopped
2 stalks celery, chopped
2 cups flour
1 pound peanut butter

1½ quarts chicken stock
1 pint heavy cream
½ cup chopped peanuts
Salt and pepper to taste

In deep soup pot, melt butter over medium heat. Add onion and celery and cook until onions are transparent. Add flour and cook 5 minutes, stirring frequently. Add peanut butter and cook 5 minutes, stirring frequently until smooth paste is derived. Add chicken stock for desired thickness and simmer 1 hour. Put mixture through fine sieve, season, add heavy cream, and serve in soup bowls. Sprinkle each bowl with chopped peanuts.

Cascades Restaurant
Williamsburg, Virginia

Miller & Rhoads' Brunswick Stew

2 5-pound stewing hens
4 quarts water
½ cup celery, diced
4 large onions, chopped
6 medium potatoes, peeled and diced
4 1-pound cans lima beans
2 1-pound cans whole-kernel corn

4 1-pound cans whole tomatoes
2 cups tomato puree
1 teaspoon salt
½ teaspoon pepper
1 stick margarine
¾ cup flour

Cut chicken into pieces and simmer in 4 quarts of water about 2¼ hours, until meat falls from the bone. Remove meat; strain and reserve stock. In same pot, simmer raw vegetables in stock until potatoes are tender. Bone chicken and pull meat apart into pieces. Add chicken meat, canned vegetables (undrained) and puree to pot. Add seasonings and simmer for 30 minutes. In small pan, melt margarine; add flour, and mix together until smooth. Continue stirring and cook for 5 minutes. Slowly add flour mixture to pot while stirring. Simmer all for 15 minutes. Remove and serve. Serves 16 to 20.

Flavor improves if made the day before and reheated.

Miller & Rhoads
Richmond, Virginia

Scotch Broth

1½ pounds lamb shoulder
2 to 3 pounds short ribs
 or chuck beef
¼ cup barley
½ cup split peas
2 large carrots, chopped
1 large onion, chopped
½ small rutabaga,
 chopped
6 to 8 leaves curly green
 kale, chopped
½ small cabbage, chopped
3 stalks celery, sliced

1 10-ounce package
 frozen peas and carrots
5 ounces Heinz "57"
 sauce
1 teaspoon salt
½ teaspoon black pepper
3 tablespoons fresh
 chopped parsley
1 bay leaf
1 pinch thyme
3 beef bouillon cubes
Snipped parsley for
 garnish

Cover meat with cold water and bring to boil. Skim foam. Cover and simmer 1 hour. Add all ingredients except frozen peas and carrots. Cook another hour. Remove meat, bone it and carve into bite-sized pieces. Return meat to pot and add frozen vegetables. Cook another 30 minutes. Adjust seasoning. Remove bay leaf and serve with snipped parsley. Preparation: 40 minutes. Serves 16.

To serve, place cooked, unpeeled, red potato in a bowl and pour broth over. After broth is eaten, potato is mashed in the bowl with a pat of butter. Broth freezes well. Flavors marry well if served the day after cooking.

Gale Cooper

Turkey Soup

Turkey Broth:

> **Leftover roasted
> turkey, bones and skin**

Remove turkey meat from bones and set aside for soup. Put bones and skin in a pot. Break up very large bones. Cover with water and simmer at least 4 hours. With large carcass, simmer 8 hours. Strain through colander and skim off excess grease.

Soup:

7 to 8 cups turkey broth	**¼ teaspoon paprika**
¼ cup carrots, chopped	**1 cup canned tomatoes,**
1 cup celery with leaves,	**chopped**
chopped	**½ bay leaf**
½ cup onion, chopped	**½ cup turnips, chopped**
¼ cup parsley, chopped	**Cooked turkey meat,**
3 tablespoons rice	**chopped**
½ teaspoon salt	

Combine all ingredients except turkey meat; simmer until vegetables are tender. Add enough chopped turkey meat to make a thick soup. Season to taste. Serves 8 to 10.

If you have leftover turkey gravy and dressing, add to soup.

Kay Williams

Beef Vegetable Soup

1 pound stew beef, cut
up
3 tablespoons oil
1 large potato, peeled
and cubed
1 large celery stalk,
chopped

1 large carrot, chopped
3 cups water
1 can succotash
1 large can tomatoes
1 15-ounce can V-8 juice
1 small can Le Sueur
peas, drained

Brown beef in oil. Combine beef, potato, carrot, celery, and water
in a large pot and simmer for 2 hours. Add succotash and
tomatoes and simmer 30 more minutes. Add V-8, peas, and
seasonings. Heat through. Serves 4 to 6.

Lyn Congdon

Swiss Cheeseburger Bisque

½ pound lean ground beef
⅓ cup onion, chopped
⅓ cup green pepper,
chopped
½ cup flour
4 cups milk

1 16-ounce can stewed
tomatoes
6 beef bouillon cubes (or
2 tablespoons granules)
1 cup Swiss cheese,
shredded

In a large saucepan, brown meat, onion, and green pepper. Stirring quickly to keep flour from lumping, sprinkle flour over meat
mixture and blend. Gradually stir in milk. Add tomatoes and
bouillon. Cook until mixture thickens, stirring occasionally. Fold
in cheese and heat until melted. Serve immediately. Preparation:
25 minutes. Yield: 1½ quarts.

Great Sunday night meal with salad and french bread.

Sue Schutt

Chilled English Stilton Soup

¼ pound butter
½ cup flour
1 tablespoon vegetable oil
2 medium onions, cut in chunks
4 stalks celery, cut in chunks
2 whole leeks, cut in chunks

½ gallon hot chicken stock
½ pound Monterey Jack cheese, grated
3 cups half-and-half
½ pound Stilton cheese, cut in small pieces
6 pears, cored and diced

In a heavy duty pot, melt butter; add flour to make roux. Cook thoroughly for 10 minutes. In a separate pot, heat oil and saute onions, celery, and leeks for 5 minutes. Add hot chicken stock to vegetables and bring to a boil. Stir boiling stock into cooked roux. Continue to stir until all stock is added and mixture is smooth. Allow to simmer for 15 minutes.

Remove pot from heat. Stir in Monterey Jack cheese. Strain soup through a china cap or a wide-meshed sieve. Cool soup in an ice bath. When soup is lukewarm, add half-and-half. When soup is thoroughly cooled, add diced Stilton. Adjust seasoning with salt and pepper. Before serving, add diced fresh pears. Yield: 8 to 12 servings.

Rather than serve crackers as an accompaniment to the soup, consider a small round flaky puff pastry with a touch of pear preserves. It all goes down quite well.

The Trellis
Williamsburg, Virginia

Leila's Cheddar Cheese Soup

4 tablespoons butter
1 medium onion, finely chopped
¼ cup all-purpose flour

3 cups chicken stock or canned chicken broth
3 cups milk
4 cups coarsely grated mild Cheddar cheese

In large saucepan, melt butter and cook onion until tender, about 5 minutes. Stir in flour and cook, stirring until blended. Add stock or broth gradually and cook, stirring constantly, until thickened. Stir in milk and bring mixture to a boil. Remove pan from heat. Add cheese, stirring until melted. If cheese does not melt completely, cook over low heat for 1 to 2 minutes. Serve immediately. Preparation: 25 minutes. Serves 6.

Leila Bristow

Wayside Inn Wine and Cheese Soup

¼ cup butter
6 leeks, trimmed, rinsed, and thinly sliced (about 5½ cups)
2 10¾-ounce cans Campbell's chicken broth
2 soup cans water

½ cup raw elbow macaroni, coarsely crushed and cooked
1 cup shredded Jarlsberg cheese
1 cup Chablis or other dry white wine

In a 4-quart saucepan over medium heat, cook leeks in hot butter until tender, about 20 minutes. Add broth and water. Heat to boiling. Reduce heat to low. Add macaroni, cheese, and wine. Heat, stirring until cheese melts. Garnish with additional cheese. Yield: 9 servings or 9 cups.

Wayside Inn
Middletown, Virginia

Clam Chowder

6 strips bacon, diced
1 medium onion, finely chopped
1 bottle clam juice
1 pint water
2 medium potatoes, finely chopped
1 pint whole milk

1½ tablespoons each melted butter and flour, mixed together to make a roux
1 quart shucked clams
2 pinches thyme
1 small can Carnation evaporated milk
Salt and pepper to taste

Saute bacon until cooked. Add onion and cook until soft. Add clam juice, water, and potato and cook until potato is soft. Scald whole milk. Stir roux mixture into milk and allow to thicken. Run clams through a coarse food chopper and add to cooked potato mixture. Add all spices and boil for 5 minutes. Turn down heat, add milk mixture and evaporated milk, and simmer 20 minutes. Preparation: 1 hour. Serves 6.

Betsy Veazey

Williamsburg Bisque of Hampton Crab

1 cup crabmeat	1¼ cups milk
1 can cream of mushroom soup	1 teaspoon Worcestershire sauce
1 can cream of asparagus soup	½ cup dry sherry
1 cup light cream	Dash of Tabasco

Blend all ingredients in blender. Heat but do not boil. Preparation: 15 minutes. Serves 8.

Becky Newman

Corn and Crab Soup

2 tablespoons oil	1½ tablespoons cornstarch (dissolved in ¼ cup water)
1 6-ounce package frozen crabmeat, thawed and drained	2 eggs, well beaten
1 teaspoon ground ginger	1 teaspoon salt (or to taste)
4 cups chicken stock	
1 16-ounce can cream-style corn	

In large pot, heat oil, crab, and ginger to enhance flavor. Add stock, corn, and bring to a boil. Stir in cornstarch mixture and cook until thickened. Remove from heat; add eggs in thin stream, beating constantly. Season with salt to taste and serve. Preparation: 20 minutes. Serves 6 to 8.

Minced green onions may be added for color.

Michael Robertson

Try one of the following combinations of flavors on your next sandwich. Instead of sliced bread, try bagels, English muffins, hard rolls, croissants, pita pockets or small loaves of French bread.

Tea Sandwiches

Cottage cheese mixed with chopped tomato or raspberries

Cream cheese and chutney or jelly

Sardines, watercress and onion

Mashed avocado, crumbled bacon and chili sauce

Ladyfingers split and spread with jam

Small canned shrimp mashed with mayonnaise and onion

Snappy cheese mixed with chopped nuts and pimento

Date nut bread with cream cheese spread

Salami and slices of cooked potato on rye

Sliced chicken, asparagus spear, olive rings and tomato slice

Hotel Roanoke ham biscuits: Prepare standard pie dough or biscuit dough recipe and roll very thin. Finely grind Smithfield ham and sprinkle with red pepper (boiled ham may be added to stretch recipe). Spread ham mixture on half of dough and fold remaining section over. Brush lightly with egg mixture (1 well-beaten egg mixed with a small amount of milk). Bake at 375° for 15 to 20 minutes.

Vegetable sandwich spread: Chop finely and mix 1 medium onion, 1 medium cucumber, 1 medium fresh tomato and 1 cup celery. Sprinkle with 2 teaspoons salt, stir and put in a collander over a bowl to drain juice (2 to 4 hours). Warm ½ cup of the juice and dissolve gelatin into it. Discard rest of juice. Mix vegetables, gelatin and mayonnaise and let sit in refrigerator overnight. Spread on 60 to 90 finger sandwiches.

Open-faced Sandwiches

Hard-cooked egg slices, tomato slices, onion rings on lettuce

Cucumber slices, sardines and chopped radishes

Sliced tongue, asparagus spear, mayonnaise, olive slices

Hard-cooked egg slices and caviar on lettuce

Smoked salmon slices, scrambled egg and chives on lettuce

Muenster cheese, tomato slice, mayonnaise, fresh dill

Combine crabmeat, grated Cheddar cheese, mayonnaise, celery, olives, green onions and garlic salt. Put mixture on buttered English muffins.

Spread pumpernickel bread with Thousand Island dressing. Add crabmeat, tomato slice and two strips of crisp bacon. Top with processed cheese and broil until cheese melts.

Sandwiches

Separate 4 English muffins into halves. On each half, place slice of tomato and half of artichoke heart. Combine 1¾ cups mayonnaise, 8 teaspoons chopped onion and 1½ cups grated Parmesan cheese. Spoon sauce on top and bake at 350° for 15 minutes.

Other Sandwiches

Camembert cheese and crisp bacon
Roquefort cheese, mayonnaise and chopped celery
Asparagus tips and chopped chives with mayonnaise
Cold meat loaf with Russian dressing
Lamb with curry mayonnaise
Pork and apple butter

Cream cheese with any one of the following: crushed pineapple, olives, dates, anchovy paste, a combination of sliced chicken and chopped green olives, a combination of deviled ham and catsup.

Chopped hard-cooked eggs and mayonnaise with one of the following: crumbled bacon, chopped olives, cooked chopped chicken livers, blanched almonds, sliced frankfurters, sliced ham, chopped green pepper on rye.

Homemade pimento cheese: 1 pound sharp cheese (grated), 1 cup salad dressing or mayonnaise, 1 tablespoon sugar, 1 7-ounce jar pimento (chopped or mashed), salt, pepper, Worcestershire sauce to taste.

Keep a stock pot in the freezer for future soups. Save the water from cooking mild-flavored vegetables and chicken.

To give a rich color to your soup or stew, brown meat first.

To thicken a stew or soup, add one slice of crustless bread and let simmer for 10 minutes. Stir.

Garnish soups with chopped parsley, sour cream, croutons, grated cheese, lemon slices or popcorn.

Make an herb bouquet by combining a pinch to a half teaspoon each of parsley, thyme, basil, marjoram, rosemary and savory. Tie mixture in cheesecloth and add to soups and stews.

Combine leftover green salad with tomato juice or bouillon in a blender for a delicious soup, hot or cold.

Tenderize stewing meat by using two cups hot tea as a cooking liquid.

Holding down paid or volunteer jobs outside their homes has cut deeply into the time women have for cooking these days. This is especially true when it comes to making extra concoctions like condiments.

But a lot of women feel their homemade pickles and jellies are better than anything sold in a store, and they make time to make grandmother's bread-and-butter pickles or momma's wine jelly.

Inns and resorts know, too, that dressings and relishes prepared in-house give their fare a better flavor. The Williamsburg Inn, in the restored town of Colonial Williamsburg, stakes its reputation on its house dressing.

Regency Dressing

1 tablespoon all-purpose flour	½ cup vegetable oil, divided
2 cups chicken stock, divided	2 tablespoons French-style prepared mustard
1 tablespoon onion, finely chopped	½ cup vinegar
1 clove garlic	1 egg yolk, lightly beaten
	Salt and pepper to taste

Mix flour thoroughly with ½ cup chicken stock. Bring remaining chicken stock to a boil and stir in flour mixture. Cook 5 minutes over medium heat, stirring constantly; remove from heat. Puree onion and garlic in ¼ cup vegetable oil in blender; transfer to mixing bowl. Add seasonings, vinegar, and egg yolk and mix. Add remaining oil very slowly, beating constantly. Add hot stock mixture while continuing to beat. Cool to room temperature before refrigerating. Yield: 3 cups.

This is our House Dressing. It goes exceptionally well with hearts of Boston lettuce, watercress, endive, or any combination of fresh vegetables.

The Williamsburg Inn
Williamsburg, Virginia

Asparagus Vinaigrette

2 pounds fresh asparagus   1 head of lettuce

Vinaigrette Dressing:

2 tablespoons lemon juice   1 teaspoon salt
2 tablespoons red wine   ½ teaspoon sugar
  vinegar   2 teaspoons Dijon
4 tablespoons olive oil   mustard
2 tablespoons vegetable   Pepper to taste
  oil

Cut asparagus into 3-inch pieces and boil slowly for 5 to 7 minutes in salted water until tender. Drain and cool. Combine dressing ingredients, and marinate asparagus in dressing for 1 hour at room temperature. Serve on a bed of lettuce. Serves 8 to 10.

Be careful not to overcook asparagus!

Linda Marks

Mushroom and Asparagus Curried Salad

2 cups asparagus, cut in-   1 teaspoon grated onion
  to 1½-inch pieces   ½ teaspoon sugar
¼ pound fresh mushroom   ¾ teaspoon lemon juice
  caps, sliced   Salt and pepper
¾ cup Hellman's   Lettuce
  mayonnaise   Fresh parsley
3 tablespoons sour cream
1½ teaspoons curry
  powder

Cook and chill asparagus. Mix remaining ingredients and combine with mushrooms and asparagus. Add salt and pepper to taste. Put on bed of lettuce and top with fresh parsley. Preparation: 15 minutes. Serves 4.

A must for curry fans!

Joan McEwan

Tasty Broccoli Salad

1 large bunch broccoli,
cut into bite-size
flowerets
½ cup Parmesan cheese,
freshly grated
½ cup sweet pickle relish
½ cup mayonnaise

½ cup sliced fresh
mushrooms
3 hard-boiled eggs,
chopped
2 tablespoons chopped
onion
Salt to taste

Combine all ingredients and mix well. Chill at least 3 hours. Serves 6 to 8.

Missy Buckingham

Fresh Broccoli Salad

1 bunch broccoli (tips
only, chopped)
1 head cauliflower
(optional)
½ cup chopped green
olives with pimento

¼ cup chopped onion
3 hard-boiled eggs,
chopped
1 bottle Italian dressing
3 tablespoons mayonnaise

Marinate all ingredients except mayonnaise in Italian dressing overnight. Drain marinade. Toss broccoli in mayonnaise and serve. Preparation: 1 hour. Serves 10.

Very unusual.

Micki Stout

Good and Easy Coleslaw

1 head cabbage
1 carrot
1 small onion
½ green pepper
1 cup mayonnaise

¼ cup vinegar
2 tablespoons sugar
1½ teaspoons celery seed
Salt and pepper to taste

Grate the first 4 ingredients and combine with the remaining ingredients, blending well. Preparation: 10 minutes. Serves 6 to 8.

Very good and very popular. A food processor makes it a quick dish.

Ann Haskell

Favorite Spinach Salad

Dressing:

1 cup oil
⅔ cup sugar
⅓ cup catsup

2 tablespoons
    Worcestershire sauce

Mix dressing ingredients together and chill.

Salad:

1 bag spinach, well
    washed
8 slices bacon, cooked
    crisp and crumbled

4 hard-boiled eggs,
    chopped
1 can sliced water
    chestnuts, drained

Tear spinach into pieces. Combine spinach, bacon, eggs, and water chestnuts in a salad bowl. Pour dressing over all and toss well. Serves 6 to 8.

Debbie Gibbs

Fire and Ice Tomatoes

6 firm ripe tomatoes,
    peeled and quartered
1 green pepper, seeded
    and cut in strips
1 red onion, cut in rings
¾ cup vinegar
1½ teaspoons celery salt

1½ teaspoons mustard seed
½ teaspoon fresh ground
    pepper
¼ cup water
6 teaspoons sugar
    Salt and Tabasco to
    taste

Combine vegetables in bowl. Mix together remainder of ingredients in saucepan and boil hard for 1 minute. Pour over vegetables and chill well. Serve in a lettuce cup or as a relish. Serves 6 to 8.

Summer tomatoes are a must!

Larkin Bynum

24 Hour Salad

1 head iceburg lettuce, chopped

1 10-ounce package frozen peas, thawed and drained

1 cup celery, sliced

1 cup green pepper, chopped

1 small onion, thinly sliced

10 strips bacon, cooked and crumbled

¾ cup Cheddar cheese, grated

Dressing:

2 cups mayonnaise

2 tablespoons sugar

¼ cup milk

1 pinch of salt

Mix dressing ingredients together and set aside.

In a large salad bowl, layer first 5 ingredients. Spread on dressing and top with bacon and cheese. Cover tightly with plastic wrap and refrigerate for 24 hours. Toss well before serving. Serves 10 to 12.

Fresh spinach may be substituted for lettuce, and fresh broccoli or cauliflower may be added if desired.

Karen Feigley

Tabouli Salad

1 cup bulghur (found in health food store)
½ cup fresh lemon juice (4 lemons)
½ cup good quality olive oil
1 pint cherry tomatoes, quartered
½ cup fresh mint, chopped
1 cup fresh parsley, minced
1 cup green onions, minced
1½ teaspoons seasoning salt
Pepper

Soak bulghur in 4 cups water about 2 hours and drain well. Add other ingredients and mix well. Refrigerate. Serves 8.

Can be made several days ahead. Good at room temperature also.

Bernice Pittman

Cucumbers in Sour Cream

2 cups vinegar
4 cups water
1½ cups sugar
¼ cup salt
4 cucumbers, sliced paper thin
1 sweet onion, sliced thin
½ cup sour cream
Fresh pepper to taste

Boil and cool the first 4 ingredients to make marinade. Place sliced cucumbers and onion in marinade overnight. Cover and chill. When ready to serve, drain marinade. Toss in sour cream and pepper. Preparation: 30 minutes. Serves 10.

Refreshing on a hot day.

Micki Stout

CC's Five Week Salad

1 cup sugar
½ cup vegetable oil
¾ cup vinegar
1 17-ounce can Le Sueur peas
1 16-ounce can French-style beans
1 small jar pimentos

1 16-ounce can shoe peg corn (small white corn)
1 cup chopped celery
1 cup thinly sliced carrots
1 cup green pepper, chopped
1 cup chopped onions

Boil sugar, oil, and vinegar until sugar dissolves. Combine remaining ingredients. Pour dressing over salad and allow to sit for several days. Serves 8 to 10.

Will keep for 5 weeks in refrigerator.

Judy Brooks

Authentic Greek Salad

3 large cucumbers
3 large tomatoes
1 large onion
8 to 10 pepperocinis (hot green peppers)
10 to 15 Kalamata olives

½ pound Feta cheese, sliced
4 to 8 tablespoons olive oil
Oregano

Chop cucumber into large cubes. Cut tomatoes into triangular pieces. Dice onion. Toss together in salad bowl. Sprinkle olives and peppers over and top with Feta cheese. Sprinkle oregano and pour olive oil over all. Toss. Preparation: 15 minutes. Serves 6 to 8.

Easy and delicious. Olives and pepperocinis can be found at an International Safeway.

Jane Helfrich

75

Potato Salad

8 medium new potatoes
⅓ cup clear Italian
   dressing
¾ cup celery, thinly
   sliced
⅓ cup green onions and
   tops, sliced

¾ cup mayonnaise
⅓ cup sour cream
⅓ cup cucumber, peeled,
   diced, and seeded
Salt and celery seed to
   taste
Pepper (optional)

Cook potatoes in jackets in slightly salted water for 30 minutes. Peel and chop potatoes while warm. Pour Italian dressing over potatoes and chill for 2 hours. Add celery and onion. Combine mayonnaise and sour cream and add to potatoes. Add salt and celery seed. Chill again for 2 hours. Add diced cucumbers and serve. Serves 6 to 8.

Dorothea Robertson

German Potato Salad

8 cups potatoes, cooked
   and sliced
1¼ cup bacon, chopped
2 large onions, finely
   chopped
¾ cup bacon drippings (or
   salad oil)

1 cup chicken stock base
3 cups hot water
¼ cup chives, chopped
1 cup apple cider vinegar

Combine the above and heat (may be served cold). Salt and pepper to taste. Serves 16.

The Hotel Roanoke
Roanoke, Virginia

Curried Rice Salad

4 cups canned chicken
  broth
2 cups uncooked rice
3 6-ounce jars marinated
  artichokes, reserve
  liquid
6 green onions, chopped
1 4-ounce jar pimento-
  stuffed green olives,
  sliced
1 green pepper, diced

3 large stalks of celery,
  diced
¼ cup chopped fresh
  parsley
2½ teaspoons curry
  powder
2 cups Hellman's
  mayonnaise
2½ teaspoons Lawry's
  seasoned salt

Bring chicken broth to a boil and stir in rice. Return to boil, then simmer 30 minutes or until liquid is absorbed. Cool. Drain artichokes, reserving liquid, and chop. Combine rice with artichokes, green onions, olives, green pepper, celery, and parsley. Combine reserved artichoke liquid, curry powder, mayonnaise, and seasoned salt. Refrigerate until serving time. Best if made 1 day ahead. Will keep for 2 days. Preparation: 45 minutes. Serves 12 to 14.

Looks pretty on a flat, leaf-lined platter decorated with parsley and paprika. Great for a party!

Bernice Pittman

Colorful Holiday Rice Salad

1 10-ounce package
  frozen peas, cooked
  and drained
3 cups cooked rice
1 4-ounce can diced
  pimento
1 cup diced baked ham
6 green onions, chopped
4 hard-boiled eggs,
  chopped

¾ cup green olives, sliced
½ cup chopped celery
⅓ cup sweet pickle relish
2 cups shredded Cheddar
  cheese
¼ cup mayonnaise

Combine all ingredients and mix well. Chill thoroughly. Serves 8.

May substitute chicken or shrimp for ham.

Jeanie Vertner

Chicken Salad Hawaiian

2½ cups chicken, cut into
    chunks
1 cup celery, diced
1 13-ounce can pineapple
    chunks
⅓ cup carrot, shredded
½ cup toasted almond
    slivers

½ cup mayonnaise
⅓ cup sour cream
1 teaspoon curry powder
1 teaspoon fresh lemon
    juice
½ teaspoon salt
Salad greens
Minced parsley

Combine chicken, celery, pineapple, carrots, and almonds; set aside. Mix mayonnaise, sour cream, curry, lemon, and salt. Pour over chicken and toss lightly. Arrange on greens and garnish with parsley. Preparation: 30 minutes. Serves 6.

Jane Helfrich

Summer Chicken Salad

¾ cup mayonnaise
½ teaspoon salt
¼ teaspoon white pepper
¼ teaspoon dry mustard
½ teaspoon granulated
    sugar
1 teaspoon cider vinegar
1 cup red apple, cubed,
    unpared
3 cups cooked chicken,
    cubed

1 cup sliced celery
1 cup seeded green
    grapes, sliced in half
½ cup pecan halves
2 apples, cut into wedges
6 small bunches of green
    grapes
Lemon juice to taste

In a small bowl, combine mayonnaise, salt , pepper, mustard, sugar, and vinegar. In large bowl, sprinkle 1 tablespoon lemon juice over apple cubes. Toss. Add chicken, celery, sliced grapes, and pecans. Stir in dressing and refrigerate. When serving, garnish chicken salad with apple wedges dipped in lemon juice and with grape bunches. Preparation: 35 minutes. Serves 6.

Becky Newman

Mary's Crab Salad

1 pound backfin
  crabmeat, fresh or
  canned
¾ cup celery, chopped
2 tablespoons chopped
  onion
2 tablespoons chopped
  green pepper

¾ teaspoon salt
1 cup shredded Cheddar
  cheese
1 cup mayonnaise
1 teaspoon Worcester-
  shire sauce
1 teaspoon Tabasco

Combine all ingredients and chill. Preparation: 15 minutes. Serves 4 to 6.

Good and very easy.

Charlotte Churchill

Shrimp and Rice Salad

2 cups shrimp, boiled,
  shelled and deveined
1 cup celery, chopped
3 scallions or green
  onions, chopped
1 bunch chopped chives,
  or 1 tablespoon dried
  chives
2 tablespoons chopped
  sweet pickle
2 eggs, hard-boiled,
  chopped (optional)

1 cup mayonnaise
½ teaspoon celery salt
½ teaspoon dried dill
  weed
1 cup rice, cooked and
  cooled
Salt and pepper to taste
Lemon juice to taste
(start with 2 tablespoons)
Toasted sesame seed
(optional)

Mix all ingredients except the shrimp. Fold in shrimp. Serve on lettuce and garnish with celery. Preparation: 20 minutes. Yield: 6 to 8 servings.

Nancy Payne

Curried Shrimp Salad

½ cup sour cream
¼ teaspoon salt
¼ teaspoon curry powder
1/8 teaspoon ground ginger

1 tablespoon fresh lemon juice
1 pound shrimp, cooked and shelled

Mix first 5 ingredients and chill ahead. Add shrimp and serve on lettuce. Preparation: 5 minutes plus chilling time. Serves 4.

Green grapes may also be added to this.

Molly Cates

Scotch Shrimp Salad

1½ pounds cooked shrimp
½ pound shell macaroni, large or small
5 celery ribs, diced

1 minced onion
1 green pepper, diced
1 cucumber, seeded and cubed

Boil shrimp with no flavoring. Cut shrimp in large chunks. Cook macaroni according to package directions; chill. Combine all salad ingredients.

Sauce:

½ cup mayonnaise (not Miracle Whip)
1 teaspoon dry mustard
1 teaspoon salt

2 tablespoons white vinegar
Pepper to taste
Green olives to garnish

Combine all sauce ingredients; mix well. Add sauce to salad. Chill for several hours, stirring one or two times. Taste again for salt. Garnish with green olives. Preparation: 30 minutes. Serves 6.

A chunky salad delight.

Carol Harding

Pasta and Seafood Salad

1 pound raw medium
shrimp, shelled
1 pound bay scallops,
rinsed
½ pound crabmeat (or
more)
½ pound pasta in in-
teresting shapes
1 cup tiny peas (fresh or
frozen)
½ cup diced sweet red
pepper

½ cup minced Bermuda
onion
½ cup good quality olive
oil
3 to 4 tablespoons lemon
juice
½ cup Basil Puree (below)
1 teaspoon salt
½ teaspoon pepper
1 cup imported black
olives

Drop scallops and shrimp in large pot of boiling, salted water. Boil 1 minute and drain. Cook pasta according to directions. Drain seafood and pasta very well and toss together. Add raw peas, red pepper, and onions and toss again. In small bowl, whisk olive oil, lemon juice, basil puree, salt and pepper. Pour over salad and toss again. Mound salad on platter and scatter olives on top. Serve at room temperature.

Basil Puree:

Blend 3 to 4 cups washed and dried fresh basil leaves or 3 to 4 cups fresh parsley leaves and 1 tablespoon dried basil with 2 to 3 tablespoons olive oil. Cover and refrigerate or freeze.

Lynn Congdon

Italian Salad

1 16-ounce can artichoke
hearts, drained
4 ounces sliced salami
¾ cup black pitted olives
¾ cup sliced fresh
mushrooms
½ cup Italian dressing
12 ounces macaroni

¾ cup sliced celery
½ green pepper, diced
1 cup cherry tomatoes
1 red onion, sliced thin
¼ cup Swiss cheese,
shredded
Salt and fresh pepper
Lettuce

In small bowl, place artichoke hearts, salami, olives, mushrooms, and dressing. Toss lightly and chill for one hour. Cook macaroni according to directions. Rinse in cold water until macaroni is cold. In large bowl, gently toss macaroni, celery, green pepper, tomatoes, salt, and pepper. Add marinated ingredients and toss. Garnish with cheese, red onions, and lettuce. Preparation: 30 minutes. Serves 10 to 12.

Ann Pastore

Pasta Salad Milanese

1 pound fresh spinach linguini, cut into 2-inch strips

⅔ pound fresh tomato linguini, cut into 2-inch strips

4 chicken breasts, boiled, boned, and cubed

1 cup finely chopped celery

1 8-ounce can sliced water chestnuts, drained

2 tablespoons soy sauce

½ cup raisins

½ cup chopped walnuts

1 11-ounce can mandarin oranges, drained

1 tablespoon lemon juice

Salt to taste

Curry dressing:

½ cup mayonnaise

1 tablespoon curry powder

Bring a large pot of water to a boil with 2 tablespoons salt. Add pasta and boil for 20 seconds. Drain immediately under cold running water. Set aside. Combine chicken, celery, water chestnuts and soy sauce in a big bowl and toss. Mix in pasta and dressing. Add remaining ingredients. Toss well and serve at room temperature. Serves 12.

Mainly Pasta, Richmond, Virginia

Party Pasta Salad

1 cooked chicken, boned and cubed

1 8-ounce package corkscrew macaroni, cooked and drained

2 tablespoons soy sauce

7 tablespoons vegetable oil

1½ teaspoons salt

2 large carrots, peeled and thinly sliced

½ pound mushrooms, washed and quartered

½ bunch broccoli, cut into bite-size flowerets

¼ head cauliflower, cut into bite-size flowerets

1 bunch green onions, cut into small pieces

Combine chicken, macaroni, soy sauce, 3 tablespoons vegetable oil, and ½ teaspoon salt. Mix and set aside. In a large frying pan or Dutch oven, saute carrots and mushrooms in 2 tablespoons oil and ½ teaspoon salt. Stir frequently until carrots are tender but crisp. Remove with slotted spoon to a large bowl. In the same pan, heat 2 more tablespoons oil. Add broccoli, cauliflower, and onions and stir to coat well. Pour in ¼ cup water and ½ teaspoon salt; cover and cook until vegetables are tender but crisp (5 to 10 minutes). Remove with slotted spoon to bowl containing carrots and mushrooms. Combine chicken mixture with vegetables and toss gently to mix. Chill well. Serves 6.

Terry Long

Zesty Pasta Salad

1 pound corkscrew
macaroni, cooked and
drained
⅔ jar McCormick's plain
Salad Supreme
seasoning
1 bottle Kraft Zesty
Italian salad dressing

1 cucumber, peeled and
diced
1 Bermuda onion, diced
1 green pepper, chopped
Cherry tomatoes,
halved

Mix all ingredients together and toss well. Refrigerate at least 1 hour before serving. Serves 12.

Any other fresh chopped vegetable may be added. Use your imagination and everyone will want the recipes! As a last-minute time saver, pasta may be cooked and mixed with seasoning and ½ bottle salad dressing the day before, adding rest of salad dressing and other ingredients prior to serving.   *Jeanie Vertner*

Spaghetti Salad

1 pound spaghetti
½ cucumber, chopped
1 bunch green onions,
chopped
½ large green pepper,
chopped
1 2-ounce can pimentos,
chopped
4 eggs, hard-boiled and
chopped
1 bunch radishes, thinly
sliced
1½ teaspoons salt

¾ teaspoon pepper
1 teaspoon sugar
½ teaspoon celery seed
1 large pinch powdered
oregano
2 cups mayonnaise
¾ cup sour cream
¾ cup half-and-half or
milk
4 tablespoons Durkee's
dressing
1 tablespoon French's
yellow mustard

Cook spaghetti according to package directions; drain and cool. Mix cucumber, green onions, green pepper, pimentos, eggs, and radishes thoroughly in a large bowl. Add spaghetti to vegetables. Add salt, pepper, sugar, celery seed and oregano. For dressing, combine mayonnaise, sour cream, half-and-half, Durkee's dressing, and mustard. Pour over spaghetti/vegetable mixture and toss until well blended. If dressing is too thick, add more milk or half-and-half. Stir well and add more half-and-half before serving. Spaghetti soaks up dressing. Preparation: 45 minutes. Serves 10 to 12.

Delicious for a large crowd. It's well worth the trouble!

Sue Reynolds

Seafood Aspic

1 large package lemon
  Jello
2½ cups hot water
2 8-ounce cans Hunts
  tomato sauce
2 tablespoons vinegar

½ teaspoon salt
¼ teaspoon garlic salt
1 cup celery, chopped
2 cups fresh medium
  shrimp, cooked and
  peeled

Dissolve Jello in water. Add tomato sauce, vinegar, and salts. Mix well. When slightly congealed, stir in celery and shrimp. Pour in 2-quart mold and chill until firm. Serves 8.

Variations: May omit shrimp for delightful tomato aspic! Can also add sliced green olives.

Gay Jewett

Two Layer Tomato Aspic

2 3-ounce packages
  lemon Jello
2 cups small curd cottage
  cheese
½ cup mayonnaise
¾ cup finely chopped
  green pepper
1 teaspoon grated onion

1½ teaspoons salt
1⅔ cups tomato juice
1 cup diced celery
1 cup boiling water
1 6-ounce jar marinated
  artichoke hearts,
  quartered

Add 1 cup of boiling water to 1 package lemon Jello. Let cool. In blender, puree cottage cheese until smooth. Combine mayonnaise, green pepper, grated onion, cottage cheese, and ½ teaspoon salt. Mix with cooled Jello and pour into 7-cup gelatin mold. Refrigerate until set, approximately 1½ hours.

Dissolve second package of lemon Jello in 1 cup hot tomato juice. Add ⅔ cup cold tomato juice, 1 teaspoon salt, and diced celery. Pour on top of first set layer. Place artichoke hearts on top. Refrigerate until set. Serves 12 to 15.

Great for buffets. Pretty and different.

Andy Bennett

Cucumber Mousse Salad

¾ cup shredded cucumber
1 3-ounce package lime Jello
¾ cup boiling water
¼ cup green onion, finely chopped

1 cup large curd cottage cheese
1 cup mayonnaise
1 teaspoon horseradish
¼ teaspoon salt

Seed and shred cucumber. Set aside. Dissolve Jello in hot water. Chill until partially set in mold. Combine shredded cucumber with other ingredients and pour into gelatin mixture. Refrigerate until set. Preparation: 30 minutes. Serves 6.

Nancy Gottwald

Molded Health Salad

1 3-ounce package lemon Jello
1 cup boiling water
1 cup pineapple juice
½ teaspoon salt
1 cup crushed pineapple, drained

2 cups raw carrots, grated
Paprika
Cottage cheese
Mayonnaise
Stuffed olives

Make Jello with boiling water, pineapple juice, and salt. When nearly set, add crushed pineapple and carrots. Pour into 8 individual ring molds (or an 8-cup mold) and chill. Unmold; fill center with cottage cheese mixed with mayonnaise. Top with stuffed olives; sprinkle with paprika. Serves 8.

Kay Williams

Blueberry Congealed Salad

2 3-ounce packages
raspberry Jello
1 16-ounce can blueberry
pie filling
1 16-ounce can crushed
pineapple

1 8-ounce package cream
cheese
1 cup sour cream
½ cup sugar
Nuts for topping

Dissolve Jello in 1 cup boiling water. Add blueberry pie filling and pineapple. Refrigerate to congeal. Mix cream cheese with sour cream until smooth. Add sugar. When salad is congealed, spread mixture on top and sprinkle with nuts. Refrigerate until ready to serve. Serves 6 to 8.

Delicious and easy!

Beth Skidmore

Bing Cherry Salad

2 16-ounce cans bing
cherries
1 3-ounce package lemon
gelatin

½ cup dry sherry
Pecans

Drain juice from cherries and bring ¾ cup of the juice to a boil. Remove and stir in gelatin to dissolve. Cool and add sherry. Arrange cherries and pecans to cover bottom of a small mold. Add gelatin mixture and refrigerate until firm. Serves 6 to 8.

Perfect combination of flavors. May top with whipped cream or whipped cream cheese.

Annette Chapman

Cranberry Buffet Salad

2 1-pound cans jellied
whole cranberry sauce
1 cup boiling water
2 3-ounce packages
raspberry Jello
1 cup rosé wine

1 cup cold water
1 cup chopped nuts
1 cup pineapple tidbits
1 cup diced celery
Lettuce
Sour cream

Crush cranberry sauce with fork and set aside. Pour boiling water over Jello and stir to dissolve. Add rosé wine, cold water, and cranberry sauce. Chill until mixture begins to thicken. Fold in nuts, pineapple, and celery. Turn into 2½-quart mold and chill until firm. Serve on crisp greens with sour cream as a topping. Preparation: 1½ hours. Serves 12.

Great for a different Thanksgiving dinner!

Jo Miller

Strawberry Pretzel Salad

2⅔ cups crushed pretzel
sticks
1½ sticks margarine,
melted
3 tablespoons sugar
1 8-ounce package cream
cheese, softened

1 cup sugar
2 cups Cool Whip
6 ounces pineapple juice
1 6-ounce box strawberry
Jello
2 10-ounce packages
frozen strawberries

To make crust, mix crushed pretzel sticks, margarine, and sugar and pat in 9 x 13-inch dish. Bake 10 minutes at 350º. Cool.

For the second layer, blend cream cheese and sugar. Add Cool Whip, blending well. Spread over crust and chill.

For the third layer, add water to pineapple juice to make 3 cups and boil. Add Jello and stir until dissolved. Add frozen strawberries. Mix well. Refrigerate for 30 minutes. Pour on top of other layers. Refrigerate for 4 hours. Serve that day or next day. (Pretzels get too soft after that.) Preparation: 1 hour. Serves 12.

Kids love it! Unusual sweet and salty flavor.

Pat Morrison

Poppy Seed Dressing

½ cup sugar (or less)
2 teaspoons dry mustard
2 teaspoons salt
⅔ cup vinegar
2 tablespoons grated
  onion (or 1 tablespoon
  dried minced onion)

2 tablespoons poppy
  seeds
2 cups Wesson oil

Blend first 6 ingredients in blender for 3 minutes. Add oil last and blend for 3 more minutes. Preparation: 10 minutes. Yield: 3¼ cups.

Especially good with spinach salad.

Jeanie Vertner

Spinach Salad Dressing

1 cup vegetable oil
5 tablespoons red wine
  vinegar
4 tablespoons sour cream
1½ teaspoons salt
½ teaspoon dry mustard

2 tablespoons sugar
2 tablespoons fresh
  parsley, chopped
2 cloves garlic, crushed
Coarsely ground pepper
to taste

Combine all ingredients and shake well. Chill. Preparation: 10 minutes. Yield: 1¾ cups.

This is enough for 2 10-ounce packages of fresh spinach. Add chopped hard-boiled eggs and crumbled bacon to spinach for a perfect salad!

Pat Short

Sweet and Sour Bacon Dressing

¾ pound lean sliced
  bacon
1 cup vinegar

¾ cup sugar
2 eggs, beaten

Cut bacon into ¼-inch pieces and fry in 2-quart saucepan until crisp. Reduce heat to low setting. Add vinegar to bacon and drippings, then stir in sugar and eggs. Cook, stirring constantly, until dressing begins to thicken. Serve warm over lettuce, spinach, or other fresh greens.

Joanne Smith

Louise's French Dressing

10 tablespoons olive oil
3 tablespoons shallot-
  flavored wine vinegar
2 tablespoons lemon juice

2 to 3 teaspoons Lawry's
  seasoned salt
Sugar (optional)

Mix ingredients and shake well. Preparation: 5 minutes. Yield: 1 cup.

Marinate vegetables for several hours. Then toss with lettuce for a delicious salad.

Stacy Fonville

French Dressing

⅔ cup catsup
⅔ cup sugar
½ cup vinegar
1 cup salad oil
2 teaspoons salt (if
  desired)

2 teaspoons paprika (if
  desired)
Grated onion to taste (if
  desired)

Mix all ingredients and chill. Preparation: 5 minutes. Yield: 2⅔ cups.

This makes a very good dressing for cole slaw.

Emily McLeod

Dressings

Tomato Salad Dressing

¾ cup salad oil
½ cup sugar
⅔ cup vinegar
1 small onion, grated
1 10-ounce can tomato
soup

1 teaspoon salt
1 teaspoon dry mustard
1 teaspoon Worcester-
shire sauce

Combine all ingredients and shake well. Refrigerate. Preparation:
5 minutes. Yield: 3¼ cups.

Beverley Shannon

Garlic Salad Dressing

2 cups olive oil
½ cup tarragon vinegar
¼ cup garlic cloves,
crushed
¼ cup fresh lemon juice
1 tablespoon Lawry's
seasoned salt

1 tablespoon dry mustard
1 teaspoon maple syrup,
honey, or sugar
Ground pepper to taste

Mix all ingredients together and shake vigorously. You may use
a blender. Chill at least 1 hour before serving. Preparation: 5
minutes. Yield: 3 cups.

Good on spinach salads.

Terry Tosh

Grandmother's Dressing for Avocados

½ cup catsup
½ cup red wine vinegar

½ cup red currant jelly
½ cup strong beef
bouillon

Combine ingredients in top of double boiler and melt. Serve warm
in bowls of fresh halved avocados. Preparation: 10 minutes. Yield:
2 cups.

Keeps for months in refrigerator.

Terry Tosh

Honey Dressing

⅔ cup sugar
1 teaspoon dry mustard
1 teaspoon paprika
¼ teaspoon salt
1 teaspoon celery seed

⅓ cup strained honey
5 tablespoons vinegar
1 tablespoon lemon juice
1 teaspoon grated onion
1 cup salad oil

Mix dry ingredients. Add honey, vinegar, lemon juice, and grated onion. Pour oil into mixture very slowly, beating constantly with rotary beater. Refrigerate. Preparation: 10 minutes. Yield: 1 pint.

Make the day before serving for best flavor. Will keep indefinitely. Very good on peaches.

Frances Harris

Poppy Seed Dressing for Fruit

½ cup vinegar
1 teaspoon salt
1 cup honey
1⅓ cups vegetable oil

1¼ teaspoons dry mustard
2 teaspoons dried poppy seeds
1 tablespoon grated onion

Mix vinegar, salt, and honey in pan. Heat until all salt granules are dissolved. Pour into quart jar. Add remaining ingredients and shake until well mixed. Keep stored in refrigerator. Always shake before using. Preparation: 20 minutes. Yield: 2½ cups.

Serve over fruit in a salad or use as a dip for fruit at cocktail parties.

Payne Tyler

Condiments

Sweet Pickles

4 quarts cucumber slices
(¼-inch thick),
unpeeled
7⅓ cups vinegar
3 tablespoons salt
1 tablespoon mustard
seed

6 cups sugar
2¼ teaspoons celery seed
1 tablespoon whole
allspice

Simmer cucumber slices in 4 cups vinegar with salt, mustard seed, and ¼ cup sugar until slices turn slightly yellow (about 15 minutes). Cook in covered pot. Do not overcook. Drain, discarding liquid. Spoon slices into hot, sterilized jars. Bring to a boil 3⅓ cups vinegar, 5¾ cups sugar, celery seed and allspice. Pour over pickles. Seal at once and process in boiling water bath in canner for 5 minutes. Remove jars from canner. Yield: 5 pints.

Susan Jenkins

Watermelon Rind Pickles

2 pounds watermelon
rind
¼ cup salt
1 quart water
2 pounds sugar
1 pint water
1 pint vinegar

1 lemon, thinly sliced
1 tablespoon ground
cinnamon
1 tablespoon whole
cloves
1 tablespoon allspice
1 tablespoon ginger root

Soak watermelon rind overnight in brine made of ¼ cup salt and 1 quart water. Drain brine and rinse in cold water 1 hour. Cook rind over medium heat in enough water to cover until tender, approximately 1 hour. Remove tender rind and drain. Combine remaining ingredients to make a hot pickling solution. Cook over medium heat for 20 minutes. Add rind and cook over medium heat until clear. Remove spices from rind and pour into sterilized jars, covering each with a slice of lemon and syrup. Seal at once. Yield: 4 pints.

Spices should be wrapped together in cheese cloth.

Dorothea Robertson

Pickled Okra

2 pounds fresh baby okra
6 cloves garlic
6 hot green peppers
3 teaspoons dill seed
1 quart vinegar
1 cup water
½ cup salt

Cut stems from okra, being careful not to open cavity of pods. Pack each sterilized pint jar tightly with okra, 1 clove garlic, 1 pepper and ½ teaspoon dill seed. Boil vinegar, water and salt and pour over okra. Cap and seal. Immerse in hot water and simmer 10 minutes. Let set 3 weeks. Yield: 6 pints.

Great hors d'oeuvre.   *Robin Traywick Williams*

Squash Pickles

4 cups yellow squash (or zucchini), thinly sliced
1 green pepper, diced
2 cups cider vinegar
3 cups sugar
2 teaspoons mustard seed
2 teaspoons celery seed
1 cup onions, sliced into rings
Salt to taste

Put squash in bowl; cover well with salt. Let stand for 1 hour. Rinse lightly with cold water to remove some of the salt. Combine green pepper, vinegar, sugar, mustard and celery seed and bring to a boil. Boil 2 minutes. Add squash and onions and bring back to a boil. Remove from heat and pack while hot into sterilized jars. Seal. Yield: 2 pints.

Frances Gordon

Apple Chutney

6 cups apples, peeled and chopped
1½ cups raisins
1 to 2 cloves garlic, minced
1 cup minced onion
2 ounces crystalized ginger, chopped, or 3 ounces fresh ginger, sliced

½ teaspoon cinnamon
½ teaspoon ground cloves
2¼ cups brown sugar
2 cups cider vinegar
Grated rind and juice of 1 lemon

In large stainless steel or enamel kettle, combine all ingredients and bring to a boil. Simmer uncovered until fruit is tender and chutney is thick. Pour into hot sterilized jars and seal. Yield: 3½ quarts.

Nice accompaniment for pork roast and ham.

Ann Gray Wood

Peach or Pear Chutney

2 cups sugar
1¼ cups white vinegar
¼ cup Sauterne
2 oranges, seeded and diced with rind
1 lemon, seeded and diced with rind
1 lime, diced with rind

1 medium onion, diced
1 clove garlic, diced
1 cup white raisins
2¾ ounces crystalized ginger, diced
2½ pounds peaches or pears, peeled and diced

Bring sugar, vinegar, and Sauterne to a boil and cook 10 to 15 minutes. Add remaining ingredients and simmer 30 minutes. Pour into sterilized jars and seal. Yield: 2½ quarts.

Michael Robertson

Cold Tomato Relish

1 gallon ripe tomatoes	½ cup black mustard seed
1 cup salt	½ cup yellow mustard
3 large onions, sliced	seed
3 large green peppers, sliced	½ cup brown sugar
1 tablespoon celery seed	Vinegar to cover tomatoes

Dip tomatoes in boiling water and remove skins. Cut tomatoes into wedges and stir in salt. Set aside for 30 minutes. Drain salt from tomatoes with hands and pour into large kettle. Add onions, green peppers, herbs, sugar and vinegar to cover all and bring to a boil. Simmer 10 minutes and pour into sterilized jars. Seal at once and store. Refrigerate overnight before serving. Yield: 5½ quarts.

A delicious old family recipe!

Jane Hall

✿ Rosy Relish

2¼ cups sugar	1½ cups vinegar (dark)
1 cup green pepper, chopped	4 cups tomatoes, peeled and chopped
4 1-inch cinnamon sticks, broken	2 cups green cooking apples, peeled and chopped
2 tablespoons mustard seed	1 cup celery, chopped
10 cloves	2 tablespoons sweet red pepper
1 tablespoon salt	

Combine all ingredients. Bring to a boil in an uncovered pot. Simmer until thick (about 4½ hours). Stir every 15 minutes. The last hour really watch your pot so that it does not burn. Cool and put in sterilized jars, leaving 1/8-inch head space. Yield: Approximately 4 half-pint jars.

This recipe can be doubled or tripled. An excellent relish for hamburgers and hot dogs. Also good as an hors d'oeuvre served on cream cheese with crackers. An old Virginia recipe.

Cabell West

Cranberry Relish

1 1-pound package fresh
   cranberries
1 orange, unpeeled,
   quartered and seeded
½ lemon, unpeeled,
   quartered and seeded

1½ cups sugar
1 teaspoon ground
   cinnamon
½ teaspoon ground cloves

Wash and clean berries. Put cranberries, orange and lemon pieces though a food grinder together. Mix sugar and spices and add to cranberry mixture. Chill and serve with meats or bread. Keeps almost indefinitely covered in refrigerator. Yield: 1 quart.

Beth Deane Gallimore

Cranberry-Orange Chutney

1 cup fresh orange
   sections
¼ cup orange juice
4 cups cranberries
2 cups sugar
1 cup apple, unpeeled
   and chopped

½ cup raisins
¼ cup walnuts, chopped
1 tablespoon vinegar
½ teaspoon ground ginger
½ teaspoon ground
   cinnamon

Combine all ingredients in a large saucepan and bring to a boil. Reduce heat and simmer 5 minutes or until berries begin to burst. Pour into hot sterlizied jars and seal. Yield: 5½ cups.

A nice change from cranberry sauce.

Jane Helfrich

Fig Preserves

5 pounds figs   3 lemons, sliced
5 cups sugar

Wash figs and remove stems. Add sugar. Add lemons and simmer uncovered for 2½ to 3 hours until cooked down and thickened. Pour in hot sterilized jars. Yield: 4 to 5 pints.

Michael Robertson

Peach Conserve

1 orange   ½ cup pecans
½ cup water   5½ cups sugar
3 pounds peaches   1 box Sure-Jell
½ cup raisins or bing
   cherries

Slice orange very thin. Simmer in ½ cup water for ½ hour. Peel and chop peaches. Place in large kettle. Add orange slices, raisins or cherries, and nuts. Stir in box of Sure-Jell. Bring to full boil over high heat, stirring constantly. Stir in sugar and bring to full rolling boil that cannot be stirred down. Boil hard 1 minute. Skim off foam. Pour into sterilized jars. Yield: 5 pints.

Gwen Weeks

Hot Pepper Jelly

6 medium green or red   3 cups cider vinegar
   peppers, chopped   2 bottles Certo
10 cups sugar   8 drops red or green food
1½ tablespoons Tabasco   coloring
   sauce

Puree peppers in blender or food processor. Pour into large saucepan and stir in sugar, vinegar and Tabasco sauce. Bring to a boil, stirring constantly, for 5 minutes. Remove from heat. Skim and add Certo. Add food coloring and boil 1 minute. Pour into hot sterilized jars and seal. Yield: 6 pints.

Pour over cream cheese and serve with crackers.

Jane Ruth

Corn syrup or honey may be substituted for ½ the amount of sugar called for in a salad dressing for fruit. Reduce the liquid by ¼.

Soak cucumbers in salt and water an hour before using. They are more digestible.

Use an egg slicer to slice raw mushrooms.

To peel oranges for a fruit salad, drop into boiling water before cutting. They peel perfectly.

Put a clove of garlic in a bottle of French dressing to improve the flavor.

Salt wilts lettuce in a short time and makes it tough. Consequently, salt should not be used on a lettuce salad until immediately before it is served.

If you slice bananas with a silver knife, they will not turn dark as rapidly.

To clean blender, put in some water and a few drops of detergent and blend.

Pickles and relishes should be subjected to a boiling water bath 15 minutes for pint jars, 20 minutes for quarts.

Because of the acids involved in pickle-making, be sure your equipment for brining is stoneware, pottery or glass, and that your pickling kettles are stainless steel or enamel.

For best results, pickle only vegetables and fruits that are in prime condition and were harvested no more than 24 hours before pickling.

Use only pickling or dairy salt, free from additives which might deter processing of pickles.

To make pickles crisp, wash unsprayed grape or cherry leaves and layer them with cucumbers during the brining process. Discard leaves when making the pickles. Lime and alum are not recommended for crisping.

To determine if fruit juice contains a sufficient amount of pectin to gel, put 1 tablespoon of the cooled fruit juice in a glass. Add the same quantity of grain alcohol and shake gently. The effect of the alcohol is to bring the pectin together in a transparent glob. If a large quantity is present, it will appear in a single mass when poured from the glass. This indicates that equal quantities of sugar and juice should be used. If the pectin does not form a mass, less sugar will be required. If it collects in two or three masses, use ⅔ to ¾ as much sugar as juice; if in smaller, more numerous particles, use ½ as much sugar as juice, unless the fruit is very tart.

Breads

Bread

Hot bread is as Southern as hot weather, although you'll get more variety with the bread than the weather.

There's the slightly sweet and cake-like Sally Lunn, a bread recipe older than the Old Dominion. The colonists brought it with them from Europe, where street vendors sold it as "sol et lune," fresh bread with a golden top and white bottom.

Then there are light biscuits and beaten biscuits. There are corn bread and corn sticks. And the garden inspires potato rolls, zucchini bread and a pastry tray full of berry muffins and nut breads.

Shoppers and sightseers in downtown Richmond often stop at Miller & Rhoads' Tea Room for lunch just to get that quintessential Southern dish, spoonbread.

Old Virginia Spoonbread

4 cups milk
1 cup yellow corn meal
1½ teaspoons salt
½ cup water

4 egg yolks, beaten
4 egg whites
1/8 teaspoon cream of tartar

Scald milk. Mix salt and corn meal with water and stir into milk. Cook until thickened. Remove from heat. Add a small amount of hot corn meal to egg yolks, then stir yolks into hot corn meal. Add cream of tartar to egg whites. Whip until stiff but moist. Fold whites into corn meal and pour into a 2 qt. casserole greased pan. Bake at 350° for 30 min. or until light brown and a knife inserted in center comes out clean.

Miller & Rhoads' Tea Room
Richmond, Virginia

Traditional Sally Lunn

1 yeast cake
2 tablespoons sugar, level
4 tablespoons butter, melted
4 to 5 cups sifted flour

1 teaspoon salt, level
3 eggs
2 cups milk, warmed and divided

Dissolve yeast and sugar in a little milk. Add butter, then flour and salt gradually, beating smooth all the time. Beat eggs well. Add milk. Beat smooth. Add to first mixture, beating until completely smooth. (This is the secret of good Sally Lunn.) Pour into greased bowl. Let rise until twice its bulk; stir down. Put in well-greased 9 to 10-inch tube pan. Let rise until doubled. Bake at 325º for 35 to 40 minutes. Yield: one loaf.

Put down at 10:30 a.m. for supper. This recipe, circa 1915, from the collection of Mildred Boyd Hayes.

Mildred Boyd Davis

Anadama Bread

7 to 8 cups unsifted flour, divided
1¼ cups yellow corn meal
2½ teaspoons salt
2 packages dry yeast
½ cup softened margarine

2¼ cups very warm tap water (120 to 130º Fahrenheit)
⅔ cup molasses (room temperature)

In large bowl, thoroughly mix 2½ cups flour, corn meal, salt and dry yeast. Add margarine. Gradually add tap water and molasses to dry ingredients and beat 2 minutes at medium speed of electric mixer. Scrape bowl occasionally. Add ½ cup flour. Beat at high speed 2 minutes. Stir in enough flour to make a stiff dough. Turn out on floured board; knead until smooth and elastic, about 8 to 10 minutes. Place in greased bowl, turn to grease top. Cover; let rise in warm place until doubled in bulk, about 1 hour. Punch dough down; halve dough. Roll each half to a 14 x 9-inch rectangle. Shape into loaves. Place in two greased 9 x 5 x 3-inch loaf pans. Let rise about 45 minutes. Bake at 375º for about 45 minutes. Remove from pan and cool on wire rack. Yield: 2 loaves.

Jane Johnson

English Muffin Bread

5½ cups flour, divided
2 packages dry yeast
1 tablespoon sugar
2 teaspoons salt
¼ teaspoon soda
2 cups milk
½ cup water
Corn meal

Mix 3 cups flour with other dry ingredients. Heat milk in water to 125°, then add to flour mixture. Mix until smooth; then add 2½ cups flour, stirring well. Grease 2 Pyrex loaf pans and sprinkle with cornmeal. Evenly divide batter between pans and let rise 45 minutes. Preheat oven to 400° and bake 25 minutes. Cool 1 minute and turn onto a rack. Yield: 2 loaves.

Sally Erickson

Irish Soda Bread

4 cups buttermilk
2 eggs
¼ teaspoon baking soda
7 cups flour
2 cups raisins
½ cup sugar
5 teaspoons baking powder
2 teaspoons salt

Beat together buttermilk, eggs, and ¼ teaspoon baking soda; set aside. In a large bowl, combine remainder of ingredients. Stir buttermilk and flour mixtures together and mix well. Pour into 3 greased and floured large loaf pans. Bake in a 375° oven for 45 minutes to an hour (till dark golden brown). Yield: 3 large loaves.

This bread has a very pleasant flavor and is a nice substitute for regular dinner rolls.

Michael Robertson

101

Yorkshire Pudding

1 cup flour, double sifted
½ teaspoon salt
3 eggs, slightly beaten
1 cup milk

Crisco
Pan drippings from
roast of beef

Preheat oven to 450°. Grease a round 1½-quart casserole dish with Crisco. Pour ¼ cup drippings into casserole dish. Place in oven to heat. Combine remaining ingredients in mixing bowl and beat just until smooth. Fill heated casserole dish half full, bake 25 minutes. Serve hot. Preparation: 20 minutes. Serves 6 to 8.

Serve with butter or gravy. Variation: Use ramekins in place of casserole.

Maria Tabb

Honey Whole Wheat Bread

3½ to 4 cups all-purpose
flour, divided
2½ cups whole wheat flour
2 packages active dry
yeast
1 tablespoon salt

1 cup milk
1 cup water
½ cup honey
3 tablespoons shortening
1 egg

In a large bowl, combine 1 cup all-purpose flour, whole wheat flour, yeast and salt; mix well and set aside. In a saucepan, heat milk, water, honey, and shortening until warm. (Shortening does not need to melt.) Add, with egg, to dry ingredients. Blend dough until moist, then beat at medium speed for 5 minutes. By hand, gradually add remaining flour. Turn dough out and knead on floured surface until smooth and elastic (About 5 minutes.) Place in greased bowl, turning to grease top. Cover and let rise until doubled in bulk (about 1 hour). Punch dough down and divide. Roll each half to 14 x 7 inches. Roll up, pinch ends and place in 2 greased large loaf pans. Cover and let rise again until double, about 30 minutes. Bake in a preheated 375° oven for 35 to 40 minutes. Yield: 2 large loaves.

Trudie Steel

Cheese Bread by Betty T.

2 cups Cheddar cheese, grated
3 tablespoons sugar
⅓ cup butter, softened
2 teaspoons salt
3 cups hot water
2 packages active dry yeast
⅓ cup lukewarm water
3 large eggs
½ cup nonfat dry milk
10 cups flour
2 medium cloves garlic
½ cup butter

Combine first 5 ingredients and stir until well blended. Set aside to cool. Dissolve yeast in warm water and stir into cooled cheese mixture. Add eggs and mix well. Sift flour and dry milk together. Stir approximately 7 cups of the flour mix into cheese batter. Blend until smooth. Add additional flour until you have a medium stiff dough. Turn dough out onto a floured surface and knead for 5 minutes. Place dough in a large buttered bowl, cover and let rise until doubled in bulk (about 60 minutes). Punch dough down, turn out again on floured surface, and divide into 5 loaves. Let loaves rest for 10 minutes. Melt the ½ cup of butter and garlic together, and butter 5 small loaf pans. Place dough in pans, and let rise again until double in bulk (about 45 minutes). Bake at 400⁰ for 30 to 35 minutes, or until brown. Yields: 5 small loaves.

Don't give all these away! Freezes beautifully.

Frances Kusterer

Corn Bread

1 cup self-rising corn-meal, or 1 box Flako corn muffin mix
1 8-ounce container sour cream
1 8-ounce can cream-style corn
4 eggs, beaten
½ cup vegetable oil

Mix all ingredients together and pour into greased 9 x 13-inch Pyrex pan. Bake approximately 25 minutes in 350⁰ oven. Cut in squares or strips and serve immediately.

After bread has cooled, it may be sliced, buttered and reheated. Delicious served with jam.

Susan Walton

103

Breads

Authentic French Bread

2 cups warm water (75°)
⅔ cup warm beer
1 tablespoon dry yeast or
  1 ounce fresh yeast
2 tablespoons whole
  wheat flour, heaping

3 to 4 cups white,
  unbleached flour
3 teaspoons salt
  Additional flour for
  kneading

Sponge Starter: 12 to 24 hours before you bake the bread, put 2 cups of warm water (75°) and ⅔ cup warm beer in a large bowl. Add yeast. Let dissolve. Stir. Add whole wheat flour, then stir in enough white, unbleached flour (3 to 4 cups) to resemble slightly watery oatmeal. Place a towel over the bowl. Let rest on a kitchen counter until needed.

When ready to make bread, take the starter and pour a thick coating of flour over it. Sprinkle on 3 teaspoons salt. Stir and mix until you can turn the dough out onto a floured surface. Begin kneading, adding more flour as you go until you have a medium firm mass that no longer will stick to your hand. Knead vigorously for 10 to 12 minutes. After bread is well kneaded, place it back in its bowl and cover with a towel. Let rise until doubled (at least one hour).

Take the dough and form it into a shape on an oiled baking pan. Make deep decorative cuts with knife. Let bread rise until almost the shape it will be after baking. Bake in a preheated 375° to 400° oven for about 1 hour. For the first 10 minutes, spray water frequently onto the bread itself and onto the oven bottom to cause steam. When done it should thump like a hollow door. Let bread rest at a tilt so that steam doesn't soften the bottom crust. Preparation: 1 day. Serves 8 or more, depending on thickness of slices.

Can be baked on a stoneware bread tile. If less than 15-inches in diameter, encircle tile with foil to prevent overflow.

Meg Roach

Michie's Christmas Bread

Biscuits:

2 cups flour
1 cup milk
3 tablespoons butter or
margarine

1 teaspoon salt
1 teaspoon baking
powder
1 teaspoon baking soda

Icing:

¾ cup walnuts, chopped
½ cup confectioners sugar
¼ cup raisins
½ cup candied red cherries, chopped

½ cup milk
½ teaspoon lemon extract

Combine first 6 ingredients, mixing well, and roll out ½-inch thick on a floured board. Cut with a biscuit cutter. Bake at 500° for 7 minutes. Remove biscuits from oven and cool.

Combine icing ingredients and mix well. Ice biscuits when they are sufficiently cool.

On the Tavern's first Christmas in the 1700's, legend claims that the doors were left open to greet friends and weary travelers. The Michies prepared a special bread as a gift for all to enjoy and it was called "The Christmas Welcoming Bread". The old inn still prepares this bread and serves it to guests during Yuletide.

Historic Michie Tavern
Charlottesville, Virginia

Monkey Bread

3 cans Pillsbury Butter-
   milk Biscuits
1½ teaspoons cinnamon
1 cup sugar

1 stick butter
¾ teaspoon vanilla
   Pecans (optional)

Preheat oven to 350°. Cut each biscuit in half; combine sugar and cinnamon in a plastic bag; coat biscuit halves with cinnamon/sugar mixture. Meanwhile, melt butter, add vanilla. Lightly grease a tube pan. Lay biscuits in pan in layers. Sprinkle with remaining cinnamon and sugar. If desired, lay pecans on top. Pour melted butter/vanilla mixture over all. Bake for 30 to 35 minutes. Yield: 1 loaf.

Looks pretty cooked in bundt pan. Variation: 1 cup Parmesan, 1 teaspoon Lawry's, 1 cup paprika in place of cinnamon, sugar and vanilla.

Suzanne Lewis

Potato Rolls

3 medium potatoes
½ cup sugar
⅔ cup shortening
2 eggs
1 package active dry
   yeast

1½ cups potato water,
   cooled
1 teaspoon salt
5 cups flour
   Butter, melted

Peel potatoes and boil until tender. Remove potatoes, reserving water, and mash. In a large bowl, cream sugar and shortening together. Add eggs and beat well. Mix in 1 cup warm mashed potatoes. In another bowl, dissolve yeast in measured potato water. Combine water and salt and mix well. Alternately add flour and yeast water to potato mixture. Knead well.

To form rolls, pinch off dough into desired shapes and let rise on a greased cookie sheet or in muffin tins for about 2½ hours. Bake at 425° for 12 minutes, brushing tops with melted butter half way through cooking time. Yield: 4 dozen.

Unrisen dough may be stored in refrigerator for 5 days. Just pinch off rolls as needed.

Susan Overton

Rolls

6 cups flour, sifted
1 cup shortening
½ cup sugar
2 packages or cakes yeast

2 teaspoons sugar
2 eggs
1 tablespoon salt

Sift flour, then dribble into measuring cup (too much flour makes heavy rolls). Cream 1 cup shortening with ½ cup sugar. Pour 1 cup boiling water over; stir and cool. Dissolve yeast in 1 cup warm water (105° to 115°) with 2 teaspoons of sugar. Set aside. Beat 2 eggs well. Add salt and the 6 cups of flour alternating with liquids; add yeast mixture last. Dough will be soft. Cover and refrigerate overnight.

Next day melt stick of butter. Roll half of dough on floured surface and cut using a large biscuit cutter. Spread each side of circle of dough with melted butter. Partially cut and fold over (envelope style). Place on greased bread pan. Cover with dry cloth. Let rise about 1 hour. Bake at 425° for 10 to 20 minutes. Preparation: Overnight. Yield: 4 dozen.

Check often, will burn quickly. May freeze after baking.

Sarah Drummond

Buttermilk Biscuits

4 cups flour
2 tablespoons baking powder
1 teaspoon baking soda
¾ teaspoon salt

1 tablespoon sugar
⅔ cup butter, softened
1½ cups buttermilk
Melted margarine

Combine dry ingredients; cut in butter. Add buttermilk, stirring until moistened. On lightly floured board, knead 4 to 5 times. Cut biscuits rather thickly and put on lightly greased cookie sheet. Brush top with margarine and bake in preheated 450° oven for 10 to 15 minutes. Yield: 24 biscuits.

Gay Jewett

Thalhimers' Richmond Room Popovers

15 eggs
10 cups of milk
10 cups of flour
2 teaspoons salt

½ cup of margarine
1 teaspoon of baking
powder

Mix well and beat for 20 minutes at medium speed. Grease regular muffin tins well with margarine or Pam. Preheat oven to 475° and preheat pans. Bake for 20 minutes. Reduce temperature to 350° and bake for 20-30 minutes or until brown.

The secret is lots of eggs and lots of beating!

Thalhimers
Richmond, Virginia

Popovers

1 cup milk
1 tablespoon salad oil
2 eggs
1 cup all-purpose flour,
   sifted

½ teaspoon salt
Crisco

Preheat oven to 425°. Using wire whisk, mix milk, eggs, and oil until well blended. Combine salt and flour in separate bowl. Add ½ dry ingredients to liquid and beat. Add remaining ½ and mix until blended, but lumpy. Grease large muffin tins with Crisco vegetable shortening. Fill tins to top with batter. Bake 20 minutes. Reduce temperature to 350° and bake for 35 minutes. Do not open oven door when temperature reduced. Preparation: 15 minutes. Yield: 6 to 9.

Serve with butter or honey. Excellent filled with seafood sauce.

Genya Glass

Crumbsnatchin' Apple Bread

½ cup butter, softened
1 cup sugar
2 eggs, beaten
1 teaspoon vanilla
½ teaspoon salt
1 teaspoon baking soda, dissolved in 2 table- spoons milk

2 apples, peeled and diced
2 cups sifted flour

Topping:

2 tablespoons butter
2 tablespoons sugar

2 tablespoons flour
1 teaspoon cinnamon

Cream together the first 6 ingredients. Add apples and flour and mix well. Turn into 2 small (or 1 large) greased and floured loaf pans. Mix together topping ingredients. Dot top of batter and bake for 1 hour at 325°. Yields: 1 large or 2 small loaves.

A real breakfast treat and exceptional with pork for supper.

Frances Kusterer

Mother's Nut Bread

3 cups sifted flour
1½ cups sugar
4 teaspoons baking powder
2 teaspoons salt

1 egg
¼ cup melted shortening
1½ cups milk
1 teaspoon vanilla
1½ cups chopped walnuts

Resift flour with sugar, baking powder, and salt. Add egg, shorten- ing, milk, and vanilla. Stir until moistened. Stir in walnuts. Bake in loaf pan for 1 hour and 20 minutes at 350°. Preparation: 20 minutes. Yield: 1 loaf.

Rosamond Lawson

109

Pear Bread

2 to 3 fresh pears or 1
16-ounce can pears
½ cup salad oil
1 cup sugar
2 eggs
¼ cup sour cream
1 teaspoon vanilla

2 cups flour
½ teaspoon salt
1 teaspoon baking soda
¼ teaspoon cinnamon
¼ teaspoon nutmeg
½ cup nuts

Cut pears in half and mash to equal one cup. Beat together oil and sugar. Beat in eggs one at a time. Add sour cream and vanilla; set aside. Sift together flour, salt, soda, cinnamon, and nutmeg. Add to oil and sugar. Beat well. Add pears and nuts. Pour in loaf pan and bake for 45 minutes at 350°. Preparation: 20 minutes. Yield: 1 loaf.

Jo Miller

Blueberry Bread

1½ cups sugar
½ cup brown sugar
½ cup melted butter
1¾ cups orange juice
2 eggs, beaten
4 cups flour
1 tablespoon baking
powder

1 teaspoon salt
1 teaspoon baking soda
2 cups nuts, chopped
1 cup oats
2 cups blueberries, fresh
or frozen
½ cup orange marmalade

Combine sugars, butter, orange juice, and eggs. Sift together flour, baking powder, salt, and soda. Add nuts and oats to dry ingredients and blend. Combine dry ingredients with orange juice mixture. Stir in blueberries and orange marmalade. Pour into 2 greased and floured loaf pans and allow to stand 20 minutes before baking. Bake at 350° for 1 hour and 15 minutes. Cool 10 minutes before removing from pan. Preparation: 30 minutes. Yield: 2 loaves.

Susanna Sauvain

Sweet Potato Bread

3 eggs
1½ cups vegetable oil
2 cups shredded sweet
   potatoes
1½ cups sugar
½ cup shredded coconut
1 teaspoon vanilla
¼ cup water

3⅓ cups all-purpose flour
2 teaspoons baking soda
1 teaspoon salt
1 teaspoon baking
   powder
1 teaspoon cinnamon
1 teaspoon cloves
⅔ cup chopped nuts

Preheat oven to 350⁰. Grease and flour two 9 x 5 x 3-inch loaf pans. Beat eggs, oil, sweet potatoes, sugar, coconut, and vanilla on low speed for 1 minute; scrape sides. Add flour, baking soda, baking powder, salt, cinnamon, cloves, and water. Beat only until moistened, then on high for 45 seconds. Stir in nuts. Spread in pans and bake 55 to 60 minutes or until wooden pick inserted in center comes out clean. Cool 10 minutes and remove from pans. Preparation: 40 minutes. Yield: 2 loaves.

Karen Feigley

Zucchini Bread

3 cups flour
2 teaspoons baking soda
1 teaspoon salt
½ teaspoon baking
   powder
1½ teaspoons cinnamon
¾ cup nuts, chopped
3 eggs

2 cups sugar
1 cup oil
2 teaspoons vanilla
2 cups zucchini, peeled
   and grated
1 8-ounce can crushed
   pineapple, drained

Sift and measure flour. Combine with soda, salt, baking powder, cinnamon, and nuts. Set aside. In a large bowl, lightly beat eggs; then add sugar, oil, and vanilla. Beat until creamy. Stir in zucchini and pineapple. Add dry ingredients, stirring only until moistened. Spoon into two greased and floured loaf pans. Bake at 350⁰ about 1 hour and 15 minutes. Cool 10 minutes before removing from pan. Yield: 2 loaves.

Margaret Bargatze

Raisin Bran Muffins

1 15-ounce box raisin
  bran cereal
1 quart buttermilk
4 eggs
1¼ cups oil
5 cups flour

2¼ cups sugar
5 teaspoons baking soda
½ teaspoon salt
1 cup wheat bran
¾ to 1 cup raisins
  (optional)

Preheat oven to 400°. Combine first four ingredients in mixing bowl and mix well. Add remaining ingredients (add extra raisins if desired) and mix. Fill greased or paper-lined muffin tins ¾ full and bake for 20 minutes. Preparation: 30 minutes. Yield: 5 dozen.

Anne Grier

Big Batch Bran Muffins

½ cup oatmeal
2½ cups Bran Buds,
  divided
½ cup butter
1 cup brown sugar
1 cup white sugar

2 eggs
2½ cups flour
2½ teaspoons soda
½ teaspoon salt
1¾ cups buttermilk
Boiling water

Combine ½ cup of the Bran Buds with the oatmeal and pour 1 cup boiling water over all. Set aside to cool. In a large bowl, cream sugars and butter together. Add eggs and beat well. Sift dry ingredients together and add to egg mixture alternately with buttermilk. Add the cooled oatmeal mixture and remainder of Bran Buds, beating until creamy. Refrigerate for 24 hours. Do not stir.

Grease large muffin tins. Pour in batter until half full. Bake at 400° for 20 minutes. Yield: Approximately 20 to 25 muffins.

Batter will keep, covered tightly, in the refrigerator for 5 weeks.

Joanne Smith

Sweet Potato Muffins

1¼ cups sugar
1¼ cups mashed cooked
    sweet potatoes (or
    canned)
½ stick butter, room
    temperature
2 large eggs, room
    temperature
1½ cups flour
2 teaspoons baking
    powder

1 teaspoon cinnamon
¼ teaspoon nutmeg
¼ teaspoon salt
1 cup milk
½ cup raisins, chopped
¼ cup pecans, chopped
2 tablespoons sugar
¼ teaspoon cinnamon

Preheat oven to 400°. Grease muffin cups. Beat sugar, potatoes and butter until smooth. Add eggs and blend well; set aside. Sift together flour, baking powder, spices, and salt. Add flour mixture to potato mixture alternately with milk. Stir just to blend. Fold in raisins and nuts. Spoon batter into muffin cups. Mix ¼ teaspoon cinnamon and 2 tablespoons sugar and sprinkle over muffins before baking. Bake 20 to 25 minutes. Yield: 24 muffins.

Use paper liners in your tins. Moist and delicious!

Ginger Chalkley

Carrot Muffins

2 sticks margarine,
    melted
4 eggs
2 teaspoons vanilla
2 cups grated carrots
3 cups flour
2 cups sugar

4 teaspoons baking
    powder
½ teaspoon baking soda
½ teaspoon salt
2 cups chopped nuts
½ teaspoon cinnamon
½ teaspoon nutmeg

Mix margarine, eggs, vanilla, and carrots; set aside. Mix flour, sugar, baking powder, soda, salt, and nuts together and add to first mixture. Combine just until mixed. Pour into two greased and floured loaf pans, or muffin tins. For bread, bake at 350° for 1 hour. For muffins, bake at 350° for 20 to 25 minutes. Preparation: 15 minutes. Yield: 2 loaves or 2 dozen muffins.

To use muffins as dessert, mix together 1 8-ounce package of cream cheese, 1 box of powdered sugar, 1 tablespoon milk, and 1½ teaspoons vanilla and spread on muffins.

Marti Thomas

113

Macaroon Muffins

Almond Macaroon Filling:

2 eggs
½ cup sugar
1 ¼ cups blanched almonds, finely chopped

1 teaspoon almond extract

Beat eggs until foamy. Gradually beat in sugar, fold in almonds and almond extract.

Muffins:

1 cup butter, softened (no substitutes!)
½ cup sugar
1 egg
½ teaspoon vanilla

½ teaspoon almond extract
2 cups flour (measured before sifting)

Cream butter and sugar. Beat in egg, flavorings, and flour. Drop by teaspoon into tiny greased muffin tins, pressing dough over bottom and up sides. Chill. Heat oven to 325⁰. Fill with almond macaroon filling and bake 25 to 30 minutes. Preparation: 30 minutes. Yield: 3 dozen muffins.

Can be frozen.

Beverley Dew

Fresh Peach Muffins

⅓ cup butter or margarine
½ cup sugar
1 egg
1 ½ cups flour, sifted
½ teaspoon salt
¼ teaspoon nutmeg

½ cup milk
1 cup fresh peaches, chopped
1 ½ teaspoons baking powder

Cream butter or margarine and sugar. Add egg and mix. Stir in baking powder, flour, salt, and nutmeg alternating with milk. Stir in fresh peaches. Fill greased muffin pan, filling each cup ⅔ full. Bake at 350⁰ for 20 to 25 minutes. Preparation: 15 minutes. Yield: 12 muffins.

Louise Mondy

Highland Inn Maple Muffins with Maple Butter Glaze

2 eggs	1 cup all-purpose flour
1 cup sour cream	1 cup bran flakes
1 cup Highland County maple syrup	1 teaspoon baking soda
	¾ cup chopped hazelnuts

Glaze:

⅔ cup Highland County maple syrup	6 tablespoons butter

Preheat oven to 400°. Beat eggs with fork in large bowl to blend. Stir in sour cream and maple syrup. Add flour, bran flakes, and baking soda. Stir until batter is moist. Mix in nuts. Line muffin tins with paper cups and fill ¾ full. Bake 15 to 20 minutes.

Glaze: Combine ingredients and stir until well blended. Dip muffins into glaze. Serve warm. Preparation: 15 minutes.

Can be prepared ahead. Let cool completely and wrap tightly and freeze. Rewarm in low oven.

Highland Inn
Monterey, Virginia

Cinnamon Nut Muffins

1 cup sugar	1 cup milk
2 cups flour	½ cup vegetable oil
3 teaspoons cinnamon	2 eggs, beaten
¼ teaspoon salt	1 cup chopped pecans
2 teaspoons baking powder	

Sift together sugar, flour, cinnamon, salt, and baking powder. Combine milk, vegetable oil, and eggs, mixing well; add to flour mixture. Add pecans. Fill greased (or lined) muffin tins and bake 15 to 20 minutes at 425°. Preparation: 10 minutes. Yield: 1½ dozen.

Becky Newman

115

Apple Muffins

½ cup milk
½ cup butter or margarine
1 cup sugar
2 eggs
2 cups flour
½ teaspoon salt

2 tablespoons baking powder
2½ cups apples, peeled and chopped
2 teaspoons sugar (for topping)

Cream butter and sugar. Add eggs one at a time, beating well. Sift dry ingredients and add to eggs alternately with milk. Beat until smooth. Add apples, mixing by hand. Pour into greased muffin tins and top each with sugar. Bake 25 to 30 minutes at 375°. Yields: 12 to 16 muffins.

Jo Miller

Stove Point Blueberry Muffins

1 stick margarine at room temperature
1 cup sugar
2 eggs
1 teaspoon vanilla
1 cup milk
5 teaspoons baking powder

1 teaspoon salt
3 cups flour, not sifted
1 16-ounce can blueberries, drained or 1 pint of fresh berries

Cream margarine and sugar in a large bowl. Mix eggs, milk, and vanilla in a separate bowl. Add liquids alternately with dry ingredients to large bowl. Fold in blueberries and fill muffin tins lined with paper baking cups. Bake at 425° for 15 to 20 minutes. Preparation: 15 minutes. Yield: 18 large muffins.

Sprinkle with granulated sugar before baking for a nice touch.

Terry Tosh

Zucchini Nut Muffins

2 eggs
1 cup sugar
½ cup vegetable oil
1 tablespoon vanilla
extract
2 cups unpeeled
shredded zucchini
2 cups all-purpose flour

1 teaspoon baking soda
¼ teaspoon baking powder
½ teaspoon salt
1½ teaspoons ground
cinnamon
¾ cup raisins
¾ cup chopped pecans

Preheat oven to 350°. Combine first 4 ingredients, mixing well. Stir in shredded zucchini; set aside. Combine next 5 ingredients in a mixing bowl. Reserve ¼ cup flour mixture and toss with raisins and pecans. Make a well in center of flour mixture. Add zucchini mixture to dry ingredients, stirring just until moistened. Stir in raisins and pecans. Spoon mixture into greased muffin cups (or paper-lined), filling ⅔ full. Bake for 20 minutes. Preparation: 10 minutes. Yield: 1½ dozen.

Anne Grier

Cream Cheese Pastries

1 8-ounce package cream
cheese
½ cup sugar

1 tablespoon lemon juice
2 cans Pillsbury Crescent
Rolls

Glaze:

½ cup confectioners sugar
1 teaspoon vanilla

1 to 2 tablespoons milk

Mix together cream cheese, sugar, and lemon juice. Set aside. Open crescent rolls; separate triangles. Spread triangles with cream cheese mixture. Fold long ends to center. Bake on ungreased cookie sheet at 350° for 20 minutes. Let cool. Mix all glaze ingredients and pour over cooled crescents. Preparation: 10 minutes. Yield: 16.

Pat Morrison

French-Style Griddle Cakes

3 eggs, separated
½ cup milk
¾ cup sifted flour
½ teaspoon salt

¼ cup sour cream
3 tablespoons butter,
melted
½ teaspoon vanilla

Beat egg whites until stiff but not dry. Set aside. Beat egg yolks in a bowl that pours. Add milk. Sift flour again with salt and mix gradually into yolk mixture, using as few strokes as possible to blend. Stir in sour cream, melted butter and vanilla. Gently fold in egg whites.

Heat lightly greased griddle until drops of water sputter when sprinkled on. Pour batter for desired size pancakes. Cook until top is bubbly; turn. Cook briefly and remove to platter. Serve with melted butter and warmed syrup. Serves 3 to 4.

Charmian Matheson

Sour Cream Waffles

2 eggs, separated
2 16-ounce containers
sour cream
1½ teaspoons baking soda

2 cups flour
4 tablespoons melted
butter

Beat egg yolks and add sour cream. Mix baking soda and flour and sift into sour cream mixture. Add melted butter. Fold in unbeaten egg whites. Preparation: 10 minutes. Yield: Approximately 6 (depending on your waffle iron).

Pamela Sexton

Moravian Sugar Cake

1 package dry yeast
½ cup warm water
⅓ cup sugar
½ teaspoon salt
1 egg, beaten (and at room temperature)
½ cup hot mashed potatoes

⅔ cup melted butter, divided
2 cups flour, sifted
¾ cup light brown sugar
1 teaspoon cinnamon
Butter

Sprinkle yeast and a pinch of sugar over water; after a few minutes, stir to dissolve. Stir sugar and salt into egg in large bowl; then add potatoes and mix well. Stir in ⅓ cup butter and yeast. Beat in flour in small portions (dough should be soft). Knead lightly on a floured board for 2 to 3 minutes until smooth and springy. Put in greased bowl, greasing top. Cover with towel and let rise until doubled (1½ hours). Press into a greased 13 x 9 x 2-inch pan (should be no thicker than ¾-inch). Butter top lightly, cover, and let rise 30 minutes. Make thumbprints 2 inches apart, and sprinkle brown sugar and cinnamon mixture over dough. Drizzle with remaining butter. Bake at 400° for 20 minutes. Yield: 24 squares.

This is an authentic Moravian recipe from Old Salem in Winston-Salem, N.C.

Larkin Bynum

Sour Cream Coffee Cake

2 cups flour
1 teaspoon baking powder
¼ teaspoon salt
2 sticks butter, softened
2 cups sugar
2 eggs

1 cup sour cream
½ teaspoon vanilla
½ cup chopped pecans
½ teaspoon cinnamon
2 tablespoons brown sugar

Sift first 3 ingredients. Cream butter and sugar; then add eggs, mixing well. Fold in sour cream, dry ingredients, and vanilla. Mix pecans, cinnamon, and brown sugar in separate bowl for topping. Spoon ½ batter in a greased and floured 10-inch tube (or bundt) pan. Cover with ½ topping and repeat. Bake at 350° for 55 to 60 minutes. Cool completely before removing from pan. Sprinkle with powdered sugar. Serves 15.

Make at least 1 day ahead. Freezes well.

Gerry Lewis

Mother's Danish Puff

Pastry:

½ cup butter or
margarine, softened

1 cup all-purpose flour
2 tablespoons water

Preheat oven to 350°. Cut butter into flour. Sprinkle water over and mix. Round into ball and divide in half. On ungreased baking sheet, pat each half into a 12 x 3-inch strip. Strips should be about 3 inches apart.

Topping:

½ cup butter or margarine
1 cup water
1 teaspoon almond
extract

1 cup flour
3 eggs

Heat butter and water to rolling boil in medium saucepan. Remove from heat and quickly stir in almond extract and flour. Stir vigorously over low heat until mixture forms a ball, about 1 minute. Remove from heat. Beat in eggs (all at once) until smooth and glossy.

Divide in half. Spread each half evenly over strips. Bake about 1 hour or until topping is crisp and brown. Cool. (Topping will shrink and fall, forming the custardy top of this puff.)

Glaze:

1½ cups confectioners
sugar
2 tablespoons butter or
margarine, softened

1½ teaspoons vanilla
1 to 2 tablespoons warm
water
Nuts

Mix ingredients until smooth and of spreading consistency. Frost coffee cakes with glaze and sprinkle generously with chopped nuts. Preparation: 45 minutes. Yield: 24 slices.

Pat Morrison

Date Nut Crescent

Pastry:

2¼ cups plain flour
2 tablespoons sugar
1 teaspoon salt

¼ cup evaporated milk
1 egg
½ cup butter

Filling:

1¼ cups butter, softened
½ cup brown sugar
½ cup chopped dates
¾ cup nuts

½ teaspoon nutmeg
1 teaspoon cinnamon
1 cup raisins (optional)

Glaze:

2 tablespoons melted
  butter
1 cup confectioners sugar

½ teaspoon vanilla
2 tablespoons milk

Mix pastry ingredients and chill for 2 hours. Divide dough into 2 parts. Roll each out to 12 x 16-inch rectangle. Mix filling ingredients and spread over pastry. Roll into 2 crescents or jellyrolls. Slit along top. Let rise 1 hour. Bake at 350° for 20 to 25 minutes. Mix glaze ingredients and spread over all. Yield: 2 pastries, each serving 10.

Kay Whitworth

Skillet Almond Coffee Cake

¾ cup butter (at room
  temperature)
1½ cups sugar
2 eggs
1½ cups sifted flour

2 teaspoons almond
  extract
Pinch of salt
Sliced almonds
Sugar

Cream butter and sugar. Beat in eggs one at a time. Add flour, extract, and salt. Mix well. Pour batter into large iron skillet (9 to 11-inches) lined with heavy-duty aluminum foil. Leave excess foil on sides. Sprinkle top with almonds and small amount of sugar. Bake for 30 to 40 minutes at 350°. Cool completely before removing foil. Preparation: 20 minutes. Serves 8.

Moist and rich!

Martha Davidson

Breads

Blueberry Coffee Cake

¾ cup sugar
¼ cup butter or
   margarine, softened
1 egg
½ cup milk
2 cups flour

2 teaspoons baking
   powder
½ teaspoon salt
2 cups fresh blueberries
   (or frozen, thawed and
   drained)

Topping:

½ cup sugar
⅓ cup flour
½ teaspoon cinnamon

¼ cup very soft butter or
   margarine

Preheat oven to 375°. Grease and flour a 9 x 9-inch pan. Mix sugar, butter, and egg well; add milk and mix; add dry ingredients, mixing again. Fold in blueberries. Spread batter in pan. Sprinkle with combined topping ingredients and bake for 30 minutes. Yield: 9 servings.

Nancy Payne

When letting yeast bread rise, always cover with a towel or a sheet of plastic wrap to prevent the surface from drying and cracking.

To speed up proofing (raising) yeast bread, use a microwave oven. Fill a 4-cup glass measure with 3 cups water. Heat on high till boiling. Place water in corner of microwave, place dough in glass bowl and cover with wax paper. Heat 20 minutes on 10 percent level. Let stand covered 20 minutes. Reshape dough as recipe directs and repeat proofing.

When dissolving yeast, use only lukewarm liquids. Hot liquids will kill yeast proofing powder.

Freshly baked bread is easier to slice if you dip the knife in hot water.

Make croutons from stale bread. Cut bread into cubes and toast at 250° until golden. Then toss lightly in butter seasoned with garlic or herbs.

Freshen dry, crusty rolls of French bread by sprinkling with a few drops of water, wrapping in aluminum foil and heating at 350° about 10 minutes.

Side Dishes & Vegetables

The nationwide interest in eating lightly has made inroads in the region of bacon grease and corn meal. While Southern cooks haven't totally foresworn those staples, they've modified menus to cut down on fat and calories—and save on the meat budget, too.

In this chapter you'll find quiches, rarebits, omelets, and rice and pasta dishes you can make a meal around. The bubbly, sharp Cheese Strata with its broccoli and ham needs only some fruit with Poppy Seed Dressing for balance. And the Pasta Primavera is a delicious vegetarian meal in itself.

There are plenty of side dishes here, too. Try Freckled Rice with your next beef roast. Or serve ham biscuits with Cheesy Garlic Grits at your next brunch.

And save room for Thalhimers' Rice Pudding. It depends on where you're from how you choose to serve it: as a vegetable or for dessert. Either way, you'll please a lot of palates.

Rice Pudding

9 eggs	1½ cups rice, cooked
1 quart milk	2½ teaspoons nutmeg
1½ cups sugar	2½ teaspoons cinnamon
1 cup butter	6 tablespoons vanilla
½ cup raisins	

Combine all ingredients and mix well. Pour into a 9-inch square pan. Bake at 300° for 25 to 30 minutes.

Thalhimers Richmond Room
Richmond, Virginia

Quick Quiche Crust

½ cup butter, very cold
1 cup flour

2 tablespoons half-and-half
Pinch of salt

Cut butter into small pieces. Place all ingredients in food processor and mix quickly. Press dough evenly into quiche pan; prick bottom with fork. Add favorite quiche filling and bake at 350° for 45 minutes or as directed. Yield: 1 crust.

Janet Peckinpaugh Rudy

Long Run Quiche

1 9-inch deep dish pie
  crust
½ cup mushrooms, sliced
1 tablespoon butter
1 cup ham, chopped
¼ cup Mozzarella cheese,
  shredded
4 ounces Muenster
  cheese, grated

4 ounces Monterey Jack
  cheese, grated
1 to 2 ounces bleu
  cheese, crumbled
3 eggs
1 cup whipping cream
Salt and pepper

Bake pie crust 10 to 15 minutes. Saute mushrooms in butter. Layer ham, mushrooms, and cheeses in pie shell. Beat eggs. Add cream, salt, and pepper. Pour into pie shell. Bake at 375° for 40 minutes or until set. Serves 4 to 6.

Robin Traywick Williams

Crabmeat Quiche

2 tablespoons flour
½ cup mayonnaise
2 eggs, beaten
1 cup evaporated milk
1⅔ cups crabmeat
⅔ cup green pepper,
  chopped

2 cups Swiss cheese,
  grated
1 9-inch deep dish pie shell
Salt
White pepper
Cayenne pepper
Paprika

Mix flour, mayonnaise, and eggs. Stir in evaporated milk. Add remaining ingredients except paprika and mix well. Pour into pie shell. Sprinkle paprika on top and bake at 350° for 40 minutes. Serves 8.

Jeanie Vertner

Spinach Quiche

8 ounces grated Gruyere cheese
2 tablespoons flour
3 eggs
1 cup half-and-half
½ teaspoon salt
10 ounces chopped spinach (fresh or frozen), cooked and well-drained

3 to 4 strips bacon, cooked and crumbled
1 tablespoon grated onion
1 unbaked deep dish pie crust
Dash pepper
Dash nutmeg

Toss cheese with flour. Combine eggs, cream, and seasonings. Add cheese and spinach and mix well. A food processor facilitates the mixing. Put bacon and onion on bottom of crust; pour egg mixture on top. Bake at 350° for 45 minutes. Serves 6.

Janet Peckinpaugh Rudy

Garden Fresh Quiche

1½ cups chopped fresh broccoli
1 cup fresh mushrooms, sliced
2 tablespoons oil (preferably peanut)
2 tablespoons soy sauce
4 eggs
1 cup half-and-half

1 teaspoon dry mustard
½ teaspoon garlic powder
1 tablespoon chopped chives
2 cups Mozzarella cheese, grated
1 deep dish pie shell, unbaked

Preheat oven to 350°. Steam broccoli until barely tender; set aside. Saute mushrooms in oil for 5 minutes; add soy sauce and stir. Beat eggs with half-and-half. Add mustard, garlic powder and chives; mix well. Place broccoli and mushrooms in pie shell and cover with cheese. Pour egg mixture over all and bake for 20 to 30 minutes. Serves 4 to 6.

A whole wheat pie shell makes this an even more nutritious dish.

Lindsey Clark

Bacon Cheese Souffle

10 slices bread, white or
    whole wheat
  8 ounces sharp Cheddar
    cheese, grated
2½ tablespoons butter,
    melted
  4 eggs
  2 cups milk
  1 teaspoon Lawry's
    seasoned salt

½ teaspoon dry mustard
½ pound bacon, chopped
    and cooked
1 medium onion, chopped
    fine or grated
½ cup green onion,
    chopped

Remove crusts from bread and cut bread into small cubes. Mix all ingredients in an electric mixing bowl until well-blended. Pour into greased, oblong Pyrex dish. Bake at 350° for 50 to 60 minutes or until golden brown. Serves 8.

Can refrigerate overnight and bake the following day. Serve on lettuce with orange slices for a tasty luncheon dish.

Terry Tosh

Hoppel Poppel Omelet

¼ cup unsalted butter
3 medium potatoes,
    peeled and cubed
⅓ cup onion, finely
    chopped
1 cup baked ham, diced
6 eggs
2 tablespoons Cognac
½ teaspoon salt

1/8 teaspoon fresh ground
    pepper
1 tablespoon parsley,
    chopped
½ cup Swiss cheese,
    grated
    Dash Worcestershire
    sauce

Melt butter in 11-inch, oven-proof frying pan. Saute potatoes and onions until tender. Add ham and saute a few more minutes. Reduce heat. Beat together eggs, Cognac, salt, pepper, and Worcestershire. Pour over frying pan mixture and sprinkle with parsley. Continuously lift cooked eggs from edges of pan, allowing liquid to run underneath and cook. When omelet is almost set, sprinkle with cheese and run under broiler until cheese is melted. Cut into wedges and serve. Serves 4.

As fun to make as it is to eat! Great for Sunday night suppers.

Trudie Steel

Ham-It-Up Potato Brunch Casserole

½ cup onions, minced
2 tablespoons olive oil
4½ tablespoons butter, divided
4 eggs
½ clove garlic, crushed
2 tablespoons parsley, minced
⅔ cup Swiss cheese, grated

4 tablespoons heavy cream
¼ teaspoon salt
1½ cups baked ham, diced
3 medium potatoes, peeled and grated
Pepper to taste

Saute onions in oil and 2 tablespoons of butter; do not brown. In a large bowl, beat eggs with garlic, parsley, cheese, cream, salt, and pepper. Blend in ham and onions. Squeeze water from potatoes and stir into egg mixture. Heat 2 tablespoons butter in baking dish. Pour in potato-egg mixture; dot with remaining butter. Bake at 375º for 30 to 40 minutes, or until brown. Serves 4.

Ann Grier

Breakfast Casserole

1 pound of sausage, hot or regular
6 eggs
2 cups milk
1 teaspoon salt

1 teaspoon dry mustard
4 to 6 slices of bread, cubed
1 cup sharp cheese, grated

Cook sausage until done, breaking it to bits as you cook it. Drain and set aside. Beat eggs; add milk, salt, and mustard. In greased baking dish, layer bread, sausage, and cheese. Pour egg mixture over these ingredients. Refrigerate overnight. Bake at 350º for 45 minutes. Serves 6.

Great breakfast for houseguests and children love it for dinner too!

Liz Thomas

127

Cheese Strata

12 slices of white bread
¾ pound processed American cheese, sliced
1 10-ounce package frozen chopped broccoli (cooked and drained)
2 cups finely diced cooked or canned ham (1½ pounds)

3½ cups whole milk
6 eggs, slightly beaten
2 tablespoons instant minced onion
½ teaspoon salt
¼ teaspoon dry mustard
1 cup grated sharp cheese

Remove crusts from bread slices. Cut 12 1-inch diameter "donut holes" from bread with biscuit cutter. Set "donut holes" aside.

Tear remaining bread into small pieces and place in bottom of a 13 x 9 x 2-inch baking dish. Place American cheese in a layer on bread, add layer of broccoli, then ham. Arrange "donut holes" on top.

Combine other ingredients and pour over casserole. Cover and refrigerate for at least 6 hours or overnight.

Bake uncovered in slow oven (325°) for 55 minutes. Sprinkle with grated sharp cheese 5 minutes before end of baking time. Before cutting into squares, let stand 10 minutes to firm. Serves 12.

Cabell West

Cheese Rarebit

2 cans condensed cheese
  soup
½ cup beer
¼ teaspoon Worcester-
  shire sauce
5 to 6 slices French
  bread, ¾-inch thick,
  toasted

5 to 6 slices bacon, halved
  and crisp-cooked
5 to 6 thick tomato slices
1 3-ounce can broiled
  mushroom crowns,
  drained
Dash dry mustard

In a saucepan, combine cheese soup, beer, Worcestershire sauce, and mustard. Stir to blend. Simmer over low heat for 10 minutes, stirring frequently.

Place toasted bread slices in shallow 13 x 9 x 2-inch baking dish. Top each with 2 pieces of bacon, a tomato slice, 2 or 3 mushroom crowns. Pour cheese sauce over all. Broil 3 to 4 inches from heat until bubbles (about 3 minutes). Yield: 5 or 6 servings.

Variations: Add hard-boiled egg slices under cheese sauce. Substitute saltine crackers for toast.

Frances Barnes

Welsh Rarebit

1 tablespoon butter
1 cup beer
1 pound yellow cheese,
  grated
1 egg
1 teaspoon Worcester-
  shire sauce

Salt
Pepper
Paprika
Red pepper
Mustard seed
Toast, cut into points

Melt butter in a double boiler. Add beer. When mixture is warm, add cheese. Beat and add egg while whisking mixture. Season with remaining ingredients and serve with dry toast points. Serves 6 to 8.

Larkin Bynum

Piperade

4 slices of bacon, in
  small pieces
1 large onion, chopped
4 slices Canadian bacon
1 green pepper, diced
1 16-ounce can tomatoes,
  drained and mashed
1 garlic clove, crushed

½ teaspoon salt
¼ teaspoon fresh ground
  pepper
1 tablespoon butter
8 eggs, slightly beaten
8 slices French bread,
  fried in butter

Heat bacon in large heavy skillet. Add onions and cook until transparent. Add Canadian bacon, peppers, tomatoes, garlic, salt, and pepper. Cook 30 minutes. In another skillet, heat butter. Add eggs and cook briskly, stirring gently with a fork until eggs are set. Stir in mixture from other skillet. Garnish with fried bread. Serves 4.

Michael Robertson

Chili Relleno Casserole

2 4-ounce cans whole
  green chilies, cut in
  strips
1 pound Monterey Jack
  cheese, grated

3 eggs
¾ teaspoon garlic salt
⅓ cup flour
  Paprika

Place ½ of chilies in bottom of medium, round casserole dish. Sprinkle with ½ of cheese. Repeat layers. Mix eggs with garlic salt and flour; beat well. Pour over chilies and cheese. Bake at 350⁰ for 40 minutes, or until set and golden brown. Garnish with paprika. Serves 6.

Missy Ryan

Cheesy Garlic Grits

7 cups water	2 sticks butter
2 teaspoons salt	4 eggs, well beaten
2 cups uncooked grits	4 tablespoons Worcester-
12 ounces sharp Cheddar	shire sauce
cheese, shredded	Salt and pepper to taste
2 to 3 cloves garlic,	Paprika
mashed	

Bring water and salt to a boil; add grits and bring to a second boil; reduce heat and cook 20 to 25 minutes. Add remaining ingredients except paprika and stir until butter and cheese have melted. Pour into greased casserole and sprinkle with paprika. Bake at 350° for 1 hour. Preparation: 30 minutes. Serves 12.

Great for brunch with ham biscuits.

Karen Feigley

Barley Pilaf

1½ pounds mushrooms,	1¾ cups uncooked medium
sliced	pearled barley
2 medium onions,	4 cups chicken broth
chopped	Salt and pepper
8 tablespoons butter,	
divided	

Saute mushrooms and onion in 4 tablespoons butter. Place in 2-quart casserole dish. In saucepan, saute barley in 4 tablespoons butter over low heat. Cook and stir until barley is almond colored. This will take 10 to 15 minutes. Add to mushrooms. Pour broth over all. Add salt and pepper to taste. Bake, covered, for 45 minutes at 350°. Uncover and bake an additional 45 minutes. Add small amount of water if barley becomes dry. Preparation: 30 minutes. Serves 8 to 10.

Excellent with poultry, lamb, or pork.

Gerry Lewis

Wild Rice and Mushrooms

¼ pound wild rice	1 pound fresh
2 medium onions,	mushrooms, sliced
chopped	½ pound butter

Cook rice according to directions; drain if necessary. Saute onions and mushrooms in butter in large, heavy skillet until onions are yellow and mushrooms dark. Add hot rice and mix well. Serves 8.

Mary Anne Burke

Rice Casserole

2 packages of Uncle Ben's Long Grain and Wild Rice	1/8 teaspoon pepper
	1½ cups Swanson's clear chicken broth
1 pound mild sausage	½ cup cream or regular milk
2 medium onions, chopped	2 small cans mushrooms
¼ cup flour	½ cup toasted almonds
1½ teaspoons salt	

Cook rice as directed on package. Saute sausage, mincing while cooking. Remove sausage and drain on paper towel; saute onions in drippings until tender. Add flour, salt, and pepper and mix well. Slowly add chicken broth and stir until thickened. Add cream, mushrooms, sausage, and rice and mix well. Place in casserole and top with toasted almonds. Bake in moderate oven until hot. Preparation: 45 minutes. Serves 12.

Freezes well.

Patti Hayden

Elegant Rice

1 10½-ounce can beef consomme	1 7½-ounce can sliced water chestnuts, drained
1 soup can water	
1 cup regular rice	1 4-ounce can sliced mushrooms, not drained
¾ stick butter, melted	
½ bell pepper, chopped	
½ small onion, chopped	1 teaspoon salt (optional)
¾ cup celery, chopped	

Combine all of the ingredients in a large casserole dish. Cook covered at 350° for 1 hour or until liquid is absorbed. Stir two or three times while cooking. Preparation: 10 minutes. Serves 6 to 8.

Variations are endless! Try substituting chicken broth, beef bouillon, onion soup, French onion soup, V-8 Juice, or any tasty combination of liquids. Change vegetables to suit your taste. Saute rice in butter before adding remaining ingredients for a different texture. May be doubled or tripled, mixed ahead and cooked later, cooked ahead and reheated later, or frozen.

Karen Feigley

Savannah Rice

6 slices bacon	1 14½-ounce can stewed tomatoes
½ cup onion, chopped	
2 cups raw rice	½ teaspoon salt
2 14½-ounce cans whole tomatoes	¼ teaspoon pepper
	1/8 teaspoon Tabasco

Fry bacon in large oven-proof skillet; remove from pan and crumble. Saute onion in bacon drippings. Add all ingredients and simmer 10 minutes. Bake at 350° for 1 hour. Serves 8 to 12.

Good with fried chicken or shish kebab.

Frances Harris

Curried Rice

3 tablespoons butter,
divided
1½ teaspoons curry
powder
1½ cups rice
3 cups chicken broth
1 cup seedless raisins
½ cup green onion,
chopped
½ cup green pepper,
chopped

½ cup celery, chopped
½ teaspoon seasoned salt
1½ tablespoons chutney
3 tablespoons pimento,
chopped
3 tablespoons pine nuts
(optional)
1½ tablespoons vinegar
1½ tablespoons brown
sugar

Melt 1½ tablespoons butter in 2-quart saucepan. Add curry powder and rice. Cook, stirring, over low heat for 5 minutes. Add chicken broth and heat to boiling. Stir and cover tightly; cook over low heat about 15 minutes or until liquid is absorbed. Meanwhile, saute raisins, onions, green pepper, and celery in remaining butter until soft. Add remaining ingredients and toss lightly together. Put hot rice on platter and spoon raisin mixture over top. Preparation: 1 hour. Serves 6 to 8.

Jane Helfrich

Rice and Green Chilies

1 cup raw rice
2½ cups boiling water
2 cups sour cream
½ pound Monterey Jack
cheese, grated
2 3-ounce cans green
chilies, diced

3 tablespoons butter
½ cup Parmesan cheese,
freshly grated
Paprika
Salt and pepper to taste

Cook rice in boiling water according to package directions. Drain if necessary and cool. Mix rice with sour cream, salt, and pepper. Place ½ of rice mixture in well-greased 1½-quart casserole. Add Monterey Jack cheese and green chilies. Cover with remaining rice mixture. Dot with butter and top with Parmesan cheese. Sprinkle with paprika. Bake at 350° for 30 minutes. Serves 4 to 6.

Marti Thomas

Freckled Rice

3 cups cooked rice (not instant)
1 cup parsley, chopped
½ cup Cheddar cheese, grated
⅓ cup onion, chopped
¼ cup green pepper, chopped
½ teaspoon garlic powder
1 14½-ounce can evaporated milk
2 eggs, beaten
½ cup vegetable oil
1 teaspoon salt
½ teaspoon seasoned salt
Juice and rind of 1 lemon
Pepper to taste
Paprika

Combine rice, parsley, cheese, onion, green pepper, and garlic powder in greased 2-quart casserole. Blend together remaining ingredients except paprika. Add to rice mixture. Sprinkle with paprika. Bake at 350° for 45 minutes or until consistency is like soft custard. Preparation: 30 minutes. Serves 8.

A suprisingly subtle flavor!

Judy Brooks

Chicken and Shrimp Fried Rice

¼ cup Kikkoman soy sauce
1 tablespoon flour, dissolved in water
¼ teaspoon ground pepper
¼ cup vegetable or peanut oil, divided
2 eggs, slightly stirred
1 cup cooked chicken, diced
1 cup cooked shrimp, diced
2 cups fresh bean sprouts
2 scallions, chopped
4 cups hot cooked rice, medium grain
1 cup lettuce, shredded

Mix soy sauce, flour, and pepper; set aside. Heat frying pan or wok on high. Add ½ of oil, turning to medium heat. Add eggs, stirring lightly to mix. Remove when slightly soft and put aside. Turn heat up and add remaining oil. Quickly add chicken, shrimp, bean sprouts, and scallions; stir-fry for 2 minutes. Add hot rice. Pour in soy sauce mixture and stir. Add eggs. Turn off heat. Add lettuce, stir, and serve. Serves 4 to 6.

Jane Johnson

Noodles Supreme

1 8-ounce package of noodles, cooked and drained
1 8-ounce carton of sour cream
1 small onion, diced
½ teaspoon Worcestershire sauce
¼ teaspoon garlic, crushed
½ teaspoon salt
Bread crumbs

Combine all ingredients except noodles and bread crumbs in the blender. Mix with noodles and place in a baking dish. Cover with bread crumbs. Bake at 350° for 25 minutes. Serves 4 to 6.

Corinne Davis

Fettuccine Alfredo

10 to 12 ounces of fettucine or other wide noodle
2 tablespoons butter

Sauce:

1½ sticks butter or margarine
1 cup half-and-half
1½ cups freshly grated Parmesan cheese
3 tablespoons minced onion (dried)
3 to 4 tablespoons minced chives
2 tablespoons fresh chopped parsley
1 cup sour cream
Dash of garlic salt

Cook noodles "al dente" according to package directions. Drain and toss lightly with 2 tablespoons of butter. Keep hot.

Melt butter on low heat and add cream. Blend in cheese and stir until melted. Add remaining ingredients and stir over low heat - do not boil. Add this sauce to hot noodles and toss well to blend. Serves 4 to 6.

Torrey Shuford

Manicotti

1 pound manicotti
  noodles
1 pound Ricotta cheese
½ pound cream cheese,
  softened
1 egg, beaten

¼ cup chives, chopped
¼ cup butter
½ pound Mozzarella
  cheese
Salt and pepper to taste
Tomato or Ragu sauce

Cook manicotti noodles according to box directions and drain. Mix together Ricotta cheese, cream cheese, egg, chives, butter, salt, and pepper. Fill manicotti shells with cheese mixture. Place in greased casserole dish. Cover with sliced Mozzarella cheese and tomato or Ragu sauce. Bake 20 to 30 minutes at 350°. Serves 6 to 8.

Corinne Davis

Pasta Primavera

1 pound pasta (spaghetti,
  vermicelli, linguini, or
  fettuccine)
1½ cups fresh broccoli
  florets
1½ cups snow peas, fresh
  or frozen, thawed and
  drained
1 cup zucchini or
  summer squash or a
  mixture of both, sliced
  and halved
1 cup frozen baby peas,
  thawed and drained
1 tablespoon olive oil

1 small onion, coarsely
  chopped
2 medium tomatoes,
  chopped
¼ cup fresh chopped
  parsley
¼ cup olive oil
3 teaspoons minced garlic
10 mushrooms, sliced
1 cup whipping cream
½ cup Parmesan cheese
⅓ cup (¾ stick) butter
⅓ cup chopped fresh basil
Salt and pepper to taste

Cook pasta and drain. Blanch broccoli, snow peas, squash, and baby peas in boiling water for 3 to 4 minutes; rinse in cold water and set aside. In medium skillet, heat 1 tablespoon olive oil and add onion, tomatoes, parsley, salt, and pepper. Saute 2 to 3 minutes; set aside and keep warm. Heat ¼ cup of olive oil in a large skillet and add garlic, mushrooms, and the previously blanched vegetables. Simmer for a few minutes. Add pasta, cream, Parmesan cheese, butter, and basil. Toss gently with a fork. Place in serving dish, top with sauteed tomatoes, and serve at once. Serves 6 to 8.

Try this for an unusually tasty and colorful dish.

Frances Kusterer

Seashell Provolone Casserole

3 medium onions, finely chopped
¼ cup butter, melted
2 pounds ground beef
1 15½-ounce jar plain spaghetti sauce
1 16-ounce can stewed tomatoes
1 4-ounce can of mushrooms, stems and pieces (optional)

1 8-ounce package seashell macaroni
1 8-ounce package Provolone cheese
3 cups commercial sour cream
1 cup (4 ounces) shredded Mozzarella cheese
¼ cup grated Parmesan cheese
Garlic salt to taste

Saute onion in butter in large skillet until tender. Add ground beef, cook until brown, stirring to crumble beef. Add spaghetti sauce, tomatoes, mushrooms, and garlic salt to meat mixture. Stir well and simmer 20 minutes. Meanwhile, cook macaroni according to package directions and drain. Place half of macaroni in a deep 4-quart, greased casserole. Layer with half of meat sauce, half of Provolone, and half of sour cream. Repeat layers and top with Mozzarella and Parmesan. Cover and bake at 350° for 30 minutes. Uncover and bake 15 minutes longer. Serves 10 to 12.

Kay Whitworth

Stuffed Pasta Provencal

1 1-pound box jumbo macaroni shells
2 10-ounce packages frozen chopped spinach
3 cups cottage cheese, well drained
¾ cup Parmesan cheese
3 eggs, well beaten
1½ teaspoons salt
2 teaspoons parsley, chopped

¾ teaspoon oregano, crushed
¼ teaspoon pepper
1 large onion, chopped
3 8-ounce cans tomato sauce
1 clove garlic, minced
1 bay leaf
1 12-ounce package shredded Mozzarella cheese
Olive oil

Cook and drain macaroni shells; set aside. Cook spinach and drain well. Combine cottage cheese, Parmesan cheese, eggs, salt, parsley, oregano, pepper, and spinach. Fill shells with this mixture. Place shells in greased 9 x 12-inch baking dish; set aside.

Saute onion in a small amount of olive oil. Add tomato sauce, garlic, and bay leaf; simmer for 10 minutes. Remove bay leaf and pour sauce over shells. Sprinkle with Mozzarella cheese and bake at 350° for 35 minutes or until thoroughly heated. Serves 8 to 10.

May be assembled ahead. A vegetarian delight served with a salad and bread.

Martha Davidson

Lasagna

Tomato Sauce:

3 **cloves garlic, minced**	1 **15-ounce can tomato**
2 **tablespoons oil**	**puree**
½ **pound Italian sausage**	1 **6-ounce can tomato**
½ **pound hot sausage**	**paste**
1 **tablespoon basil**	**Pinch of salt and**
1 **28-ounce can Italian**	**pepper**
plum tomatoes	

Saute garlic in oil. Add sausage (casings removed and crumbled) and saute a few minutes longer. Add remaining ingredients and simmer until sauce thickens (at least ½ hour).

Spinach filling:

2 **packages frozen**	½ **cup grated Parmesan**
chopped spinach (cooked	**cheese**
and well drained)	1 **pound Ricotta cheese**
3 **eggs, lightly beaten**	

Cool spinach slightly. Add remaining ingredients and mix well.

Lasagna:

½ **pound lasagna noodles**	¼ **cup Parmesan cheese, grated**

Cook lasagna noodles according to package directions. Grease a 9 x 13 x 2-inch pan. Layer noodles, spinach filling, tomato sauce (in that order); repeat layers, finishing with sauce. Top with Parmesan cheese. Bake at 425° for 15 minutes or until bubbly. Serves 8.

Freezes beautifully!

Kitty Bayliss

Spaghetti Carbonara

3 eggs, beaten
1 cup grated Parmesan
 cheese, divided
½ cup cream or
 half-and-half
8 slices bacon, cooked
 and crumbled
¼ cup fresh parsley,
 chopped

¼ teaspoon basil
1 garlic clove, crushed
1 pound spaghetti
 noodles, cooked and
 drained
¼ cup butter, cut into
 chunks

Stir together eggs and ½ cup cheese; set aside. Heat cream and stir in bacon, parsley, basil, and garlic. In a large serving bowl, combine hot noodles, egg and cream mixtures, and butter. Toss until butter is melted and all ingredients are combined. Top with remaining cheese. Serves 8.

May add more bacon for a heartier meal. Great with a salad for a crowd.

Terry Tosh

Spaghetti Sauce

1 pound ground beef
⅓ cup chopped onion
2 cloves garlic, minced
1 28-ounce can tomatoes
1 12-ounce can tomato
 paste
½ pound sliced fresh
 mushrooms (or 4-ounce
 can mushrooms,
 drained)

1 tablespoon salt
1 tablespoon sugar
2 teaspoons oregano
1 bay leaf
2 tablespoons chopped
 parsley
½ teaspoon basil

Brown ground beef. Drain. Add onion and garlic; saute 2 to 3 minutes. Add all remaining ingredients. Bring to a boil. Reduce heat and simmer 1½ hours. Serve over spaghetti noodles. Serves 6 to 8.

More sugar may be added if desired.

Wycliffe McClure

Italian Spaghetti Sauce

1½ pounds hamburger meat and Italian sausage combined (more sausage than meat)
3 medium onions, chopped
3 tablespoons fresh parsley, chopped finely
3 garlic cloves, chopped finely
1 10½-ounce can tomato puree
1 15-ounce can tomato sauce
18 ounces tomato paste
1½ teaspoons oregano
2 to 3 teaspoons fresh basil
3 teaspoons Worcestershire sauce
¼ cup water
½ cup red wine
12 ounces mushrooms, sauteed in butter

Brown meat in olive oil. Add onions, parsley, and garlic and saute until limp. Add all other ingredients and simmer, covered, approximately 2 hours. Serves 8.

Use hot or mild Italian sausage, according to your own taste. Can be frozen.

Charmian Matheson

Eggplant Spaghetti

1 medium eggplant, pared and cubed
1 clove garlic, minced
¼ cup olive oil, 100% pure
1 28-ounce can peeled Italian tomatoes
2½ teaspoons salt
2 teaspoons sugar
2 teaspoons basil
1 8-ounce package spaghetti, cooked and drained
½ cup freshly grated Parmesan cheese

Saute eggplant and garlic in oil. Add tomatoes with juice, salt, sugar, and basil. Stir and mix well. Break up tomatoes over high heat until boiling. Reduce heat. Cover and simmer 20 minutes or until eggplant is tender. Serve over hot spaghetti; sprinkle with Parmesan cheese. Serves 4.

This is a good side dish to serve with beef or a main dish with salad and Italian bread.

Ann Bray Pastore

When cooking rice, add a spoonful of vinegar or lemon juice to make it light, separated and fluffy.

When rice has burned, place a fresh piece of white bread crust on top of the rice and cover the pot again. Within a few minutes the scorched taste will disappear. Discard bread.

To prevent pasta from sticking together while cooking, add a tablespoon of oil to the water.

To preserve egg yolks for several days, put in a small bowl, cover with water and refrigerate.

Break eggs one at a time into a cup instead of directly into your recipe. That way if one of them is spoiled you haven't ruined the recipe.

Add 1 tablespoon of salt to water to keep egg white from escaping a cracked shell while boiling.

A tablespoon of vinegar added to the water when poaching eggs will help set the whites so they don't spread.

To keep egg yolks from crumbling when slicing hard-cooked eggs, wet the knife before cutting.

If you run eggs under cold water before putting them in boiling water, it helps prevent cracking.

Allow egg whites to reach room temperature before beating to achieve greatest volume.

Recipes are written for regular or large eggs. Extra large and jumbo eggs will add too much liquid to recipe.

Separate egg yolks from whites by using fingers as sieve.

When making a quiche, pre-cook the crust for 10 minutes at 350°, then brush with egg white, egg yolk or Dijon mustard and put back in the oven for 2 minutes. Then fill with filling. This will prevent a soggy crust.

To rectify curdled Hollandaise sauce, remove from heat and add 1 teaspoon of hot water a few drops at a time.

To clean up a broken egg on the floor, sprinkle heavily with salt and leave it alone for 10 minutes. Sweep dried egg into dustpan.

Put leftover pieces of cheese into a jar with a small amount of wine. After cheese has collected, blend in blender for a nice spread to serve with salads.

When recipe calls for cream cheese, it should be softened to room temperature first.

Being blessed with four seasons means Virginians have a variety of fresh fruits and vegetables nearly all year round, from hardy green vegetables in spring to apples in autumn.

In the summertime, vegetable stands selling all the bounty of local gardens line rural roads. Chief among the vegetables is the Hanover tomato, which is fast becoming as famous for its sweet taste as Georgia's Vidalia onion.

Some think summer vegetables, like eggs or bourbon, need little in the way of enhancement. Others, like chef Alain Vincey, like to combine all the fresh flavors in one dish.

Vincey, who has cooked at New York's famed Lutece and for Jacques Cousteau on the Calypso, likes to use fresh Virginia produce for the ratatouille he serves at La Maisonnette.

Ratatouille

1 **large eggplant**	4 **tablespoons olive oil**
4 **medium zucchini**	½ **head garlic, minced**
1 **large onion**	¼ **teaspoon thyme**
6 **fresh tomatoes (or 2**	**Basil, salt, pepper to**
16-ounce cans whole	**taste**
tomatoes)	

Chop the vegetables into small pieces the same size. Do not peel. One at a time, saute the vegetables in "a good soup spoon" of olive oil until they are light brown. Drain each vegetable in a colander while you are cooking the next. You can put the vegetables on top of each other in the colander.

While the vegetables are draining, lightly saute the garlic. Combine vegetables, garlic, and other seasonings and cook slowly on the stove about an hour. Serves 4.

Refrigerating overnight and reheating improves flavor.

La Maisonnette
Richmond, Virginia

Green Vegetable Medley

1½ cups mayonnaise
2 hard-boiled eggs, finely chopped
1 small onion, finely chopped
1 tablespoon Worcestershire sauce
1 tablespoon prepared mustard
¼ teaspoon salt

1/8 teaspoon garlic salt
2 packages frozen green peas
2 packages frozen baby lima beans
2 packages frozen French-style green beans
Dash of hot sauce
Juice of 1 lemon

Combine first 7 ingredients with hot sauce and lemon juice, stirring well. Chill several hours. When ready to use, bring to room temperature. Cook frozen vegetables according to package directions and drain. Combine vegetables; add sauce, stirring gently to coat. Serve hot. Preparation: 30 minutes. Serves 10 to 12.

Can be halved successfully. Try it cold! Substitute ½ cup sour cream for ½ cup mayonnaise.

Jeanie Vertner

Vegetable Hash

2 peeled carrots
1 egg-size onion
1 cup celery
1 green pepper
2 cucumbers

1 envelope gelatin
1 tablespoon lemon juice
½ teaspoon salt
¼ teaspoon white pepper
1½ cups mayonnaise

Chop vegetables very fine (preferably in a food processor). Drain chopped vegetables for 45 minutes, reserving juice. Add gelatin to 4 tablespoons of heated vegetable juice. Combine with vegetables, lemon juice, salt, pepper, and mayonnaise. Refrigerate overnight.

Connie Barry

Italian Asparagus

1 pound fresh asparagus	¼ pound fresh Parmesan
½ stick butter, melted	cheese, grated
	Juice of ½ lemon

Cook asparagus and drain. Place in 13 x 9 x 2-inch dish. Pour butter and lemon over asparagus. Top with Parmesan cheese. Place under broiler until brown.

This can be done in microwave.

Cabell West

Almond Asparagus

1 pound fresh asparagus	½ cup blanched, slivered
2 tablespoons butter or	almonds, toasted
margarine	Salt and pepper
1 tablespoon lemon juice	

Wash asparagus; cut into 1-inch diagonal slices. Heat butter in skillet. Add asparagus and saute 3 to 4 minutes. Cover skillet and steam about 2 minutes or until tender-crisp. Toss asparagus with lemon juice and almonds; salt and pepper to taste. Serves 4.

Robin Ware

Asparagus Loaf

1 egg	1 16-ounce can asparagus
1 cup milk	and liquid
1 cup cracker crumbs	¼ cup grated sharp cheese
2 tablespoons butter,	Salt and pepper
melted	
1 tablespoon minced	
onion	

Beat egg slightly. Heat milk and gradually add to egg. Add crumbs, butter, and onion and let stand until crumbs absorb milk. Cut asparagus into small pieces with scissors and fold asparagus and cheese into milk mixture, adding salt and pepper. Spoon into greased loaf pan. Bake at 350° for 25 to 30 minutes. Serves 6 to 8.

Gwen Weeks

Asparagus-Carrot Casserole

6 medium carrots	1 cup evaporated milk
½ teaspoon salt	½ cup asparagus juice
½ stick butter	1 cup grated sharp Cheddar
3 tablespoons flour	cheese
1 large can asparagus	Dash of pepper

Scrape carrots and slice lengthwise. Boil until tender in water to which ½ teaspoon salt has been added. Set aside. Melt butter. Add flour and mix well. Slowly add milk; mix to a smooth paste. Add asparagus juice and pepper. Cook over low heat until thick. Add grated cheese. Butter a baking dish and arrange a layer of carrots and a layer of asparagus. Cover with sauce and repeat until all are used. Bake at 350⁰ for 20 to 30 minutes, until heated through. Serves 6.

Cindy Vogel

Green Beans Vinaigrette

¾ pound fresh green beans	1 tablespoon red wine vinegar
⅓ cup chopped green onion	1 teaspoon Dijon mustard
2 tablespoons snipped fresh parsley	3 tablespoons olive oil or cooking oil
2 cloves garlic, minced, or ¼ teaspoon garlic powder	Salt and pepper

Trim beans. Cook beans and onions, covered, in small amount of boiling salted water 5 to 6 minutes or until crisp-tender. Drain vegetables well.

Combine parsley, garlic, vinegar, and mustard. Gradually add oil, stirring with whisk or fork. Add dash of salt and pepper. Stir until well blended. Pour over green beans and heat through or refrigerate and serve cold.

Good either hot or cold, but I prefer them served cold - great for cold plate lunch or dinner! French-cut beans would also be nice.

Patsy Barr

Baked Limas with Sour Cream

1 pound dried lima beans (or 4 cans, drained)	¾ cup brown sugar
3 teaspoons salt	1 tablespoon dry mustard
¾ cup butter or margarine	1 tablespoon molasses
	1 cup sour cream

Soak dried beans in water overnight. Next day, drain; cover with fresh water to which 1 teaspoon salt has been added; cook until tender. (If using canned beans, heat until boiling; drain; rinse under hot water.) Put in medium-size casserole. Dab butter over hot beans. Mix brown sugar, mustard, and 2 teaspoons salt in a bowl. Then sprinkle over top. Stir in molasses and sour cream. Mix gently. Bake at 350° for 1 hour.

This is a delicious accompaniment for ham.

Mary Anne Burke

Calico Baked Beans

½ pound hamburger meat	1 16-ounce can pork and beans
½ pound bacon, cubed	½ cup catsup
1 cup onion, chopped	1 teaspoon salt
1 16-ounce can kidney beans	1 teaspoon dried mustard
1 16-ounce can butter beans	¾ cup light brown sugar
1 16-ounce can lima beans	2 teaspoons vinegar

Brown onion and bacon in a skillet; add hamburger meat and brown. Drain off grease and put meat and onion in large, deep baking dish. Add rest of ingredients partially draining beans. Mix well. Bake 40 minutes at 350°, or until very hot. Serves 10 to 12.

This is excellent as a main dish with cornbread and a salad.

Margaret Gentil

147

Broccoli Stuffed Onions

3 medium Vidalia onions
1 10-ounce package
  frozen chopped broccoli
½ cup Parmesan cheese
⅓ cup mayonnaise
2 tablespoons lemon juice

2 tablespoons butter
2 tablespoons flour
¼ teaspoon salt
⅔ cup milk
1 3-ounce package cream
  cheese

Peel and halve onions. Parboil in salted water 10 to 12 minutes. Drain. Remove centers, leaving ¼-inch edges. Chop center portions to equal 1 cup. Cook and drain broccoli. Mix broccoli, chopped onion, Parmesan cheese, mayonnaise, and lemon juice. Spoon into center of onion. Melt butter; blend in flour, salt, and milk. Cook until thick. Remove from heat; blend in cream cheese. Spoon over broccoli mixture in onion halves. Bake, covered, at 375⁰ for 20 minutes. Serves 4 to 6.

Great with chicken.

Jill Traywick

Broccoli Oriental

1 bunch broccoli, sliced
1 clove garlic, minced
1 teaspoon sugar
1 teaspoon flour or
  cornstarch
2 tablespoons soy sauce

½ cup water
1 cube bouillon, beef or
  chicken
¼ cup vegetable oil
1/8 teaspoon salt
2 tablespoons sherry

Wash and slice broccoli; set aside. Combine sugar, flour, soy sauce, water, and bouillon; stir to dissolve bouillon; set aside. Heat oil in wok or frying pan, add garlic and brown. Add broccoli and stir-fry 2 minutes. Add sherry and salt, cover, and cook 2 minutes. Lift cover and add sauce; stir thoroughly. When sauce has thickened, remove and serve. Serves 4.

This recipe is also good with cabbage, green beans, or a combination of vegetables.

Jane Johnson

Broccoli with Cashews

2 tablespoons butter
2 tablespoons minced
   onion
1 cup sour cream
2 teaspoons sugar
1 teaspoon vinegar
½ teaspoon poppy seeds

¼ teaspoon salt
½ teaspoon paprika
1 cup cashew nuts,
   chopped
1 large bunch broccoli,
   broken into florets
   (save stems for soup)

Saute onion in butter until soft and pale yellow. Remove from heat and stir in sour cream, sugar, vinegar, and seasonings. Pour over cooked broccoli and sprinkle with cashews. Serve hot. Serves 4 to 6.

Connie Garrett

Carrots Vichy

1½ pounds carrots, peeled
   and cut into 2-inch
   pieces
1½ cups canned beef
   bouillon
2 tablespoons sugar

6 tablespoons butter
½ cup heavy cream
   (optional)
Pinch of pepper
Minced parsley

Boil carrots slowly in covered saucepan with bouillon, sugar, pepper, and butter for 30 to 40 minutes or until carrots are tender and liquid has been reduced to a syrupy glaze. Toss with parsley. Cream may be added just before serving; warm but do not boil. Serves 6.

Marti Thomas

Marinated Carrots

2 pounds carrots, peeled
and cut on diagonal
into small pieces
1 medium onion, sliced
in rings

1 large green pepper, cut
in thin strips

Cook carrots until tender but firm. Add onion and green pepper.

Marinade:

1 cup tomato soup
½ cup salad oil
1 cup sugar
¾ cup vinegar
1 teaspoon prepared
mustard

½ teaspoon pepper
1 teaspoon Worcester-
shire sauce
1 teaspoon salt

Mix well and pour over vegetables. Refrigerate 12 hours. Serves 10.

Recipe can be halved.

Michael Robertson

Glazed Carrots

4 tablespoons butter
4 tablespoons brown
sugar

2 cans Belgian tiny
carrots

Melt butter in saucepan. Add brown sugar and cook over medium heat until sugar dissolves. Drain carrots and add to butter/sugar mixture. Gently roll carrots until they turn golden brown. Add more butter and sugar if necessary. Serves 6.

Delightful touch for a colorful plate.

Anne Grier

Sweet 'n Sour Red Cabbage

3 heads firm red cabbage, about 3 pounds	¼ bay leaf
3 tablespoons lard, chicken fat, or duck fat	1 teaspoon caraway seeds
1 tablespoon finely minced onion	½ cup vinegar, or more, to taste
1 teaspoon salt	Freshly ground black pepper to taste
½ cup sugar	Very light sprinkling of nutmeg (optional)

Remove outside leaves of cabbage. Split each head in half and remove core from each half. Split halves into quarters. Cut quarters into ¼-inch strips, or thinner, crosswise. Quickly wash cut cabbage in cold water. Place in colander and drain well. Melt lard or fat in large pot. Add onions and cook until glossy. Add cabbage, salt, pepper, sugar, bay leaf, nutmeg, and caraway seeds. Pour in vinegar. Gently toss mixture together. Cook cabbage over medium heat, uncovered, until it starts to steam. Continue cooking over medium heat, stirring. When liquid starts to boil, reduce heat to low and cook until tender, stirring occasionally. All liquid must slowly evaporate; this is the only way to make cabbage sweet-sour, tender, and a pretty purple. Taste a few strips and add more sugar or vinegar to taste. Remove bay leaf. Serves 12.

Buying red cabbage is similar to buying white cabbage. Look for firmest, hardest heads. If three or four leaves are bursting through or have burst in the same place, watch out - cabbage is oversoaked with water, which adds additional weight.

Joanne Smith

Corn Souffle

1 10-ounce package frozen whole-kernel corn	3 eggs
½ pint whipping cream	2½ tablespoons sugar
	Pinch of salt
	Butter

Blend corn, whipping cream, eggs, sugar, and salt in a blender. Pour into a greased casserole and dot with butter. Bake at 325° for 1 hour and 5 to 10 minutes. Serves 4.

Elizabeth Bradshaw

Vegetables

Corn Timbale

12 ears of fresh corn
6 eggs
2 to 3 tablespoons grated onion
1 teaspoon salt
4 to 5 tablespoons fresh parsley
⅔ cup lightly pressed-down white bread crumbs
⅔ cup lightly pressed-down grated cheese (Swiss or Cheddar)
6 drops Tabasco (or 1/8 teaspoon cayenne pepper)
8 to 10 grinds of fresh pepper
⅔ cup cream

Scrape or grate corn. Beat eggs in mixing bowl. Add remaining ingredients, including corn. Butter a mold and cover bottom with buttered wax paper. Stir mixture and pour into mold. Set mold in larger dish filled with water ⅔ up mold. Preheat oven to 350º. Bake in lower part of oven 30 minutes. Reduce heat to 325º and bake 45 to 60 minutes longer. Dish is done when it almost fills mold and top has cracked. Let rest 10 minutes with oven off and door ajar. Remove and unmold. May be served hot or cold. Serves 12.

Corinne Davis

Corn Pudding

2 16-ounce cans cream-style corn
2 16-ounce cans regular corn
5 eggs, beaten slightly
1 pint half-and-half
1 cup cream
2 tablespoons flour
2 tablespoons cornmeal
2 tablespoons sugar
¼ cup butter, melted
Salt
Pepper

Combine all ingredients in a 2½ to 3-quart casserole. Bake at 325º to 350º for 1 hour or until set. Serves 12 to 14.

Can be halved (use 3 eggs).

Robin Traywick Williams

Eggplant Casserole

2 medium eggplants	1½ cups grated Cheddar
3 medium tomatoes, sliced	cheese
	Olive oil
1 large onion, thinly sliced	Buttered bread crumbs

Peel eggplant and cut in slices ¼ to ½-inch thick. Saute until light brown in oil. (You will have to keep adding oil for each batch as eggplant soaks it up.) In a 9 x 12-inch casserole, layer ⅓ eggplant, ½ tomatoes, onions, and cheese. Repeat and end with top layer of eggplant. Top with buttered crumbs. Cover and bake at 350° until bubbly all through, about 45 minutes. Preparation: 45 minutes. Serves 10.

Wonderful with lamb, poultry, or fish. A family favorite!

Gerry Lewis

Aunt Em's Eggplant Casserole

4 eggs (2 hard-boiled)	½ cup saltine cracker
1 medium eggplant	crumbs
1 small onion, finely chopped	13 ounces evaporated milk (1 can)
3 tablespoons margarine	Juice of ½ lemon

Hard-boil 2 eggs and chop. Peel and slice eggplant. Soak in salt water for 15 minutes; cook until tender. Drain and mash. Add other ingredients with milk last. Bake in greased dish at 300° for 30 to 40 minutes, or until knife comes out clean when inserted. Serves 4 to 6.

Emily McLeod

Vegetables

Eggplant Parmesan

¼ cup margarine
½ cup cornflake crumbs
¼ cup grated Parmesan
cheese
1 small to medium
eggplant
1 egg, slightly beaten
1 8-ounce can tomato
sauce

½ teaspoon dried oregano,
crushed
½ teaspoon sugar
1/8 teaspoon onion salt
4 to 6 ounces Mozzarella
cheese, grated
Pepper

Melt margarine in oblong baking dish. Combine cornflake crumbs, Parmesan cheese, and a dash of pepper. Wash eggplant and slice into ¼-inch thick slices. Dip in egg, then in crumb mixture. Place in baking dish. Bake at 400° for 10 to 15 minutes. Turn eggplant over; bake 10 minutes more. Meanwhile, combine tomato sauce, oregano, sugar, and onion salt; heat to boiling, stirring frequently. Pour sauce over cooked eggplant, top with cheese. Return to oven to melt cheese. Serves 4.

Nancy Perrow

Baked Vidalia Onions

Beef bouillon cubes
Butter

Vidalia onions

Place bouillon cube in center of each cored and peeled onion. Dot with butter. Set in baking dish, cover tightly, and bake at 425° for 30 to 40 minutes. (They can be wrapped individually in foil, if desired.)

Use only Vidalia, Georgia onions. They are available in May, June, and July.

Margaret Bargatze

End-of-the-Rainbow Onion Rings

1½ cups plus 2 tablespoons (13 ounces) beer
1 tablespoon baking powder
1 tablespoon Lawry's seasoning salt
1 egg
1½ cups flour
2 large golden or Spanish onions, cut in ¼ to ½-inch slices
Oil for deep frying

Combine beer, baking powder, salt, and egg in large bowl and blend. Gradually add flour, stirring to form loose paste. Heat oil to 375º. Separate onion slices into rings. Dip rings into batter, coating well. Fry in batches (do not crowd) until golden brown, turning once (a few seconds after you put rings in oil). Drain on paper towels. Serve hot. Makes 30 to 60 rings.

This recipe would also work well for mushrooms.

Terry Tosh

Gorgeous Fries

6 baking potatoes
½ cup butter (1 stick)
1 8-ounce wedge of fresh Parmesan cheese, grated
Onion salt
Paprika

Wash potatoes and cut into ½-inch wide sticks. Put in ice water for ½ hour; drain and dry. Arrange on cookie sheet. Slice butter and scatter over potatoes. Sprinkle onion salt to taste. Bake at 350º for 1 hour, tossing with a spatula every 10 to 15 minutes. Five minutes before removing, sprinkle with Parmesan cheese and paprika. Preparation: 30 minutes. Serves 6 to 8.

Pamela Sexton

Creamed Cauliflower and Peas

1 large cauliflower, separated into florets, or 3 packages frozen cauliflower	3 tablespoons flour
	¼ teaspoon pepper
	¼ teaspoon nutmeg
	1 teaspoon salt
1 package frozen peas	1 cup light cream
¼ cup butter	¼ cup dry bread crumbs
¾ cup finely chopped onion	Milk

Cook cauliflower in 1½ cups water. Drain. Cook peas as directed. Save pea liquid to add to milk to make 2 cups. Preheat oven to 400°. Saute onion in ¼ cup butter until golden. Remove from heat and stir in flour, salt, pepper, and nutmeg. Gradually stir in milk and cream. Cook until thickened. In a 3-quart casserole, gently combine peas and cauliflower and sauce. Add melted butter to crumbs and sprinkle over top. Bake casserole covered for 30 minutes; uncover and bake 20 minutes longer or until bubbly. Serves 8 to 10.

Anne Grier

Green Pea and Water Chestnut Casserole Supreme

1 package frozen green peas	1 can water chestnuts, sliced
¾ stick butter or margarine	1 4-ounce can mushrooms, whole or sliced; reserve juice
2 medium onions, chopped	1 tablespoon flour
2 ribs of celery, chopped	½ cup herb stuffing mix

Cook peas just slightly. Drain. Saute onions and celery in butter. Add mushroom juice and flour. Stir until thickened. Mix in remaining ingredients, including peas. Place in buttered casserole and sprinkle with herb stuffing mix. Dot with butter. Bake at 350° until hot. Serves 6 to 8.

Louise Mondy

Mushroom Florentine

1 pound fresh
  mushrooms, caps and
  stems, sauteed in butter
2 packages frozen,
  chopped spinach,
  cooked and drained
1 teaspoon salt

¼ cup chopped onion
¼ cup butter, melted
1 cup grated Cheddar
  cheese
  Garlic salt
  Pepper

Line 10-inch greased pie or quiche pan with spinach seasoned with salt, onion, and melted butter. Sprinkle with ½ cup cheese. Arrange sauteed mushrooms over spinach. Season with garlic salt and pepper. Cover with remaining cheese. (May be refrigerated at this time.) Bake at 350° for 20 minutes. Serves 6.

Nancy Morris

Creamy Mushroom Bake

1 pound mushrooms,
  stems removed
½ cup butter
2 tablespoons flour
½ cup half-and-half
¼ cup rich beef or
  chicken stock
½ cup grated sharp
  Cheddar cheese

½ cup Monterey Jack
  cheese, grated
¼ cup cooking sherry
½ cup fresh fine or
  Italian bread crumbs
½ cup freshly grated
  Parmesan cheese
  Dash of freshly ground
  pepper

Preheat oven to 350°. Butter shallow baking dish. Arrange mushrooms in dish stem side down. Melt butter in saucepan over low heat. Increase heat to medium-high, blend in flour, and cook 3 minutes, stirring constantly. Pour in half-and-half and bring to a boil. Mix in beef or chicken stock, and pepper and return to a boil. Reduce heat to low; add Cheddar and Monterey Jack cheeses. Add ¼ cup sherry. Let cook until sauce is smooth. If sauce is not thick enough for your taste, add more Cheddar cheese. Pour sauce over mushroooms. Sprinkle with bread crumbs. Bake uncovered 30 minutes. Sprinkle with Parmesan and continue baking until cheese melts, about 5 minutes. Serve hot. Serves 4 to 6.

Chicken stock is tastier.

Terry Tosh

Mashed Potato Casserole

8 to 10 medium boiling
 potatoes
1 8-ounce package cream
 cheese, softened
2 eggs, lightly beaten
2 tablespoons flour
2 tablespoons minced
 parsley

2 tablespoons minced
 chives or grated onion
1 3½-ounce can French-
 fried onions (optional)
 Salt and pepper to taste

Peel potatoes and boil until tender; drain and put in large bowl of electric mixer. Beat until smooth; add salt, pepper, and cream cheese; and beat again. Blend in eggs, flour, parsley, and chives, and beat thoroughly. Turn into a buttered 2-quart casserole. Spread slightly crushed onions over top and bake uncovered at 325° for 30 to 40 minutes, until puffy. Serves 6 to 8.

Can be made in advance and refrigerated. Add onion topping before placing in oven. May be frozen before baking.

Pat Morrison

Creamy Taters

2 to 2½ potatoes, diced
1 large green pepper,
 diced
1 large onion, diced
1 tablespoon flour
4 tablespoons chopped
 parsley

4 ounces grated Cheddar
 cheese
¼ pint hot milk
¼ pint heavy cream
2 tablespoons butter
 Pinch paprika, nutmeg,
 salt, and pepper

Preheat oven to 400°. Sprinkle potatoes, green pepper, and onions with flour, cheese, and spices. Spread potato mixture in 3-quart oven-proof dish. Pour milk and cream over top and dot with butter. Bake 1 hour or until potatoes are soft with crisp, golden brown topping. Serves 6.

Pooh Steele

Sweet Potato Souffle

2 cups mashed sweet potatoes (put through ricer)
1 to 1½ cups sugar
¾ stick butter or margarine
½ cup milk

½ teaspoon nutmeg
½ teaspoon cinnamon
¾ cup crushed cornflakes
½ cup chopped pecans
½ cup light brown sugar
¾ stick butter or margarine

Preheat oven to 400°. Mix first 6 ingredients and put in 1½-quart casserole. Bake for 20 minutes. Mix remaining ingredients and place on top of casserole. Bake for 10 minutes more. Serves 4.

Lucy Meade

Mrs. Strupe's Sweet Potatoes

3 cups mashed sweet potatoes (cooked and mashed in food processor or ricer)
1 cup sugar
1/8 teaspoon salt
⅓ stick butter or margarine

1 teaspoon vanilla
1 teaspoon rum
2 eggs, beaten
1 small can crushed pineapple, drained
1 cup miniature marshmallows

Combine all above ingredients and top with the following topping:
1 cup brown sugar
⅓ cup flour
⅓ stick butter (or margarine)

1 cup pecans, chopped

Bake in 350° oven for 35 minutes. Serves 8.

Nancy Gottwald

Super Spinach Souffle

1 package frozen chopped spinach	⅓ cup milk
½ cup butter	2 eggs, separated
¼ cup flour	½ cup grated Swiss or
⅓ cup liquid from cooking spinach	Cheddar cheese
	Salt and pepper

Cook spinach according to package directions; drain very well, saving liquid. Melt butter; add flour, cooking several minutes, stirring continuously. Add liquid and milk, cooking over low heat and stirring until thick. Add spinach and beaten egg yolks. Beat egg whites and fold in. Add salt and pepper. Pour into greased 1½-quart casserole. Top with cheese. Set in pan of water. Bake at 350° for 35 to 40 minutes or until knife inserted in middle comes out clean. Serves 4 to 5.

Charmian Matheson

Creamed Spinach Crunch

2 packages frozen chopped spinach	1 small onion, chopped
1 stick butter, softened	Salt and pepper
1 8-ounce package cream cheese, softened	Plain bread crumbs
1 can sliced water chestnuts	Grated fresh Parmesan cheese

Cook spinach according to package directions. Drain. Mix butter, cream cheese, water chestnuts, salt, pepper, and onion with hot spinach. Put into 2-quart casserole. Top with mixture of bread crumbs and Parmesan cheese. Bake uncovered at 350° for 30 minutes. Serves 6 to 8.

Variation: Line bottom of 13 x 9 x 2-inch casserole with drained and halved artichoke hearts (not marinated) and proceed with recipe above.

Cabell West

Spinach Casserole

2 10-ounce packages
frozen spinach
½ cup butter
½ onion, finely chopped
1 14-ounce can
artichokes, quartered

1 pint sour cream
½ cup grated Parmesan
cheese
½ teaspoon salt
¼ teaspoon pepper

Cook spinach. Drain and squeeze dry. Saute onion in butter. Add remaining ingredients. Add spinach. Put in 1½-quart casserole and bake 25 to 30 minutes. Preparation: 15 minutes. Serves 6 to 8.

Janet Dennis

Bettina's Spinach Casserole

3 medium red onions,
sliced
2½ sticks butter, divided
½ pound fresh
mushrooms, sliced
2 tablespoons flour
1 cup milk
2 10-ounce packages
frozen chopped
spinach, thawed and
drained

10 ounces Mozzarella
cheese, grated
3 to 4 firm tomatoes,
thinly sliced
¾ cup bread crumbs
Salt and pepper
Nutmeg to taste

Saute onions in ½ cup butter until soft; set aside. Saute mushrooms in ½ cup butter; add salt and pepper to taste; set aside. Melt 2 tablespoons butter in saucepan. Blend in flour. Slowly add milk, stirring constantly to make a cream sauce. Mix in spinach. Add salt, pepper, and nutmeg to taste. Place spinach mixture in bottom of greased, 3-quart oblong casserole dish. Layer with sauteed onions, Mozzarella cheese, and sauteed mushrooms. Season tomato slices with salt and pepper, dip into bread crumbs, and place on top of casserole. Dot with 2 to 3 tablespoons of butter. Bake at 350° for 40 minutes or until brown and bubbly.

Great with roast beef!

Ann Reed

Squash Casserole with Sage

2 pounds summer squash, sliced	2 eggs, beaten
1 medium onion, chopped	1 teaspoon sage, ground
1 cup Cheddar cheese, grated and divided	1 teaspoon sugar
	Salt and pepper
	Paprika

Cook squash in lightly salted water until tender. Combine all ingredients, reserving half the cheese and the paprika. Mix gently with drained, cooked squash and place in a slightly greased 2-quart casserole or flat dish. Top with remaining cheese and paprika. Bake at 350° for 25 to 30 minutes. Serves 6 to 8.

This may be done the day before and baked just before serving. Don't leave out the sage! It's the magic ingredient of this dish.

Nancy Penick

Squash and Corn Casserole

4 medium yellow squash	1 16-ounce can cream-style corn
1 tablespoon butter	Salt and pepper
1 small onion, diced	Additional dressing for topping
⅓ cup Pepperidge Farm cornbread dressing	
3 eggs, well beaten	

Slice squash about ½-inch thick. Cook until done, about 10 to 15 minutes. Drain well; mash with butter, salt, pepper, and onion. Add dressing, eggs, and corn. Put in casserole. Sprinkle dressing on top and bake at 350° for 1 hour. Serves 6 to 8.

Good family fare.

Lynn Congdon

Baked Squash

7 small summer squash, sliced
1 small onion, diced
½ cup light cream

¼ cup saltine crackers, crushed
2 tablespoons butter
Bread crumbs

Boil squash in salted water until tender. Drain and mash. Saute onion in butter. Add cream, crackers, and squash. Pour into greased casserole and top with butter dots and a few bread crumbs. Bake at 400° for 30 minutes or until done. Serves 6.

Battletown Inn
Berryville, Virginia

Zucchini Boats

Zucchini, sliced in half lengthwise
Sour cream

Grated Parmesan cheese

Pierce meat of zucchini with fork or knife. Spread top with sour cream and sprinkle generously with cheese. Bake about 45 minutes at 325° or until cheese is browned.

Mary Garrison

Zucchini Parmesan

4 cups thinly sliced zucchini
1 onion, sliced
1 tablespoon water
2 tablespoons butter

1 teaspoon salt
Pepper
Parmesan cheese, freshly grated

Put first 6 ingredients in skillet. Cover and cook 1 minute. Uncover and cook, turning with spatula until barely tender (about 5 minutes). Sprinkle with Parmesan cheese; toss. Serves 4.

If doubling, do not increase salt.

Nancy Morris

Quick Zucchini

6 to 7 zucchini, small
3 to 4 tablespoons butter,
    melted

Dill to taste

Cut zucchini into bite-sized pieces. Saute zucchini in melted butter with dill for 1 to 2 minutes. Mix and coat well. Cover pan and cook slowly for 1 to 3 minutes. Zucchini should be crunchy. Serves 6 to 8.

Margaret Bargatze

Baked Zucchini

3 long zucchini
4 to 5 strips raw bacon
Grated Parmesan
cheese

Pepper to taste

Cut each zucchini in half and then cut halves lengthwise. Place cut side up in 2-quart rectangular Pyrex dish. Sprinkle Parmesan cheese liberally onto each slice. Cut raw bacon into pieces to fit on top of each piece of zucchini and sprinkle with pepper to taste. Bake uncovered at 350° for 40 minutes, or until tender, and cheese turns light brown. Serves 4.

Zucchini dish may be prepared in advance and refrigerated until time to cook. Recipe may be doubled or tripled.

Mary Miller

Zucchini Casserole

2 to 3 fresh zucchini,
    sliced
2 ripe tomatoes, peeled
    and sliced
2 medium onions, thinly
    sliced
½ cup melted butter or
    margarine

1 8-ounce package
    Mozzarella cheese, sliced
    or grated
Basil
Parmesan cheese,
    grated

Preheat oven to 450°. Layer zucchini, tomatoes, and onions in a 2 to 3-quart Pyrex dish. Drizzle butter over top. Sprinkle with basil. Cook for 20 minutes. Remove and put Mozzarella on top. Sprinkle with Parmesan cheese. Cook another 10 minutes until cheese is melted. Serves 6.

Debbie Dunlap

Lucy's Fried Tomatoes

Half ripe tomatoes   **Salt and pepper**
Cornmeal   **Butter**

Grease frying pan with butter and preheat. Mix cornmeal, salt, and pepper. Slice tomatoes ¼-inch thick and roll in cornmeal mixture. Simmer tomatoes for approximately 10 to 15 minutes, turning once.

Keith Wylie

Tomato Pie

3 cups Bisquick   1 cup grated Cheddar
¾ cup milk   cheese
6 to 7 tomatoes   1 cup mayonnaise
1 tablespoon chives   Salt and pepper
1 tablespoon sweet basil

Mix first 2 ingredients, roll out, and fit into two 9-inch or 10-inch pie pans. Freeze one to use later or double remaining ingredients to make two pies. Peel tomatoes. Cut into thick slices and fill pie shell, sprinkling with salt, pepper, chives, and sweet basil so that spices are distributed evenly throughout. Cover with topping made by blending last 2 ingredients. Bake at 400° for 25 to 30 minutes. Serves 6.

This can be prepared one-half day ahead and stored in refrigerator until one hour before baking. Even good as a leftover.

Wilton Dunn

Curried Baked Fruit

1 1-pound can pear halves	13 maraschino cherries
1 1-pound can cling peaches	⅔ cup blanched, slivered almonds
1 1-pound can pineapple chunks	⅓ cup butter, melted
1 1-pound can apricot halves	¾ cup light brown sugar
	3 tablespoons curry

Drain all fruit. Arrange fruit and nuts in layers in casserole. Melt butter in saucepan; add sugar and curry powder and blend. Pour butter mixture over fruit and nuts and bake at 325⁰ for 1 hour. Refrigerate overnight. Reheat at 350⁰ before serving. Serves 12.

Carroll Cottrell

Fresh Cranberry Casserole

½ cup white sugar	1 teaspooon cinnamon
½ cup light brown sugar	1½ cups fresh cranberries
1 cup quick oatmeal, uncooked	3 medium apples, diced
3 tablespoons flour	1 cup pecans, chopped
	1 stick margarine

Combine sugars, oatmeal, flour, and cinnamon. Add fruit and nuts, mixing well. Spread in casserole. Top with margarine. Bake at 350⁰ for 30 minutes.

This is a marvelous side dish at Thanksgiving and Christmas or to perk up a leftover dinner.

Sara Drummond

Bourbon Apples

1 can apple pie filling
⅓ cup bourbon
¼ cup brown sugar
1/8 cup white sugar

2 tablespoons butter
Cinnamon and nutmeg
to taste

Mix all ingredients except butter and let set in refrigerator 24 hours to mellow. Remove and dot with butter. Bake at 350º for 1½ hours. May need to put under broiler to crystalize top.

This dish is an excellent accompaniment for game and may also be used for brunch. Could also be a tasty dessert.

Dorothy Gentil

Pineapple Casserole

½ cup butter or
    margarine, softened
1¾ cups sugar
3 eggs
1 20-ounce can pine-
    apple, undrained

½ cup milk
½ teaspoon vanilla
8 to 9 slices white bread,
    cubed

Preheat oven to 325º. Lightly butter a 9-inch square glass baking dish or 1½-quart casserole. Cream butter and sugar with mixer. Beat in eggs. By hand, stir in pineapple, milk, and vanilla. Fold in bread. Bake 1 hour. Serve hot or at room temperature. Serves 8.

This can be made ahead and is a good accompaniment for ham.

Margaret Bargatze

Sauces

Holiday Mayonnaise

2 egg yolks, lightly
  beaten
½ teaspoon salt
1 pint Crisco oil, chilled

Dash cayenne
Dash paprika
Juice of 1 lemon (add
  more if necessary)

Mix egg yolks, lemon juice, and seasonings. Add Crisco very slowly.
Yield: 2¼ cups.

Delicious on tomato aspic or cooked vegetables.

Alice Burke

Sour Cream Hollandaise

¼ cup butter, melted
1 cup sour cream
1 tablespoon flour
1/8 teaspoon salt
2 to 3 tablespoons fresh
  lemon juice

2 egg yolks, slightly
  beaten
Dash pepper

In small saucepan, combine butter, sour cream, flour, salt, and
pepper. Gradually stir in lemon juice. Over medium heat, bring
mixture to boiling, stirring constantly. Let boil 1 minute. Stir some
of hot mixture into egg yolks; then pour egg mixture back into
saucepan. Over low heat, cook, stirring just until thickened again.
Be very careful not to curdle sauce. Yield: 1½ cups.

May be reheated in double boiler.

Molly Cates

Blender Hollandaise Sauce

1 cup butter or margarine
4 egg yolks
2 tablespoons lemon juice
¼ teaspoon salt or
  seasoned salt

Pinch red pepper
Pinch cayenne

Place butter in a small saucepan and heat until it bubbles; do not
brown. Place remaining ingredients in blender (cover and turn
on low speed). Remove cover and pour in bubbling-hot butter
in a slow, steady stream. Serve immediately. Yield: 1½ cups.

*To keep sauce warm, place blender jar in pan filled with 2 or
3 inches very warm water. Blend briefly before serving.*

Edie Cabaniss

Garlic Butter Sauce

¾ cup butter
3 garlic cloves, minced
¼ cup water

½ teaspoon chopped parsley

Combine all ingredients and cook about 10 minutes. Yield: 1 cup.

Super over vegetables and homemade pasta.

Jane Johnson

Cleiland Carter's Fresh Herb Butter

2 sticks butter or margarine
3 tablespoons fresh chives
3 tablespoons fresh marjoram
3 tablespoons fresh sage
3 tablespoons fresh peppermint

3 tablespoons fresh thyme
3 tablespoons fresh parsley
3 tablespoons fresh basil
3 tablespoons fresh oregano
1 tablespoon minced garlic

Soften butter to room temperature. Finely chop all herbs and measure after chopping. Mix all ingredients thoroughly and chill. Yield: 1½ cups.

Vary herbs and amounts to taste. Serve on toasted french bread. Excellent on all vegetables.

Cleiland Donnan

Sauces

Fresh Basil Pesto Sauce

2 cups packed fresh basil
  leaves
2 large garlic cloves
1 small bunch fresh
  parsley (optional)

½ cup pine nuts (or un-
  salted, blanched almonds)
¾ cup fresh Parmesan
  cheese, grated
⅔ to 1 cup good olive oil

Place basil, garlic, and parsley in blender or food processor; chop finely but do not puree. Add nuts and cheese and process until smooth. Slowly pour in oil with machine running and process only until oil is incorporated. Sauce should be the consistency of creamed butter. Place in jar and cover with 1/8-inch oil. May be stored in the refrigerator for several months or in the freezer for up to a year. Yield: 2 cups.

Use pesto sparingly! Toss with buttered pasta and freshly grated Parmesan cheese or with cooked spring vegetables. A wonderful addition to clam or tomato sauce or to minestrone soup.

Joan McEwan

When cleaning spinach, add salt to the first rinse water and let it soak a minute. This will remove the grit.

Cut down on the odor of cabbage, cauliflower, etc., when cooking by adding a small amount of vinegar to the water.

A small amount of bacon drippings or ham leftovers can be added to greens as they cook to give them a good flavor.

Wrap green tomatoes in newspaper to keep during the winter. Store in a cool, dry place and tomatoes will gradually ripen.

Peel an onion under running water to keep back the tears.

To freshen wilted greens, douse quickly in hot water, then in iced water with a little vinegar added.

To make your mashed potatoes fluffier, add hot milk with melted butter and a pinch of baking powder.

Always add a pinch or two of sugar to vegetables to improve their flavor.

To cut even onion rings, slice before peeling and slip the peel off each ring. Always slice the mustache end last.

Roll lemons, oranges and grapefruit on a counter before extracting juice.

Meat

Beef

Game

Lamb

Pork

Veal

Sauces

In Virginia, the first choice for holiday meals, picnics, or cocktail parties featuring "heavy hors d'oeuvres" is often ham.

The country ham tradition, synonymous with a Southside town called Smithfield, goes back to colonial days. English settlers brought wild boars to Virginia in the early 1600's and let the razorbacks run wild.

The settlers learned how the Indians salt-cured and smoked venison for preservation, and they adapted the process to pork. Over the years, the process has been perfected for making the world-famous Smithfield hams.

The Homestead, built around the natural waters of Hot Springs in the Allegheny Mountains, is internationally known for its gracious atmosphere and elegant table. Chef Albert Schnarwyler frequently draws on Virginia's larder for his creations, as in this recipe for ham with a fruit sauce.

Virginia Ham and Fruit Dressing

Wash ham thoroughly and place in a large pan or roaster, skin side down. Cover completely with water. Bring to a boil and simmer 15 to 20 minutes per pound. Remove ham from water. Remove skin. Sprinkle ham with plenty of light brown sugar and dot with cloves. Bake in 375° oven until glazed. Two cups of dry sherry may be added when baking ham (baste several times during baking). Glaze can also be made of the rind from two oranges mixed with brown sugar.

Homestead Fruit Dressing:

1 16-ounce can sliced yellow cling peaches	3 ounces raisins
	3 ounces walnuts
1 16-ounce can sliced pears	6 ounces brown sugar
	½ pound butter, sweet or lightly salted, melted
1 16-ounce can pineapple chunks	1 teaspoon vanilla
1 16-ounce can apricot halves	5 slices white bread, toasted

Drain fruits in a colander, keeping the apricots separate. Put fruits (except apricots) in a large bowl and add raisins, walnuts, 4 ounces brown sugar, and vanilla. Mix lightly. Pour into a baking pan and place apricots evenly on top. Cut toast in ½-inch squares and place on top of fruit. Pour melted butter and the 2 ounces remaining brown sugar over entire mixture. Bake at 325° for 30 minutes. Serves 8 to 10 people.

The Homestead
Hot Springs, Virginia

Filet of Beef

1 filet of beef, 5 to 6
  pounds
¾ stick unsalted butter or
  margarine, softened

Garlic salt
Crushed pepper

Bring meat to room temperature and pat dry with paper towel. Place in a greased or aluminum foil lined shallow pan. Spread margarine or butter over top and sides of meat. Sprinkle with garlic salt and crushed pepper, rubbing into meat.

Preheat oven to 450⁰. Cook meat for 15 minutes. Reduce heat to 350⁰ and cook for an additional 30 minutes. Remove meat from oven and let sit for 20 minutes. Meat will be medium rare. Slice and serve as an entree or cool completely and serve as an hors d'oeuvre, thinly sliced, with party rye and mayonnaise or horseradish sauce on the side. Preparation: 10 minutes. Serves 8 as an entree.

Delicious!

Missy Ryan

Steak Diane

2 3-ounce center cut filets
  of beef, thinly sliced
1 ounce chopped onion
1 ounce mushrooms
½ ounce brandy
1 ounce red wine

Salt
Pepper
Mustard
Worcestershire sauce
Steak sauce

Saute meat, onions, and mushrooms together. Flame with brandy, season to taste, and simmer 5 minutes in red wine. Serves 1.

The Hotel Roanoke
Roanoke, Virginia

Fool Proof Rib Roast

1 standing rib roast   **Salt and pepper**

Let roast stand at room temperature 30 minutes per pound. Season with salt and pepper. Place rib side down in shallow baking dish and place in preheated 500° oven. Cook 5 minutes per pound. Turn off heat and leave in oven for 2 hours, but not more than 3 hours. Do not open oven door. Roast will be crusty and brown outside and rare and juicy inside. Preparation: 5 minutes. Serves 2 per rib.

Judy Brooks

Marinated Rare Beef

2½ to 3 pounds rolled   1½ teaspoons dry mustard
rump roast   Dash pepper
1⅓ cups cooking oil   Cherry tomatoes
½ cup red wine vinegar   (optional)
2 small cloves garlic,   Asparagus or broccoli
crushed   (optional)
2 teaspoons sugar   Sliced fresh mushrooms
1½ teaspoons salt   (optional)

Have meat at room temperature. Place on rack in shallow pan. Roast at 325° until thermometer reads 140° (approximately 1 hour). Cool. Cut in ¼-inch slices. Arrange in baking dish. In jar combine oil, vinegar, garlic, sugar, salt, dry mustard, and pepper; shake well (do not blend). Pour over meat. Chill 2 to 3 hours. May also marinate tomatoes, asparagus or broccoli, and mushrooms. Drain marinade; arrange meat and vegetables on platter. Serves 6.

Especially nice because it can be done ahead; cook meat the day before! Can easily be doubled or tripled.

Annette Chapman

Ginger Marinade for London Broil

¼ cup water	¼ teaspoon ginger
¼ cup honey	Garlic salt
¼ cup soy sauce	London Broil

Pierce meat with sharp knife and sprinkle with garlic salt. Place meat in plastic bag and cover with marinade. Refrigerate for 24 hours, turning bag occasionally. Cook meat as desired and heat marinade before serving. Preparation: 5 minutes.

Liz Thomas

Bourbon Marinated Eye of Round

2½ pounds eye of round	Pepper
1 stick butter	Worcestershire sauce
¾ cup bourbon	A-1 sauce
Garlic salt	Juice of ½ lemon

Place meat in Dutch oven. Melt butter in separate pan. Sprinkle garlic salt over roast until white and then pepper until black. Pour butter over roast, wash off butter with Worcestershire sauce and A-1 sauce. Pour enough bourbon to wash off these sauces and pour lemon juice on top of this. Boil on top of stove until alcohol is burned off, about 2 minutes. After it reaches a boil, remove from heat and let marinate about 4 hours, basting occasionally. Cook on grill, basting with marinade for 30 to 40 minutes for rare. Check for preference. Preparation: 10 minutes. Serves 8 to 10.

Lynn Congdon

Lemon Marinated Flank Steak

1 ½ pounds flank steak
½ cup lemon juice
Seasoned salt
Fresh ground pepper

Place flank steak in dish suitable for marinating. Pour lemon juice over steak and sprinkle generously with salt and pepper. Turn steak over and repeat salt and pepper. Refrigerate at least 3 hours, turning at least once. Grill over gas or charcoal approximately 15 minutes or to desired doneness. Preparation: 5 minutes. Serves 4.

Kathy Adair

Barbecued Beef Brisket

1 5-pound beef brisket
1 cup Kraft regular barbecue sauce
½ cup water
1 large onion
Fresh ground pepper
Seasoned salt

Place brisket in a large piece of aluminum foil in a shallow pan or a broiler pan. Season with pepper and seasoned salt to taste. Slice onion over top of brisket and pour barbecue sauce over all. Add ½ cup water around sides of meat inside foil. Close tightly keeping all liquids inside. Bake at 275° for 5 hours.

Allow brisket to cool slightly and chop for barbecue sandwiches or place brisket in refrigerator overnight and remove the next day and slice. Chopped barbecued meat may be reheated using some of the pan drippings and additional sauce. Preparation: 10 minutes. Serves 6 to 10.

Kathy Adair

Marinated Barbecued Beef Brisket

6 to 8 pounds lean
boneless brisket
1 4-ounce bottle Liquid
Smoke
Garlic salt to taste

Onion salt to taste
Celery salt to taste
Worcestershire sauce to
taste
Salt and pepper to taste

Sauce:

1 14-ounce bottle catsup
½ cup brown sugar
½ tablespoon salt
½ teaspoon dry mustard
3 cloves garlic
1 catsup bottle of water
¾ tablespoon Worcester-
shire sauce

1/8 teaspoon cayenne
pepper
¼ tablespoon Liquid
Smoke
½ teaspoon vinegar
¼ teaspoon pepper
½ tablespoon A-1 sauce

Place meat in long, shallow pan. Cover with 4 ounces Liquid Smoke and sprinkle generously with garlic salt, onion salt, and celery salt. Refrigerate overnight. Remove from refrigerator and sprinkle generously with Worcestershire sauce, salt, and pepper. Cover with foil and bake at 275° for 5 hours. Combine sauce ingredients in saucepan and simmer 30 to 40 minutes. Cover brisket with sauce and bake 1 hour. Cool before slicing.

This sauce is out of this world and freezes well!

Sue Reynolds

Delicious Corned Beef

4 pounds corned beef	1 carrot, sliced
1 tablespoon pickling spice	1 tablespoon mustard
1 rib celery, sliced	⅓ cup brown sugar
1 onion, quartered	½ cup sweet pickle juice

Place beef, spices and vegetables in large pot; cover with cold water. Bring to boil and simmer, covered, for 4 hours. Cool beef in broth. Drain and place in shallow baking dish. Coat beef with mixture of mustard and brown sugar. Pour pickle juice in pan. Bake at 300° for 1 hour, basting occasionally. Serves 8 to 10.

Delicious with sauerkraut and rye bread.

Ann Bray Pastore

Spinach Meatballs

1 small onion, finely chopped	1 10¾-ounce can mushroom soup
1 package frozen spinach, thawed and well drained	½ soup can water
	½ soup can white wine
1 pound ground round	Oil
1 egg, beaten	Flour
1 tablespoon Parmesan cheese	Salt and pepper

In a large skillet, saute onion in oil until transparent. Transfer with slotted spoon to a large bowl. Add spinach, salt and pepper, meat, egg, and Parmesan cheese; mix well. Shape into meatballs and roll in seasoned flour. Saute in oil until outsides are brown. Place in casserole. Combine soup, water, and wine. Bake 35 minutes at 350°. Serve over rice or spinach noodles. Preparation: 1 hour. Serves 4.

Be sure to squeeze thawed spinach of any excess water.

Julie Goodell

Zucchini Stuffed Flank Steak

2 to 3 pounds flank steak	¾ cup oil
1 clove garlic, minced	1 teaspoon freshly
2 tablespoons soy sauce	ground pepper
3 tablespoons red wine	½ teaspoon nutmeg
vinegar	Zucchini stuffing
1 tablespoon Dijon	
mustard	

Score steak and pound to ½-inch thick. Mix together next 7 ingredients in a small bowl. Place steak in shallow roasting pan and cover with marinade. Let meat marinate at least 4 hours, turning often.

Lay steak on a large cutting board and spread zucchini stuffing on steak to within 1-inch of each side. Roll jelly roll fashion, tying with string to secure. Place meat in shallow roasting pan and baste with marinade. Roast in preheated 450° oven for 20 minutes for rare, 35 minutes for medium rare. Baste and turn meat 2 to 3 times during cooking. Slice in ½-inch slices through meat and stuffing. Serves 6 to 8.

Zucchini Stuffing:

½ pound bulk sausage	1 egg, slightly beaten
1 large onion, chopped	½ cup fresh bread crumbs
1½ cups zucchini, grated	½ cup slivered almonds
½ teaspoon salt	Marinade or beef broth

Cook sausage until brown. Drain well, reserving 1 tablespoon of fat. Saute onion in remaining fat for 5 minutes. Add zucchini and saute another 5 minutes. Drain all fat and remove from heat. Add salt, egg, bread crumbs, almonds, and 3 tablespoons of marinade to sauteed mixture. Stuff flank steak and cook as directed above.

Marti Thomas

Beef and Snow Peas

2 tablespoons sherry
4 tablespoons soy sauce
5½ teaspoons cornstarch
1 clove garlic, crushed
1 pound top sirloin, thinly sliced
4 tablespoons oil

¼ pound fresh mushrooms, thinly sliced
1 8-ounce package snow peas, thawed
1 teaspoon sugar
1 cup beef consomme
1 tablespoon water
Salt and pepper to taste

Combine sherry, 2 tablespoons soy sauce, 4 teaspoons cornstarch, and garlic. Add beef and mix well. Let stand 15 minutes. Saute beef quickly in 3 tablespoons hot oil, stirring constantly until color barely disappears. Add mushrooms and cook 2 minutes. Remove meat and mushrooms. Add remaining oil and peas to pan. Add remaining soy sauce, sugar, consomme, and remaining cornstarch dissolved in water. Simmer until sauce thickens. Return meat and mushrooms to sauce, salt and pepper to taste, and mix until thoroughly heated. Preparation: 45 minutes. Serves 4.

Carol Colby

Sukiyaki

1½ pounds sirloin tip steak
2 tablespoons cooking oil
½ cup soy sauce
⅔ cup water
3 tablespoons sugar
1 5-ounce can bamboo shoots, drained
1 cup green onions, cut in ½-inch pieces

1 8-ounce package frozen broccoli, thawed, dried, and cut in 1-inch pieces
1 16-ounce can bean sprouts, drained
1 5-ounce can water chestnuts, sliced and drained
1 cup fresh mushrooms, cut in half
Cooked rice

Cut steak into paper-thin slices across the grain, then into 1-inch wide strips. Brown meat in cooking oil in a large skillet or wok 2 to 3 minutes. Combine soy sauce, water, and sugar. Pour over meat. Push meat to one side of skillet. Keeping the ingredients separate, add bamboo shoots, green onions, and broccoli. Cook 5 minutes, turning vegetables and keeping separate. Push vegetables to one side. Add bean sprouts, water chestnuts, and mushrooms, keeping each separate. Cook 2 minutes until hot. To serve, place 1 cup rice in the center of each plate. Surround rice with meat and vegetables, keeping each separate. Pour a small amount of gravy over rice. Preparation: 15 minutes. Serves 6 to 8.

Kathy Brasington

179

Eggplant Parmigiana

2 tablespoons butter or margarine
½ cup onion, chopped
1 clove garlic, minced
1 pound ground beef
1 16-ounce can tomatoes
1 6-ounce can tomato paste
2 teaspoons dried oregano
1 teaspoon basil
1½ teaspoons salt
¼ teaspoon pepper
½ cup water
1 tablespoon brown sugar
1 large eggplant
2 eggs, slightly beaten
1 tablespoon water
½ cup dry Italian bread crumbs
¼ cup salad oil
1¼ cups Parmesan cheese
6 to 8 ounces Mozzarella cheese, shredded

In a large skillet, saute onion, garlic, and ground beef in butter until meat is no longer red. Add tomatoes, tomato paste, oregano, basil, salt, and pepper. Stir well. Add ½ cup water and brown sugar. Bring all ingredients in skillet to a boil. Simmer uncovered 20 minutes.

Heat oven to 350°. Grease baking dish well. Peel and cut eggplant into ½-inch slices. Combine eggs and 1 tablespoon water; mix well. Dip eggplant in egg, coating well. Dip in bread crumbs and coat well. Saute eggplant in oil until brown and arrange in bottom of baking dish. Sprinkle with half of the Parmesan cheese. Top with half of the Mozzarella cheese and cover with half of the tomato sauce. Repeat. Bake uncovered or until Mozzarella is melted and slightly brown. Preparation: 1 hour. Serves 6.

Nancy Payne

Beef Stroganoff

Sauce:

1 large onion, diced
4 ounces butter
2 ounces tomato paste
1/8 teaspoon oregano
¼ bay leaf
2 tablespoons flour
3 cups chicken or veal broth, boiling (more if needed)

1 cup sour cream, room temperature
½ cup mushrooms, precooked
Pinch thyme
Salt and pepper

Smother onions in butter lightly. Add tomato paste and seasonings. Smother on low heat for a few minutes. Add flour, mix well, then add boiling broth. Cook 30 minutes. Strain; blend in sour cream and mushrooms.

1½ pounds beef tenderloin, minced

Noodles or rice, cooked

Saute beef in hot skillet until done, 3 to 4 minutes. Pour sauce over it and mix lightly. Serve over noodles or rice. Serves 5.

Executive Chef Albert Schnarwyler says this "is one of my favorite recipes I use here at The Homestead. Hope your users of the cookbook enjoy the Beef Stroganoff."

The Homestead
Hot Springs, Virginia

Beef

Beef Stew with Red Wine

2 pounds beef chuck, cut
  into 1½-inch cubes
2 short beef ribs
2 tablespoons oil
4 cups boiling water
1 tablespoon meat extract
  (Wilson's BV)
1 teaspoon
  Worcestershire
½ teaspoon Tabasco
1 clove garlic
1 medium onion, sliced

1 tablespoon salt
½ teaspoon pepper
1 cup dry red wine
6 carrots, quartered
½ pound small white
  onions
3 medium potatoes,
  quartered
1 pound canned tomatoes
½ pound fresh mushrooms
  Butter

Dry meat by wrapping in paper towels repeatedly until most of the moisture is absorbed. Thoroughly brown meat on all sides in hot oil. Add boiling water, meat extract, Worcestershire sauce, Tabasco, garlic, onion, salt, pepper, and wine. Simmer slowly, covered, for 2 hours.

Add carrots, onions, potatoes, and tomatoes. Continue to cook for 30 minutes more. Saute mushrooms in butter; add to stew and heat until simmering again. Preparation: 30 minutes. Serves 8 to 10.

Charmian Matheson

Bill's Chili

1 large onion, chopped
1 tablespoon margarine
  or butter
1 pound ground beef
1 clove garlic, pressed
2 8-ounce cans tomato
  sauce

2 tablespoons chili
  powder (Mexene if
  available)
1 teaspoon ground cumin
1 teaspoon salt
1 16-ounce can kidney
  beans, drained

Saute onion in butter until clear. Add meat and stir until brown. Add remaining ingredients and simmer at least 30 minutes, stirring occasionally to keep from sticking. Add kidney beans 15 minutes before serving. Preparation: 15 minutes. Serves 4.

This freezes well.

Janet Dennis

Italian Meat Pie

1½ pounds ground chuck
¾ cup dry oats (uncooked oatmeal)
1 cup tomato sauce
1 egg, beaten
1 teaspoon salt
2 teaspoons oregano
½ cup Parmesan cheese, grated

1 package chopped spinach, cooked and drained
1 16-ounce can peeled tomatoes, drained and sliced
12 ounces Mozzarella cheese, grated

Brown and drain meat. Add oats, tomato sauce, egg, seasonings, and ¼ cup Parmesan cheese. Pack ½ mixture into 9 x 12-inch baking dish. Spread spinach over mixture then slice tomatoes over spinach. Put remaining meat mixture over tomatoes. Top with Parmesan cheese and Mozzarella cheese. Bake at 350° for 30 minutes. Preparation: 30 minutes. Serves 6.

Sue Schutt

Tamale Pie

1 pound ground beef
1 cup onion, chopped
1 cup green pepper, chopped
1 clove garlic, crushed
2 8-ounce cans tomato sauce
1 8-ounce can tomatoes, loosely broken
1 12-ounce can corn, drained
½ cup raisins

½ cup pitted ripe olives
1 tablespoon sugar
1 teaspoon salt
2 teaspoons chili powder
2 to 3 dashes Tabasco
½ teaspoon pepper
1 6-ounce package sharp Cheddar cheese, grated
¾ cup yellow cornmeal
½ teaspoon salt
2 cups cold water
1 tablespoon butter

Cook meat, onion, green pepper, and garlic in large skillet until meat and vegetables are lightly done. Stir in tomato sauce, tomatoes, corn, raisins, olives, sugar, 1 teaspoon salt, chili powder, Tabasco, and pepper. Simmer 20 to 25 minutes or until mixture is thick. Add cheese and stir until melted. Turn into greased 14 x 7-inch baking dish.

Stir cornmeal and ½ teaspoon salt into water. Cook, stirring constantly, until thick. Add butter and mix well. Spoon over meat mixture. Bake 40 minutes at 375°. Preparation: 45 minutes. Serves 6.

Jane Johnson

Beef

Bleu Cheese Burgers

2 to 3 pounds lean
 ground beef
1 teaspoon salt
½ teaspoon freshly
 ground pepper
¾ package large cream
 cheese, softened with a
 small amount of milk
2 tablespoons bleu
 cheese, crumbled

2 tablespoons onion,
 minced
2 teaspoons creamy
 horseradish sauce
2 teaspoons mustard
½ pound fresh
 mushrooms, sliced and
 sauteed in butter

Combine beef, salt, and pepper in a large bowl and blend. Shape into 12 to 16 patties about 4 inches in diameter (each is thin and will be ½ the final burger).

Combine cheeses, onion, horseradish, and mustard, mixing until smooth. Put filling on top of half of the patties, spreading to within ½-inch of edge. Top with the remaining patties, pressing edges together to seal. Broil to desired doneness. Top with sauteed mushrooms and serve with hot French or Italian bread. Burgers may be made and filled one day ahead. Preparation: 25 minutes. Serves 6 to 8.

Connie Garrett

Creamy "Getti"

8 ounces spaghetti
1½ pounds ground beef
2 15-ounce cans tomato
 sauce
1 large onion, chopped
1 large green pepper,
 chopped
1 teaspoon oregano

½ cup cottage cheese
8 ounces cream cheese,
 softened
8 ounces sour cream
1 small onion, chopped
 Salt and pepper
 Butter

Cook spaghetti, adding salt to taste. Set aside. Brown ground beef; drain grease; add salt and pepper to taste. Add tomato sauce, large onion, green pepper, and oregano. Simmer 30 minutes. In separate bowl, mix, with electric mixer, cottage cheese, cream cheese, sour cream, and small onion until combined. In greased 9 x 13-inch casserole, layer half the cooked spaghetti, then cheese mixture, then remaining spaghetti. Top with meat sauce, dot with butter. Bake 1 hour at 350°.

Frances Gordon

184

Bearnaise Sauce

2 egg yolks
1 stick butter, cut in
  pieces
1½ teaspoons tarragon
  vinegar

1½ teaspoons lemon juice
¼ teaspoon salt
½ teaspoon parsley flakes

Put egg yolks in cup (Pyrex is good) and place cup in pan of very warm water. Beat with wire whisk and gradually add pieces of butter, melting each piece before adding more. When all butter is melted, remove cup from water and add vinegar, lemon juice, salt, and parsley. Serve immediately or allow to cool to room temperature. Yield: 1 cup.

Excellent with beef, fish, and vegetables. Do not try to reheat sauce; butter and eggs will separate.

Sue Reynolds

Palmour Sauce

1 16-ounce can tomatoes
1 large onion, chopped
1 cup sugar
1 cup vinegar
1 teaspoon ground cloves

1 teaspoon ground
   cinnamon
1 teaspoon salt
   Dash cayenne

Combine ingredients. Cook slowly for 45 to 60 minutes or until sauce is thick and onions are transparent. Serves 6 to 8.

Absolutely delicious on roast beef or venison. Keeps well in refrigerator.

Georgia Luck

Soy Marinade

¼ cup soy sauce
¼ cup salad oil
¼ cup lemon juice

½ teaspoon parsley flakes
½ teaspoon salt
Dash of pepper

Combine all indredients and pour over meat. Refrigerate several hours or overnight.

This is a good marinade for beef, pork, and poultry. Our favorite is London Broil.

Carolyn Gard

Ellen's Mushroom Gravy

2 sticks margarine
3 to 4 green onions, tops and bottoms, finely chopped
1 large can sliced mushrooms
2 tablespoons Worcestershire sauce

2 tablespoons Kitchen Bouquet
½ cup red wine (or more)
1 teaspoon cornstarch (or more)
¼ bunch parsley, finely chopped

Cook all ingredients except parsley for about 5 minutes; then add parsley. Serves 8 to 10.

Serve over tenderloin or any steak.

Karen Feigley

Sauce for Beef

1 stick butter
1 large onion, grated
½ cup fresh parsley, finely chopped
1 tablespoon dried tarragon, finely chopped

1 tablespoon vinegar
Juice of 2 fresh lemons
Salt
Pepper

Heat butter and onion on low heat for about 2 minutes. Add lemon juice, parsley, tarragon, and vinegar; simmer (do not boil) about 5 minutes. Add salt and pepper to taste. Serves 4.

Nancy Gresham

Cooking Country Ham

1 country ham   2 cups Coke or Pepsi

Preheat oven to 400°. Wash ham and scrub pepper off. Make
a tin foil bag and put in roaster. Wrap ham in foil, leaving a small
opening at the top. Pour in Coke or Pepsi. Seal. Put ham in oven
for 30 minutes. Turn oven off for 3 hours. Refire 30 minutes.
Turn off 3 hours or overnight. Refire 30 minutes. Bone ham while
hot. Cut off skin and excess fat; ready to bake with brown sugar
or whatever you customarily use, or ready to serve as is.

*NEVER OPEN OVEN DOOR! Makes ordinary country ham taste
like more expensive kind.*

Robin Traywick Williams

Ham Loaf with Horseradish Sauce

1 cup milk	¼ cup horseradish
1 cup dry bread crumbs	1½ tablespoons vinegar
2 eggs, slightly beaten	1 tablespoon prepared
2 pounds ground smoked	mustard
ham	½ teaspoon salt
½ pound ground lean	4 drops Worcestershire
pork	sauce
¾ cup brown sugar	½ cup heavy cream,
¼ cup water	whipped
¼ cup vinegar	Dash cayenne
2 teaspoons dry mustard	Dash paprika

Thoroughly combine first 5 ingredients and shape into loaf. Place
in a 10 x 5 x 3-inch loaf pan and invert on a shallow baking dish.
Score top of loaf with handle of wooden spoon or knife. Bake
for 1½ hours at 350°. Baste occasionally with glaze made of
brown sugar, water, vinegar, and dry mustard. Preparation: 30
minutes. Serves 12.

Horseradish sauce: Combine remaining ingredients except cream.
Whip cream and fold into horseradish mixture. Chill and serve
with ham loaf. Yield: 1 cup.

Frances Barnes

Innkeeper's Ham and Apple Pie

6 to 8 large tart apples,
  peeled and thinly sliced
1 cup cooked western
  ham, diced
¾ cup brown sugar

2 tablespoons flour
½ teaspoon salt
½ teaspoon pepper
  Pie dough for a 10-inch
  double crust

Preheat oven to 325⁰. Grease a 10-inch pie plate and add bottom crust. Cover with a third of apple slices and ½ cup diced ham. Sprinkle with one half of sugar, flour, salt, and pepper. Layer with another one third apple slices and remaining ham and seasonings. Top with remaining apples. Cover with pastry and pierce. Bake about 1 to 1½ hours or until crust is brown and apples are tender. Serves 6.

Highland Inn
Monterey, Virginia

Apple Stuffed Pork Chops

2 thick pork chops
½ cup bread crumbs
¼ teaspoon salt
1 teaspoon parsley,
  minced
1/8 teaspoon sage

1 teaspoon onion, grated
¼ cup apples, diced
3 tablespoons milk
  Dash of pepper
  Oil

Cut pockets in sides of pork chops. Brown chops in oil. Mix remaining ingredients and stuff chops. Bake 45 minutes to 1 hour at 350⁰. Preparation: 50 minutes. Serves 2.

Betty Williams

Orange Glazed Pork Chops

4 ¾-inch pork chops
1 tablespoon vegetable oil
½ cup orange juice
2 tablespoons orange marmalade
2 tablespoons brown sugar
1 tablespoon vinegar
Salt and pepper to taste
All-purpose flour

Sprinkle pork chops lightly with salt and pepper; dredge in flour. Heat oil in heavy skillet; brown pork chops on both sides. Combine remaining ingredients, mixing well; pour over pork chops. Reduce heat; cover and simmer 40 to 45 minutes, basting periodically. Serves 4.

Kay Whitworth

Sweet and Sour Pork

2 whole butterfly pork chops
2 eggs
¾ cup flour
½ teaspoon salt
2 tablespoons water
1½ cups apple juice
⅓ cup vinegar
¼ cup sugar
¼ cup catsup
2 tablespoons soy sauce
¼ teaspoon salt
½ cup carrots, sliced
½ cup green pepper, diced
¼ cup onion, sliced
2 tablespoons cornstarch
Oil for browning pork
Rice

Cut pork chops into 1 x 2-inch pieces. Mix eggs, flour, salt, and water. Dip meat into batter and fry in hot oil until golden brown. Set meat aside. Bring apple juice, vinegar, sugar, catsup, soy sauce, and salt to a boil. Add carrots and simmer 15 minutes. Add green pepper and onion, simmering 10 minutes. Thicken with cornstarch that has been dissolved in apple juice. Add pork and mix well. Serve over rice. Serves 4.

Peggy Crowley

189

Loin of Pork Vouvray

2 boneless pork loin
  roasts (rolled and tied)
20 large prunes
1½ cups Vouvray wine
12 large dried apricots
3 tablespoons butter
2 tablespoons oil
6 tablespoons cognac or
  brandy
4 tablespoons flour
  (beurre manie)

4 tablespoons butter
  (beurre manie)
1¼ cups beef bouillon
1 cup heavy cream
3 tablespoons elderberry
  jelly
2 tablespoons orange
  juice

Soak prunes in wine 1 hour, then stuff prunes and apricots in bone pocket of roast. Reserve wine. Brown meat in butter and oil in large pan. Pour cognac over meat and flame. Place in 325° oven for 1½ hours. Let rest for 20 minutes after cooking. Make beurre manie by blending flour and butter until resembles peas. Combine bouillon, wine from prunes, cream, jelly, and orange juice in saucepan. Reduce by boiling. Skim pan juices to remove fat and add juices to sauce. Add ¼ beurre manie at a time, whisking well, until thickened. Simmer 3 minutes, whisking occasionally. Glaze roast with sauce and serve remainder with roast. Serves 10.

Gwen Weeks

Pork Tenderloin with Cinnamon

2 pounds pork tenderloin
4 tablespoons sugar
¼ teaspoon salt
4 tablespoons soy sauce
1½ teaspoons cinnamon

2 tablespoons sherry
1 teaspoon powdered
  ginger
2 teaspoons dry mustard
2 teaspoons lemon juice

Place pork in roasting pan. Combine all ingredients and pour over pork. Bake for 1 hour at 325°, basting frequently with sauce. Preparation: 15 minutes. Serves 4 to 6.

This is also good thinly sliced and served on rolls for cocktail parties.

Torrey Shuford

Braciola

1 pork tenderloin	½ large Spanish onion,
1 clove garlic, finely	chopped
chopped	2½ cups canned tomatoes,
2 tablespoons parsley,	sieved
chopped	½ teaspoon salt
2 tablespoons Parmesan	¼ teaspoon pepper
cheese, grated	1 bay leaf
½ pound Mozzarella	1 pound thin spaghetti,
cheese	cooked
¼ cup olive oil	

Slice pork about ½-inch thick and pound to make cutlets. Combine garlic, parsley, and Parmesan cheese. Cut Mozzarella into strips and place 1 strip on each cutlet with 1 teaspoon of Parmesan mixture. Fold ends over cheese and roll up. Secure with twine. Brown rolls in olive oil; remove and brown onion. Add tomatoes, salt, pepper, and bay leaf. Return rolls to sauce and cook about 1½ hours. Serve with hot spaghetti and Garlic Butter Sauce.

Garlic Butter Sauce:

¾ cup butter	½ teaspoon chopped
3 garlic cloves, minced	parsley
¼ cup water	

Combine and cook 10 minutes.

Jane Johnson

Pork

Down South Barbecue

4 to 5-pound pork roast
2 onions, sliced
5 to 6 whole cloves
2 cups water

1 16-ounce bottle
barbecue sauce (mild or
hot according to taste)
1 large onion, sliced

Put ½ of onions in bottom of Crock-Pot and add meat along with other ingredients. Place remaining onions on top. Cover and cook overnight or 8 to 12 hours on low. Drain and remove all fat and bone from meat. Put back in Crock-Pot and shred with fork. Add barbecue sauce and large onion sliced. Cover and cook additional 1 to 3 hours on high or 4 to 8 hours on low, stirring 2 or 3 times. Serve on large buns. Serves 12.

Pat Morrison

Ratatouille with Sausage

2 large eggplants, peeled
and cut into strips
8 zucchini, sliced
5 medium onions, sliced
6 green peppers, sliced
6 garlic cloves, minced
8 large tomatoes, cut into
strips
1 cup parsley, chopped

2 teaspoons oregano
2 teaspoons thyme
2 teaspoons basil
12 mild Italian sausages
(about 1½-inches long)
Salt and pepper
Flour to coat vegetables
Olive oil

Dredge eggplant and zucchini in flour. Heat a small amount of olive oil in skillet and saute in batches. Drain on paper towels. Saute onions, green pepper, and garlic in same skillet. (Add more oil if needed, but use as little as possible.) Preheat oven to 350°. In a 9 x 13-inch casserole, layer sauteed vegetables, tomatoes, parsley, and seasonings. Stir gently to mix. Saute sliced sausage in skillet; add to vegetables. Bake 45 minutes. Serves 12.

Flavor improves by preparing 24 hours ahead and refrigerating. Bring to room temperature before cooking.

Cristy Jarvis

Spanish Spare Ribs

2 whole heads of garlic
⅔ cup sweet orange juice
⅓ cup lime juice

3 teaspoons oregano
3 pounds pork spare ribs

Peel garlic and press into orange juice, lime juice, and oregano. Pour all together over ribs and marinate 24 hours. Drain all juice off before cooking for at least 1 hour at 450° or on the grill. As ribs cook, baste with juice frequently. Serves 6.

The secret is in marinating for 24 hours and basting while cooking.

Jane Christian

Empanadas (Mexican Meatpies)

1 small onion, finely chopped
1 small bell pepper, finely chopped
3 tablespoons butter
½ pound ground pork
1 tablespoon parsley, finely chopped

3 tablespoons raisins
2 tablespoons sweet relish
½ teaspoon sugar
½ teaspoon salt
Dough for 3 standard pie shells

Saute onion and pepper in butter. Brown pork, drain fat, and combine with onion and pepper. Stir in remaining ingredients (except pastry) and mix well. Cut 3 to 4-inch circles from pastry shells, rolled flat. Place about 1½ tablespoons of pork mixture on each circle. Fold over and press edges together. Bake on cookie sheet at 425° for about 12 minutes or until brown. Makes about 20.

These are also good dipped in a mix of sour cream and hot picante sauce.

Mary Garrison

Sauces

Mustard Sauce for Ham

1 8-ounce jar red currant jelly
1 8-ounce jar Dijon mustard

Dry mustard (optional)

Empty jar of jelly into mixing bowl. Beat mustard into jelly to the consistency desired (about ½ to 1 jar depending on how spicy you want it). Add a bit of dry mustard if you like it hot. Serve cold.

Torrey Shuford

Teriyaki Marinade

1 cup soy sauce
¾ cup sugar
3 to 4 tablespoons fresh ginger, crushed

2 to 3 cloves garlic, crushed

Combine above ingredients. Marinate beef, pork, chicken, or fish for at least 1 hour; then prepare as usual. Baste meat with marinade, if desired, or serve as a hot sauce over cooked meat. Yield: 1½ cups.

To make barbecued spare ribs: parboil ribs; then marinate in sauce for 1 hour. Barbecue on grill, basting with sauce.

Anne Grier

Piquant Sauce

3 tablespoons brown sugar
¼ cup catsup

¼ teaspoon nutmeg
1 teaspoon dry mustard

Mix and heat until bubbling in saucepan. Yield: ⅓ cup.

Good on pork chops, meatloaf, chicken, or ribs.

Beth Skidmore

Rack of Lamb for Four

1 lamb rack, French
  finished, weighing 1½
  to 2 pounds
1 cup red wine
½ cup butter

½ cup parsley, chopped
Salt
Pepper
Oregano
Garlic powder

Rub lamb rack with salt, pepper, oregano, and garlic powder and brush with oil. Roast at 400° for 30 to 35 minutes, brushing with oil as needed. When lamb is at desired doneness, remove to serving platter. Drain off excess fat, retaining pan juices.

Deglaze pan with wine, stirring over low heat on top of stove. Add softened butter and simmer until well blended. Pour over lamb rack and sprinkle with chopped parsley. Serves 4.

The Hotel Roanoke
Roanoke, Virginia

Lamb Chops en Papillote

4 shoulder lamb chops,
  ½-inch thick, trimmed
  of fat
1 teaspoon celery salt
¼ teaspoon crumbled
  chervil (1 teaspoon
  fresh)
2 onions, peeled and
  sliced

3 to 4 zucchini, quartered
  lengthwise
3 to 4 carrots, peeled,
  quartered, 2 inches long
4 new potatoes, peeled
  and sliced
Salt
Few twists of fresh
  pepper

Preheat oven to 350°. Cut four 16-inch squares of heavy-duty foil. Place a chop on each; sprinkle each side with celery salt, pepper and chervil. Top with vegetables and sprinkle lightly with salt. Wrap tightly and place on jelly-roll pan. Bake for 1 hour. Can be served in packet. Serves 4.

Trudie Steel

Butterflied Leg of Lamb with Tarragon

1 8-pound leg of lamb, bone-in, or 5½-pound butterflied and well trimmed	1 tablespoon garlic, finely minced
¼ cup olive oil	¼ cup tarragon vinegar
3 tablespoons whole white mustard seeds	6 tablespoons butter
3 tablespoons fresh tarragon, finely chopped	Salt to taste
	Freshly ground pepper

Preheat charcoal grill or if broiler is used, preheat to high. Sprinkle lamb generously with pepper on all sides. Place oil in baking dish and add lamb, coating well with mustard seeds, tarragon, garlic, vinegar, and salt.

If grilling, place lamb flat on the grill and heat marinade briefly when ready to serve. If broiler is used, place lamb 4 to 5 inches from source of heat and let cook 10 minutes. Turn and cook 10 minutes on other side. Transfer lamb back to marinating dish. Dot with butter and let meat rest 10 to 20 minutes before slicing. Preparation: 20 minutes. Serves 6.

The longer lamb marinates, the better it is. If it is refrigerated after preparation, bring to room temperature before cooking.

Martha Wheeler

Butterflied Leg of Lamb on Grill

1 whole leg of lamb, butterflied	1 cup dry white wine
2 garlic cloves, minced	1 bottle Cross and Blackwell mint sauce
¾ cup olive oil	

Pierce lamb with fork several times. Marinate lamb in all ingredients for 24 hours, turning frequently. Cook on grill until pink inside.

Pooh Steele

Lamb Marinade

½ cup lemon juice
2 large garlic cloves,
   slivered
2 tablespoons Dijon
   mustard
2 tablespoons olive oil

1/8 teaspoon powdered
   ginger
1 6-pound leg of lamb,
   butterflied
Salt
Freshly ground pepper

Mix lemon juice, garlic cloves, mustard, oil, and ginger. Season with salt and pepper. Marinate lamb 6 hours or overnight in refrigerator. Grill 20 minutes on each side. Serves 12.

May be used on lamb kebabs.

Priscilla Alexander

Braised Lamb Rosemary

1 boned leg of lamb (7 to
   8 pounds with fat
   removed)
3 or 4 garlic cloves,
   thinly sliced
1 large onion (white or
   yellow), peeled and
   thinly sliced

3 medium carrots, diced
   finely
2 tablespoons dried
   rosemary, powdered
2 tablespoons arrowroot
   or cornstarch
Cracked pepper

Preheat oven to 350°. Rest lamb at room temperature for 30 minutes before preparation. Make small incisions on surface and ends of leg and in bone pocket. Insert a slice of garlic into each incision. Spread vegetables over bottom of a roasting pan which is just large enough to hold leg of lamb. If desired, lamb may be browned in pan before vegetables are added. Apply powdered rosemary to entire surface of lamb and inside pocket. Place lamb on top of vegetables and sprinkle with pepper. Cover and roast lamb to desired degree of doneness (1¼ hours to 1½ hours for medium rare roast).

After roasting, remove lamb to a rack and let rest for 15 to 20 minutes. While lamb is resting, strain vegetables from pan juices. Deglaze juices. Mix a small amount of juices with 2 tablespoons of arrowroot or cornstarch to make a paste. Thicken remaining juices with paste using hot water to establish and maintain desired consistency. Add reserved vegetables to sauce. Carve roast and serve with sauce. Serves 8.

Kathy DeLoyht

Veal Picatta

16 1-ounce scallopini of
    veal
12 ¼-inch slices cucumber
1 cup white wine
3 ounces capers
3 tablespoons fresh
    parsley, chopped

½ pound butter, melted
Salt and pepper
Flour for dredging
Oil for frying
Juice of 2 lemons

Sprinkle veal and cucumber with salt and pepper; dredge with flour. Saute in oil in frying pan until browned on each side; set aside. Drain off fat; deglaze pan with wine, lemon juice, capers, and chopped parsley over low heat. Add melted butter and simmer slowly about 5 minutes. Place scallopini and cucumbers back in pan. Bring to a boil and serve on heated plates. Serves 4.

The Hotel Roanoke
Roanoke, Virginia

Lemon Veal with Parsley

1½ pounds thin veal steak,
    round or sirloin
 2 tablespoons flour
 ¼ cup butter
 1 clove garlic, minced
 ½ pound fresh
    mushrooms, sliced (or
    1 4-ounce jar)

½ teaspoon salt
1 tablespoon lemon juice
⅓ cup dry white wine
2 tablespoons snipped
    fresh parsley or 1
    tablespoon dried
Dash of pepper

Flatten veal with meat mallet until ¼-inch thick. Cut into 2-inch squares and flour. Melt butter and saute veal, a few pieces at a time, until golden brown on both sides. Return all meat and the garlic to skillet and heap mushrooms on top. Sprinkle with salt, pepper, and lemon juice. Pour on white wine, cover, and cook over low heat for 20 minutes or until veal is fork tender. Add a little more wine if needed. Sprinkle with parsley just before serving. Preparation: 30 minutes. Serves 4.

This dish can be prepared ahead of time and reheated in the oven when ready to serve.

Martha Davidson

Veal Vermouth

2 pounds veal for
scallopini, sliced tissue-
thin and cut into bite-
size pieces
½ cup unsalted butter or
more if needed
2 large onions, chopped
5 carrots, sliced ¼-inch
thick
½ to 1 pound fresh
mushrooms, sliced

3 to 4 chicken bouillon
cubes
1½ cups boiling water
½ cup dry vermouth
Grated Parmesan
cheese
Salt and freshly ground
pepper

Sprinkle veal with salt, pepper, and Parmesan cheese. Melt half of the butter in a skillet and brown veal quickly, adding more butter if necessary. Place veal in a large casserole dish and add remaining butter to skillet. When melted, add onions, carrots, and mushrooms, cooking until almost tender. Dissolve bouillon in water, add vermouth, and pour over vegetables and veal in casserole. Refrigerate at least 12 hours or overnight. Remove from refrigerator at least ½ hour before baking. Bake covered 1 to 1¼ hours in a 325⁰ oven. Preparation: 30 minutes. Serves 6.

This recipe can be easily doubled.

Trudie Steel

Wiener Schnitzel

4 veal cutlets, beaten flat
1 egg, slightly beaten
3 tablespoons butter
2 lemons
8 anchovy fillets

Salt and pepper
Flour
Seasoned bread crumbs
Capers
Parsley

Sprinkle cutlets with salt and pepper. Dip each into flour, then into egg, and then into bread crumbs. Heat butter in skillet and brown on each side (about 3 minutes). Sprinkle with juice of 1 lemon and arrange on platter. Garnish with lemon slices, anchovies, capers, and parsley. Preparation: 10 minutes. Serves 4.

Nancy Gresham

Veal Parmigiana

1½ pounds veal cutlets
2 eggs, beaten slightly
½ cup Italian bread crumbs

½ cup Parmesan cheese, grated
Cooking oil

Sauce:

2 cloves garlic, minced
1 medium onion, finely chopped
1 16-ounce can whole tomatoes

1 24-ounce can tomato sauce
¼ teaspoon dried thyme
¾ teaspoon dried oregano
8 ounces sliced Mozzarella cheese

Cut and pound cutlets into 5 or 6 serving pieces. Dip each piece into beaten egg. Combine bread crumbs and Parmesan cheese; dip cutlet in this mixture. Brown each cutlet in hot cooking oil and place in greased 13 x 9-inch baking dish. Saute garlic and onion. Add tomatoes, breaking them into small pieces; simmer 10 minutes. Add tomato sauce and spices; simmer 30 to 45 minutes. Place half the sauce over the browned cutlets. Cover with Mozzarella cheese. Cover cheese with remaining sauce. Sprinkle well with Parmesan cheese. Bake uncovered at 375° for 30 minutes.

To save time, prepare the sauce before preparing the veal. This dish is better if made ahead. It freezes well after assembling. For a more economical dish, use eggplant instead of veal. Peel and slice thinly, and then follow same directions.

Betsy Worthington

Veal Scaloppini Bolognese

1½ pounds veal, thinly
  sliced for scaloppini
6 tablespoons unsalted
  butter
½ cup Marsala wine

1 cup chicken broth
½ cup grated Parmesan
  cheese
Flour
Salt and pepper

Have butcher slice veal when frozen (thinner than he thinks he can). Dip veal into flour and shake off excess. Over medium heat, melt 2 tablespoons butter in skillet. Saute veal quickly, adding butter for each new skilletful. Keep veal warm on a heat-proof serving platter.

Discard skillet butter, add wine, and stir with wooden spoon to scrape sides. Add chicken broth and simmer until sauce is reduced to about half.

Season meat lightly with salt and pepper. Cover each veal slice with Parmesan cheese and dot with butter. Broil until cheese is melted, pour sauce over veal, and serve. Preparation: 30 minutes. Serves 6.

Trudie Steel

Saltimbocca

12 slices veal (about 1½
  pounds)
½ cup olive oil, divided
4 tablespoons butter
¾ pound tomatoes, peeled
  and chopped
2 or 3 sprigs parsley,
  finely chopped

1 teaspoon oregano
12 slices of Smithfield
  ham, thinly sliced
12 slices of Mozzarella
  cheese, thinly sliced
¼ cup grated Parmesan
  cheese
Salt and pepper

Flatten out veal as thinly as possible. Heat 5 tablespoons of olive oil and all the butter, and lightly fry veal on both sides. Sprinkle with salt and pepper and keep hot.

Heat remaining oil in another pan. Add the tomatoes, salt, pepper, parsley, and oregano, and cook quickly for 10 minutes, or until tomatoes are reduced to a pulp. On each veal slice, put a slice of ham and a slice of Mozzarella cheese. Next spread a spoonful of tomato sauce and top with Parmesan cheese. Place in a shallow, greased baking dish. Preheat oven to 425°. Bake until cheese melts. Preparation: 20 minutes. Serves 6.

Cabell West

Sweetbreads Crillon

2 pair sweetbreads
1 quart cold water
1 bay leaf
1 carrot, scraped and diced
2 onions, peeled and sliced, divided
4 slices lean bacon
2 tablespoons flour
1 tomato, peeled and sliced

2 tablespoons finely cut parsley, or 2 teaspoons dried parsley
¼ teaspoon thyme
1 teaspoon salt
½ teaspoon pepper
1 cup dry white wine
8 triangle toast points
1 cup chicken broth (optional)
Juice of 1 lemon

Soak sweetbreads in cold water 20 minutes. Drain. Combine 1 quart water, bay leaf, carrot, 1 onion, and lemon juice in kettle (enamel if you have it) and bring to boil. Add sweetbreads. Simmer 20 minutes. Drain. Cover sweetbreads with cold water 5 minutes. When cool, cut skin, fat, gristle, and veins from sweetbreads and break into serving size pieces. Cook bacon in skillet until crisp. Break with fork in pan. Remove large pieces of bacon, leaving bits and the fat. Roll sweetbreads in flour. Brown in bacon fat on each side over high heat. Lower heat and add remaining onion, tomato, parsley, thyme, salt, and pepper. Add crumbled bacon. Blend all. Cook over medium heat 5 minutes. Add wine. Simmer uncovered 15 minutes. Serve on toast. Serves 4.

Sweetbreads must be fresh and used the same day. One cup of chicken broth may also be added with the wine if more sauce is desired.

Grace Deane

Boar Pie

1½ pounds diced boar
(pork shoulder may be
substituted by the less
daring)
3 cups pork stock or
water
3 tablespoons butter
4 tablespoons flour
⅓ cup raisins

½ cup prunes
½ cup dates
⅓ cup diced apples
½ teaspoon ginger
½ teaspoon nutmeg
½ cup mincemeat
½ teaspoon cloves
Salt and pepper
Pastry for double pie

Simmer the meat in the stock or water until ⅔ done. Melt the butter in a saucepan and add flour, cooking gently for 1 minute. Drain the hot stock off the meat and stir into a well-blended roux.

Put the meat and all other ingredients in the sauce and pour into an 8 or 9-cup deep pie dish lined with pastry dough. Top with dough and bake at 375° for 45 minutes or until well browned.

The Boar's Head Inn
Charlottesville, Virginia

Venison Roast

1 haunch venison
½ pound bacon
1 onion, chopped

1 cup hot water
Salt and pepper

Trim meat of most fat. Wash in tepid water; dry thoroughly with cloth. Make dressing with onion, salt, and pepper. Cut slits into meat and stuff with dressing. Cover with strips of bacon. Pour in 1 cup hot water, cover, and cook until done in a slow oven, allowing 25 minutes per pound. Baste often. Preparation: 2 hours. Serves 8-12.

Soaking venison overnight in vinegar water or Worcestershire sauce will help remove some of the gamey taste. Also remove as much fat as possible.

Lynn Congdon

Barbecued Venison

1 hindquarter venison, boned	2 cups vinegar
	1 cup onion, minced

Barbecue sauce:

1 cup onions, minced	½ cup brown sugar, packed
5 tablespoons bacon drippings	
2¼ cups catsup	¼ cup prepared mustard
11/8 cups white vinegar	2¼ teaspoons salt

Make sauce first. Saute onions in drippings until translucent. Drain. Combine with remaining ingredients and store in refrigerator until ready for use. Yield: 1 quart.

Place 2 cups vinegar and venison in crockpot, and cook on low for 24 hours. Remove and discard liquid. Shred venison and combine with onion and 1 quart sauce until completely moistened. Cook in crockpot on low for 1 to 3 hours. Serve on hamburger rolls or dinner rolls. Yield: 1 gallon.

Venison has very little fat so it requires a great deal of sauce. This can serve 50 to 75 for a cocktail party.

Susan Jenkins

Broiled Venison Steaks

1 haunch of young buck	Butter
Salt and pepper	Water
Flour	

Cut haunch of young buck into steaks. Sprinkle with pepper and lightly flour. Dot with butter and cook in sizzling hot iron frying pan. Sprinkle with salt as you turn. Cook 10 to 15 minutes with enough water in pan to make gravy. Serve hot with wild rice. Preparation: 30 minutes. Serves 4.

Lynn Congdon

Roast Venison

4 pounds venison roast	1 teaspoon mustard
2 tablespoons flour	¼ cup vinegar or lemon
2 cloves garlic, minced	juice
1 large onion, sliced	1 pound can tomatoes
2 tablespoons brown	Salt
sugar	Oil
1 tablespoon Worcestershire sauce	

Marinade Sauce:

½ cup vinegar	Cold water to cover
2 cloves garlic, minced	game
2 tablespoons salt	

Let venison (can be frozen) stand overnight in marinade sauce. Season venison with salt, roll in flour and brown in hot skillet. Place in crockpot and add other ingredients. Cover and cook on low for 12 hours. Serves 8.

Rabbit may be substituted for venison. Tastes like chicken!

Susan Jenkins

In buying meat with some bone, allow ⅓ to ½ pound per serving. These cuts include rib roasts, steaks, chops and ham. For bony cuts, allow ¾ to 1 pound per serving. Roast beef: 2 to 3 servings per pound. Tenderloin of beef: 3 servings per pound. Pork spareribs: 1 serving per pound.

Salting meat before browning draws the juices, with their considerable natural salt content, out of the meat and into the pan.

Seasoning meat: rub with garlic, onion, herbs or spices about a half hour before cooking, or insert slivers of garlic or onion near the bone of a roast.

Always handle ground meat lightly to avoid a dense finished texture.

Before roasting meat, brush the pan with a small bit of fat to prevent charring the drippings, which results in a bitter taste in the juices used later for gravy.

Do not store meat in hot gravy in quantities larger than 3 cups. Drain off gravy and allow it to cool separately.

If meats are stuffed, unstuff leftovers and store them separately.

Ham and other cured meats should be desalted before cooking. Soak 12 hours, allowing 1 quart of water to 1 pound of cured meat, or parblanch before cooking.

Variety meats are highly perishable. Use them at once.

Cooking liver too long or too fast will make it tough.

Never handle any wild meat without using gloves, because of the danger of tularemic infections.

Always make sure the meat of wild animals is sufficiently cooked, because any omnivorous, warm-blooded animal could be harboring trichinosis.

Care must be taken to remove all fat from any fresh game, as it grows rancid quickly.

Do not use game fat to grease pans or for sauteing or browning.

Before washing a meat grinder, run a piece of bread through it.

To clean a burned pan: Immediately fill pan with cold water for starchy foods or milk, with hot water for greasy foods. Soak for an hour or so. Put some water and baking soda in pan and boil for a few minutes.

206

Poultry and Seafood

Which came first, the Kentucky fried chicken, the Maryland fried chicken, the Carolina fried chicken or the Virginia fried chicken?

Who cares? What matters is what tastes good. The world has learned how good Southern fried chicken is, but don't stop there. We think you'll enjoy other poultry dishes from our part of the world—some we claim credit for and some we've adopted.

The woods and fields and waterways of the Old Dominion teem with game birds, so, in addition to recipes for orange chicken and Virginia ham-and-chicken, we've included local recipes for potted dove breasts, smoked goose and breasts of wild duck.

After you've tried this traditional approach by the chef at the Historic Michie Tavern, take a gander at the rest of the selection. The Michie Tavern, located on Monticello Mountain near Thomas Jefferson's old home, was opened in 1784 and continues to attract travelers with its daily colonial-style buffet.

Michie Tavern's Colonial Style Chicken

1 2 to 3-pound fryer, cut up	1½ teaspoons paprika
3 cups shortening	1 teaspoon garlic salt
¾ cup all-purpose flour	¼ teaspoon pepper

Combine flour and seasonings and roll the chicken in this mixture. Using a Dutch oven or other heavy deep pan, fry chicken in shortening at 350° for 12 to 15 minutes on each side, or until tender. Preparation: 30 minutes. Serves 4 to 6.

"Fried chicken was a very popular dish in the 1700's."

Historic Michie Tavern
Charlottesville, Virginia

Chesapeake Bay Chicken

4 whole chicken breasts, skinned, halved, and boned
½ cup chopped onion
½ cup chopped celery
3 tablespoons butter
3 tablespoons white wine
8 ounces crabmeat (fresh or canned)
½ cup herb-seasoned stuffing

2 tablespoons flour
½ teaspoon paprika
2 tablespoons melted butter
¼ cup white wine
1 cup shredded Swiss cheese
Hollandaise sauce
Salt and pepper to taste

Pound chicken breasts to flatten and season with salt and pepper. Cook onion and celery in 3 tablespoons butter until tender. Remove from heat and combine with wine, crabmeat, and stuffing mix. Divide mixture onto chicken breasts, roll up and close with a toothpick. Roll each breast in flour-paprika mixture. Place in baking dish and drizzle with 2 tablespoons butter. Bake uncovered for 1 hour at 375°. Combine Hollandaise sauce, ¼ cup white wine, and cheese over low heat until cheese melts. Spoon over chicken. Preparation: 45 minutes. Serves 8.

Mary Roach

Mustard Grilled Boneless Chicken Breasts

6 whole chicken breasts, skinned and boned
1 7-ounce jar sweet and rough mustard (by the Silver Palate)

¾ cup lemon juice
1 heaping tablespoon Worcestershire sauce

Paint chicken breasts on both sides with mustard. Place in large dish. Sprinkle lemon juice and Worcestershire sauce over chicken, cover, and allow to marinate overnight in refrigerator. Remove from refrigerator and let return to room temperature before grilling. Preheat broiler or outdoor grill. Grill chicken 4 minutes per side or until just tender, basting with left-over marinade. Preparation: Overnight. Serves 6.

The Tides Lodge
Irvington, Virginia

Chicken Fishing Bay

2 tablespoons margarine
1 teaspoon Worcester-
shire sauce
1½ teaspoons Old Bay
seasoning

4 boneless chicken
breasts
Juice of 1 large slice of
lemon

Combine margarine, Worcestershire sauce, Old Bay, and lemon juice in a small saucepan over medium heat and cook until margarine is melted. Place chicken over charcoal fire and baste with sauce until chicken is white and done. Serves 4.

Paula Dennison

Chicken Rollatine Gourmet

2 whole chicken breasts,
skinned, boned, and
halved
2 teaspoons unsalted
butter
4 tablespoons grated
Mozzarella cheese
4 teaspoons freshly
grated Parmesan cheese
4 slices prosciutto (or
Smithfield ham)

4 large mushrooms,
thinly sliced
1 teaspoon unsalted
butter
2 tablespoons unsalted
butter
1 tablespoon unsalted
butter
½ cup dry white wine
Minced fresh parsley
Flour

Flatten chicken breasts between sheets of wax paper until they are ½-inch thick. Spread top of each breast with ½ teaspoon softened butter. Sprinkle with 1 tablespoon grated Mozzarella and 1 teaspoon Parmesan. Arrange 1 slice prosciutto over each breast and sprinkle with minced parsley. Roll up each breast, secure with wooden toothpicks and dust with flour. In small skillet, saute mushrooms in 1 teaspoon butter until golden. In large skillet, cook chicken in 2 tablespoons butter over moderately low heat, turning occasionally, for 20 minutes, or until golden brown. Pour off the butter. Add mushrooms, 1 tablespoon butter, and white wine to chicken and simmer for ten minutes. Remove the wooden picks, transfer chicken with a slotted spatula to a heated platter, and spoon the mushroom mixture over it. Preparation: 1 hour. Serves 2 to 4.

Celie Gehring

209

Chicken Breasts in Cream

6 chicken breasts,
skinned and boned
¼ cup butter or margarine
1 cup cream
1 cup chicken broth

½ cup onion, chopped
½ cup green pepper,
chopped
Salt, pepper, and garlic
powder to taste

Brown chicken breasts in butter. Place in baking dish. In same skillet, combine cream, broth, onion, green pepper, and spices and warm. Pour over chicken. Bake at 325° for 1 hour or until most of liquid has evaporated. Preparation: 20 minutes. Serves 6.

This recipe can be assembled in advance, then baked at proper time. Easily doubled or tripled.

Terry Tosh

Virginia Ham and Chicken

4 to 6 boneless chicken
breasts
4 to 6 medium thin slices
ham (Smithfield or
Virginia baked)
1 can cream of
mushroom soup

1 8-ounce container sour
cream
Garlic salt
Pepper

Mix soup, sour cream, garlic salt, and pepper to taste. Spread ½ cup on bottom of small casserole. Wrap each chicken breast with ham and arrange, seam side down, in dish and cover with rest of sauce. Meat may touch; sauce should cover. Bake at 325° for 1½ hours. Preparation: 15 minutes. Serves 4 to 6.

Great for microwave - do on low power.

Larkin Bynum

Chicken in the Pot with Tarragon

1 3 to 4-pound roasting
   chicken
1 lemon, thinly sliced
1 teaspoon crushed dried
   tarragon

3 tablespoons butter
1 teaspoon salt

Preheat oven to 300°. Rub chicken inside and out with butter and salt. Place in deep oval casserole (glass or crockery preferable). Place lemon slices on chicken and sprinkle with tarragon. Cover and bake for 1½ hours. Serve directly from pot.
Preparation: 15 minutes. Serves 4 to 6.

Virginia Ritchie

Chicken Paprika

2 fryer chickens, cut up
1 teaspoon salt
1 teaspoon pepper
4 tablespoons unsalted
   butter
4 small onions, chopped

3 cloves garlic, minced
2 tablespoons Hungarian
   paprika
1 cup chicken broth
   Hot cooked noodles
   (optional)

Rub chicken with salt and pepper. In skillet heat butter and add onions, garlic and 1 tablespoon paprika. Stir and cook 7 minutes over medium heat. Add chicken and brown quickly. Cover pan and cook 30 minutes. Add chicken broth and simmer 15 minutes. Sprinkle remaining paprika over all. Good served over noodles (especially spaetzle). Also good reheated. Serves 6 to 8.

Trudie Steel

Chicken Breasts Dijon

6 whole chicken breasts
skinned and boned
1 16-ounce jar Dijon
mustard

1 16-ounce carton sour
cream
1 stick butter
Seasoned bread crumbs

Preheat oven to 400°. Rinse chicken and pat dry. Combine sour cream and Dijon mustard. Dip chicken breasts in mixture. Roll heavily in bread crumbs. Line baking dish with aluminum foil. Place chicken on top and dot with butter. Cover chicken with foil and bake for 30 minutes. Remove top layer of foil, increase oven temperature to 450°, and bake for 15 minutes until brown. Preparation: 15 minutes. Serves 6.

Kathy Piette

Chicken and Asparagus

2 whole chicken breasts,
skinned, boned, and
cut into 2 x 4-inch
pieces
½ cup oil
2 10-ounce packages
frozen asparagus
1 can cream of chicken
soup

½ cup mayonnaise
1 teaspoon lemon juice
½ teaspoon curry powder
1 cup grated sharp Ched-
dar cheese
Pepper

Sprinkle pepper on chicken. Saute chicken in oil until white and opaque, about 6 minutes. Drain on paper towels. Cook asparagus 5 minutes. Drain asparagus and arrange in a 9 x 9 x 2-inch pan. Place chicken on top. Mix soup, mayonnaise, lemon juice, and curry powder. Pour over the chicken and asparagus. Sprinkle cheese on top. Cover with foil and bake at 375° for 30 minutes. Preparation: 30 minutes. Serves 4.

Betty Williams

Chicken, Artichoke and Cheddar

2 sprigs parsley
1 celery top
1 carrot, quartered
1 onion, chopped
2 3-pound broiler chickens, cut in pieces
1 tablespoon salt
2 10-ounce packages frozen artichoke hearts
¼ cup butter
¼ cup flour
3 cups Cheddar cheese, shredded
½ cup fine bread crumbs
3 tablespoons butter

Make a bouquet garni of the first four items. Place chicken pieces, bouquet garni, salt-pepper, and water to cover in a large pan. Cover and simmer about an hour or until chicken is tender. Cool chicken stock and reserve. Remove meat from bones in good sized pieces. Arrange chicken and artichokes in 3-quart casserole.

Melt butter in saucepan and blend in flour until smooth. Gradually add 2 cups of chicken stock. Cook, stirring constantly until thick and smooth. Stir in cheese, and pour over chicken and artichoke hearts. Sprinkle with bread crumbs and dot with butter. Bake uncovered at 350° for 30 minutes or until golden brown. Preparation: 45 minutes. Serves 8.

Nel Laughon

Stuffed Chicken and Artichoke

2 whole chicken breasts, boned, skinned, and halved
¾ cup freshly grated Parmesan cheese
¾ cup Italian bread crumbs
1 6-ounce jar marinated artichoke hearts
4 lemon slices
4 tablespoons butter
Salt
Pepper
McCormick Lemon Herb Seasoning
Garlic powder
Paprika

Preheat oven to 350°. Wash chicken parts; sprinkle with salt, pepper, lemon herb seasoning, and garlic powder. Mix Parmesan cheese and Italian bread crumbs with oil from marinated artichoke hearts. Slit chicken breasts and stuff center with dressing, reserving a small amount of mixture for garnishing. Arrange stuffed breasts in an 8 x 8-inch ungreased baking dish. Toss artichoke hearts in remaining stuffing mixture and place on top of chicken breasts. Top each with a slice of lemon, a tablespoon of butter, and a dash of paprika. Bake in covered dish at 350° for 30 minutes. Uncover and bake an additional 30 minutes. Preparation: 40 minutes. Serves 4.

Barrie Barnett

213

Cheesy Chicken and Artichoke

4 whole chicken breasts, skinned, boned, and halved
1 cup margarine
½ cup flour
3½ cups milk
¼ teaspoon cayenne pepper
1 teaspoon monosodium glutamate (MSG)
1 clove garlic, minced
2 ounces sharp Cheddar cheese, cubed

3 ounces Gruyere cheese, cubed
8 ounces fresh mushrooms, sliced
1 to 2 tablespoons butter
2 cans (8½-ounce) artichoke hearts packed in water
1 cup Rice Krispies
2 tablespoons butter, melted
Lemon pepper
Salt

Sprinkle chicken breasts with lemon pepper and salt. Place in 9 x 12-inch casserole and bake at 350° for ½ hour.
Combine margarine and flour in saucepan. Add milk and cook, stirring constantly, until thick and smooth. Add seasonings and cheeses. Cook until cheese melts and bubbles. In separate pan, saute mushrooms in butter. Add to milk/cheese mixture.
Layer artichokes on top of chicken, pour sauce over all and top with Rice Krispies that have been mixed with butter. Bake at 350° for 30 minutes. Preparation: 1 hour. Serves 8.

Cabell West

Artichoke Chicken with Water Chestnuts

3 whole chicken breasts, split and skinned
¼ cup vegetable oil
2 or 3 carrots, cut in 2-inch pieces
½ pound fresh mushrooms, sliced
1 14-ounce can artichokes, drained and halved

½ cup green onion, chopped
½ cup water chestnuts, sliced
1/8 teaspoon thyme
½ teaspoon salt
1/8 teaspoon pepper
1½ cups chicken broth
½ cup sherry
2 tablespoons cornstarch

Brown chicken in hot vegetable oil in large skillet; add carrots. Cover and simmer 5 minutes. Add mushrooms, artichokes, onion, water chestnuts, thyme, salt, and pepper; cover and simmer 10 minutes. Combine broth, sherry, and cornstarch in a small saucepan; stir well. Cook over medium heat, stirring constantly, until sauce is thickened. Place chicken and vegetables in a greased 9 x 13-inch baking dish. Pour sauce over top. Bake at 375° for 45 to 55 minutes, basting with pan drippings. Serves 6.

Jeanie Vertner

Chicken Crepes Parsley

Basic Crepe Batter:

1 cup sifted flour	3 large eggs, beaten
½ teaspoon salt	2 cups milk

Mix batter ingredients together. Refrigerate 1 hour before making crepes. To make crepes, pour 2 to 3 tablespoons batter in small greased skillet, allow to brown lightly on one side only, remove. These can be stored in refrigerator until ready to use by placing them between wax paper and storing in an airtight container.

Stuffing for Crepes:

½ stick butter	¾ cup milk
½ cup flour	¾ cup chicken broth
½ cup green onions, chopped	1 cup sliced mushrooms
½ cup white onions, chopped	4 chicken breasts, boned, cooked, and sliced
1 tablespoon parsley, chopped	1 cup water chestnuts, sliced

Melt butter in a large sauce pan. Saute onions and parsley for several minutes and gradually add flour, stirring constantly. Slowly add liquids, chicken, mushrooms, and chestnuts to mixture, which should be sticky and thick. Place 2 to 3 tablespoons of stuffing in each crepe, roll up, and place seam side down in shallow Pyrex baking dish. Top with sauce and bake at 350° for 30 minutes.

Sauce for Crepes:

4 tablespoons butter	Salt
4 tablespoons flour	Cayenne pepper
2 cups milk	Worcestershire sauce
1 cup chicken broth	
2 tablespoons green onions, chopped	

Make a rather thin cream sauce out of the above ingredients. Season well with salt, cayenne pepper, and Worcestershire Sauce. Preparation: 1 hour. Serves 8.

Karen Feigley

Chicken, Sausage and Wild Rice

1 pound pork sausage
1 pound mushrooms, sliced
1 large onion, chopped
4 whole chicken breasts or a 2½ to 3 pound chicken, cooked, boned, and cut in bite-size chunks

1 6-ounce box Uncle Ben's Wild and Long Grain Rice
¼ cup flour
½ cup heavy cream
2½ cups chicken broth
1 tablespoon salt
1/8 teaspoon pepper
Pinch each of oregano, thyme and marjoram

Saute sausage in large skillet or Dutch oven; drain and set aside. In fat, saute mushrooms and onions; add sausage and chicken and set aside. Cook wild rice according to package directions. (Sherry can be substituted for part of the water in rice.) Mix flour with heavy cream in a medium saucepan until smooth; add chicken broth and cook until thickened. Add seasonings and combine with rice, sausage, chicken, and vegetables. Put in a greased casserole dish and bake 25 to 30 minutes in 350° oven. Serves 10 to 12.

Just as delicious when made ahead and frozen.

Sue Reynolds

Chicken Divan with Nutmeg

3 whole chicken breasts, split, boned, and cooked
3 boxes frozen broccoli
3 tablespoons butter
3 tablespoons flour
1½ cups milk
¾ cup mayonnaise
2 teaspoons Worcestershire sauce

1 teaspoon dried nutmeg
4½ tablespoons dry sherry
1 10½-ounce can cream of celery soup
¾ cup heavy cream, whipped
¾ cup buttered bread crumbs
1 cup grated Parmesan cheese

Cook chicken breasts. (Suggest roasting in butter to preserve moist flavor.) Cook broccoli according to package directions. Melt butter. Stir in flour and cook 2 minutes. Slowly add milk, stirring constantly with a wire whisk. Add soup, mayonnaise, Worcestershire sauce, and nutmeg. Mix well. Add sherry. Place broccoli in 9 x 12-inch glass casserole. Layer chicken on top. Add whipped cream to the cream sauce and pour over chicken. Cover with thin layer of bread crumbs and Parmesan cheese. Bake in preheated oven at 400° for 30 minutes. Serves 6.

Cook chicken and broccoli ahead of time. One hour before dinner do remainder of casserole recipe and then bake. Can easily double. Be sure to whip cream and add it at the last minute. Nutmeg flavor and sherry are delicious.

Susan Dull

Southern Cornbread Chicken Sandwich

1 baked hen or 8 baked
  boneless chicken
  breasts, sliced

Bread:

2 cups cornmeal
½ teaspoon baking soda
1 cup buttermilk
1 teaspoon salt
2 eggs, beaten

1 teaspoon baking
  powder
6 tablespoons melted
  shortening

Combine bread ingredients, thin with sweet milk, if necessary. Bake in greased iron skillet at 400° for 20 minutes. Cut into squares.

Sauce:

2 tablespoons onion,
  minced
2 tablespoons celery,
  minced
½ cup butter

4 tablespoons flour
3 cups strong chicken
  broth
¾ cup cream
Salt and pepper to taste

Brown onion and celery in butter to a light golden color. Add remaining ingredients and cook until sauce thickens.

To assemble: put slices of chicken between 2 slices of cornbread and cover with sauce. Preparation: 1 hour. Serves 8.

This recipe can easily be doubled. It is very rich. A salad is all you need to accompany this dish. Any recipe for good cornbread can be used.

Elaine Davila

Overnight Chicken Souffle

8 slices of day old bread
1 chicken or 4 chicken
  breasts, cooked and
  chopped
½ cup mayonnaise
1 cup celery, diced
¾ cup onion, finely
  chopped

¾ cup green pepper, finely
  chopped
4 eggs, beaten
3 cups milk
1 can cream of
  mushroom soup
1 cup shredded sharp
  Cheddar cheese

Grease 10½ x 7 x 1½-inch pan. Cut 4 slices of bread into cubes. Remove the crust from the remaining slices. Line bottom of pan with bread cubes. Combine chicken, mayonnaise, celery, onion, green pepper, and seasoning. Spread mixture over bread cubes; cover with bread slices. Mix eggs and milk; pour over ingredients in pan. Cover and refrigerate overnight. Bake uncovered for 15 minutes at 350°. Pour undiluted soup over mixture. Bake for 30 minutes. Sprinkle top with cheese. Bake 15 minutes. Preparation: 25 minutes and overnight in refrigerator. Serves 10 to 12.

Robin Ware

Chicken Pot Pie

1 3-pound fryer chicken
3½ cups water
1 teaspoon salt
½ teaspoon coarsely
  ground pepper
3 cups chicken broth
5 slices bacon
3 tablespoons bacon
  drippings
½ cup green onion,
  chopped

½ cup celery, chopped
½ cup flour
3 eggs, hard-boiled and
  sliced
1 10-ounce package frozen
  peas and carrots
½ teaspoon salt
1/8 teaspoon white pepper
1/8 teaspoon thyme
12 biscuits, unbaked
  Leaves of 2 stalks celery

Combine chicken, water, celery leaves, salt and pepper in a Dutch oven. Bring to boil; cover and simmer 1½ hours. Remove chicken from broth and cool. Discard skin, bone meat and shred into small pieces. Reserve 3 cups chicken broth. Cook bacon crisply and crumble. Saute onions and celery for 5 minutes in bacon drippings. Gradually add flour, stirring until well blended. Add reserved broth and cook, stirring constantly, until thickened. Stir in chicken, bacon, eggs, peas and carrots, salt, white pepper, and thyme. Pour into 3-quart casserole and bake at 425° about 10 minutes. Place biscuits on top and continue cooking until biscuits are golden, about 10 to 12 minutes. Serves 8.

Sandy King

Sue's Sour Cream Chicken Enchiladas

12 corn tortillas
½ cup vegetable oil
2 cups sour cream
2 cups cooked chicken, chopped
½ pound Cheddar or Monterey Jack cheese, grated

1 cup green onions, chopped
1 4-ounce can whole green chili peppers, rinsed, seeded, and cut into 12 strips
Salt

Fry tortillas in hot oil until soft (3 seconds per side). Drain and salt lightly. Layer each tortilla with sour cream, chicken, cheese, onion, and a chili strip. (Reserve some sour cream and cheese for the top.) Roll up each tortilla and place, seam side down, in an ungreased casserole dish. Top with remaining sour cream and cheese. Bake covered at 350° for 45 minutes. Serves 6.

Look for large tortillas, often found in the dairy section. They are much easier to roll.
Mildred Davis

Chicken Curry

1 small onion, chopped
1 small green pepper, chopped
½ cup celery, chopped
¾ cup margarine
½ teaspoon salt
2 tablespoons curry powder
½ cup flour
2 cups chicken stock

1 cup milk
3 pound fryer, cooked, boned, and chopped
2 tablespoons sherry
2 tablespoons brown sugar
½ cup raisins
Dash cayenne pepper
Cooked rice

Condiments:

Chopped peanuts
Chopped hard-boiled eggs

Chopped cooked bacon
Chutney

Saute onion, green pepper, and celery in margarine. Combine salt and curry powder with flour; blend into vegetable mixture. Slowly stir in stock and milk until thickened. Add chicken, sherry, brown sugar, raisins, and cayenne pepper. Simmer for 15 minutes. Serve hot over rice and garnish with accompanying condiments. Preparation: 30 minutes. Serves 8.
Jeanie Vertner

Chicken Parmigiana

6 boned chicken breast halves

2 eggs, lightly beaten

1 teaspoon salt

1/8 teaspoon pepper, coarsely ground

¾ cup Italian seasoned bread crumbs (fine, dried)

½ cup vegetable oil

1 15½-ounce jar Ragu Homestyle Spaghetti Sauce with Mushrooms

1 6-ounce can V-8 Juice

1 cup stewed tomatoes

¼ teaspoon sugar

¼ teaspoon basil, dried and crushed

1½ teaspoon Italian herb seasoning, dried and crushed

¼ teaspoon oregano, dried and crushed

1 tablespoon butter or margarine

1 cup freshly grated Parmesan cheese

4 ounces Mozzarella cheese, sliced and cut into triangles (1 per breast)

Pepper to taste

Preheat oven to 350°. Combine eggs, salt, and 1/8 teaspoon pepper. Dip chicken into egg mixture and then crumbs. Heat oil until very hot in large skillet. Quickly brown chicken on both sides and remove to shallow casserole dish. Pour excess oil from skillet. Add Ragu, V-8 Juice, stewed tomatoes, sugar, basil, Italian seasoning, oregano, and pepper to skillet. Heat to boiling, stirring occasionally; simmer 10 minutes. Stir in butter. Pour over chicken; sprinkle with Parmesan cheese; cover. Bake for 30 minutes; uncover. Place Mozzarella triangles over chicken. Bake 10 minutes longer or until cheese melts. Serves 4 to 6.

Missy Ryan

Italian Chicken

1 egg	½ teaspoon garlic powder
4 whole chicken breasts	½ teaspoon basil
½ cup Italian flavored bread crumbs	½ teaspoon crushed oregano leaves
2 tablespoons shortening	Shredded Mozzarella cheese
1 10¾-ounce can tomato soup	Parmesan cheese (optional)
¼ cup water	
¼ cup onion, chopped	

Beat egg with 1 tablespoon water. Roll chicken in egg mixture, then crumbs. In skillet, brown chicken in shortening; pour off fat. Stir in soup, water, onion, and seasonings. Cover and cook over low heat 45 minutes or until done, stirring occasionally. Sprinkle with cheese; heat until cheese melts. If desired, serve with grated Parmesan cheese and additional oregano leaves. Preparation: 15 minutes. Serves 4.

Susan Jenkins

Christian's Parmesan Chicken

Parmesan Coating:

1½ cups grated Parmesan cheese	2 cups crushed Pepperidge Farm stuffing mix (herb seasoned)
½ cup dehydrated parsley flakes	2 to 3 cloves garlic, peeled

Mix in plastic container and let sit in refrigerator 5 to 6 days.

Christian's Chicken:

6 chicken breast halves, boned	½ cup butter, melted

If time permits, soak chicken for a few hours in lightly salted water. Dry with paper towels or cloth. Dip chicken in butter, letting excess drip back in pan. Dredge well in Parmesan coating. Place in shallow baking pan; do not let pieces touch. Drizzle excess butter over chicken and coat any "bare spots". Bake uncovered for 45 minutes at 350° to 375°. Serves 6.

A sure-fire winner for kids and adults. It looks beautiful over rice, garnished with "sugared" green grapes. Parmesan coating will keep forever in the refrigerator, and can be used to top casseroles, coat fish, etc.

Marti Shield

221

Paella Valenciana

1 cup olive oil
1 stewing chicken, cut for fricaseeing
4 cloves garlic, sliced
1 green pepper, diced
3 tomatoes, fresh or canned, drained and chopped

1 pound cooked shrimp
2 cups rice
4 cups chicken broth
1 package frozen peas
Salt to taste
Pinch of saffron
Pinch of rosemary

In large, deep frying pan or kettle, heat olive oil. While frying chicken, add sections of garlic and green pepper; do not burn. Add tomatoes, cook a few minutes, and add enough boiling water to cover all. Stir in salt to taste. Season with pinch of saffron and pinch of rosemary. Cook over low heat for 1 hour. Add more water if necessary. When chicken is about done, add shrimp. Add rice and chicken broth and continue cooking until broth is absorbed and you see original olive oil. When rice is half done, add package of peas. Keep simmering and do not stir rice. May be kept warm until ready to serve. Even better the next day! Serves 6.

Anne Fox

Chicken Ratatouille

4 tablespoons olive oil
8 tablespoons vegetable oil
1 clove garlic
1 medium onion, chopped
½ green pepper, diced
10 mushrooms, sliced
1 zucchini, sliced ¼-inch thick
2 tomatoes, diced
1 eggplant, skinned and diced

1 6-ounce can tomato paste
3 6-ounce cans water
1 teaspoon salt
¼ teaspoon chervil
¼ teaspoon sweet basil
4 chicken breasts, boned and skinned
1 can chicken broth
2 tablespoons butter
Pinch of rosemary
Pinch of marjoram

In a large skillet, heat ½ of oils and saute garlic, onion, and green pepper. Add remaining oils and saute mushrooms, zucchini, tomatoes, and eggplant for 15 minutes. Add tomato paste, water, salt, herbs. Simmer covered 1 hour. Twenty minutes before sauce is done, put chicken in frying pan. Add broth and butter. Boil, then simmer, covered, 5 minutes on each side. Pour sauce over chicken. Serves 4.

Anne Grier

Chicken in Tomato Vinaigrette

2 tablespoons olive oil	½ teaspoon sugar
1 clove garlic, crushed	1 tablespoon wine
1/8 teaspoon red pepper	½ teaspoon salt
1 tablespoon fresh basil	2 tablespoons parsley
1 3-inch strip lemon peel	4 halves chicken breasts,
1 16-ounce can tomatoes,	skinned and boned
drained and chopped	1 tablespoon butter

In medium saucepan over medium heat, combine 1 tablespoon olive oil, garlic, red pepper, and basil and cook 1 minute. Add lemon peel, tomatoes, and sugar. Simmer 20 minutes. Remove from heat. Stir in vinegar, salt and parsley. Remove lemon. Pound chicken to ½-inch thickness. In large skillet cook chicken 3 minutes on each side in 1 tablespoon olive oil and butter. Remove to platter and keep warm. Add tomato mixture to skillet and cook 1 minute, stirring constantly. Pour over chicken. Serves 4.

Mims Powell

Chicken Tetrazzini

2 pounds chicken breasts	1 can cream of
1 stalk of celery with	mushroom soup
leaves	1 cup light cream
1 carrot, sliced	1½ teaspoons salt
1 onion, chopped	¼ teaspoon pepper
1 bay leaf	¼ teaspoon dry mustard
1 5-ounce package	¼ teaspoon paprika
noodles	2 tablespoons sherry
¼ pound fresh	1 2-ounce package
mushrooms	slivered almonds,
2 tablespoons water	lightly toasted
½ stick butter or	Peppercorns
margarine, melted	Pinch of thyme
2 tablespoons flour	Parmesan or Romano

Simmer about 1 hour in water to cover: chicken, celery, carrot, onion, bay leaf, peppercorns, and thyme. Cube chicken. Boil noodles in strained chicken broth and strain again. Saute mushrooms in 2 tablespoons water and drain. Melt butter in large skillet. Stir in flour until mixed; add soup and cream. Cook slowly, stirring constantly, until sauce thickens. Add salt, pepper, mustard, paprika, and sherry. Stir in mushrooms, noodles, chicken, and almonds. Pour into 1½-quart casserole, sprinkle with Parmesan or Romano cheese and bake at 350° until bubbly. Serves 6.

Staige Nolley

223

Golden Chicken Nuggets

4 whole chicken breasts, boned and skinned
½ cup unseasoned dry bread crumbs
¼ cup grated Parmesan cheese
2 teaspoons monosodium glutamate (MSG)
1 teaspoon salt
1 teaspoon dried leaf thyme or ¼ teaspoon powdered thyme
1 teaspoon dried leaf basil
½ cup margarine or butter, melted

Cut chicken into 1½-inch "nuggets". (Cut in smaller pieces if using as an appetizer). Combine bread crumbs, cheese, seasonings, and herbs. Dip chicken nuggets in melted butter, then in bread crumbs. Place in single layer on foil-lined baking sheet. Bake at 400° for 10 minutes. Preparation: 20 minutes. Yield: 4 to 5 dozen nuggets.

Delicious as an appetizer served with sauces such as honey, mustard, or sweet and sour.

Karen Feigley

Korean Chicken Wings

8 chicken wings
5 green onions, chopped
3 large garlic cloves, crushed
1 tablespoon sesame oil
1 teaspoon sugar
3 tablespoons soy sauce
3 tablespoons water
Small piece of ginger root, sliced
Pepper
Paprika

Cut chicken wings into 3 sections. Discard the small tips of each wing. Put chicken in a large bowl. Add chopped onions and crushed garlic cloves. Sprinkle chicken with a dash of paprika and pepper. Add sesame oil, sugar, soy sauce, water, and sliced ginger root. Let marinate overnight in refrigerator, turning chicken several times. Right before cooking, discard ginger root. Arrange chicken in a casserole dish. Broil 15 minutes on 1 side and 10 minutes on other side. Be careful not to burn. Brush on sauce while broiling. Preparation: 15 minutes and overnight marinating. Serves 2 to 3.

Use as much chicken as you want, making sure that you have enough marinade sauce to completely cover. Serve with rice and green vegetable for dinner or use just the chicken wings for an appetizer.

Becky Newman

Chinese Walnut Chicken

¾ cup walnut halves or quarters

2 cups shredded Chinese cabbage (or Romaine or iceberg lettuce)

3 stalks celery

1 onion (optional)

1 8½-ounce can bamboo shoots

1 can water chestnuts

2 pounds chicken breasts, skinned and boned

6 tablespoons salad oil

3 tablespoons soy sauce

2 tablespoons cornstarch

¾ teaspoon salt

1 teaspoon sugar

¾ cup chicken broth

Cooked rice

Place walnuts in small saucepan. Cover with cold water. Bring to boil; boil for 3 minutes and drain. Wash and drain cabbage; cut crosswise into 1/8-inch thick slices to make 2 cups shredded. Wash celery and cut into 1½-inch pieces, then cut into julienne strips to make 1 cup. Slice onion paper-thin to make 1 cup. Drain bamboo shoots and chestnuts, and cut into julienne strips or slices. Wash and dry chicken breasts. Remove and discard skin and bones. Cut meat into julienne strips.

In a large skillet heat 3 tablespoons salad oil; add vegetables and saute until tender/crisp. Remove from skillet and set aside. Add walnuts to skillet and saute until brown. Remove and add to vegetables.

In a bowl, combine soy sauce, cornstarch, salt, sugar and mix. Add chicken pieces and toss until coated with mixture. Add remaining 3 tablespoons oil to skillet and saute chicken until tender. Add chicken broth and cook, stirring constantly until broth comes to a boil. Add vegetables and nuts and heat stirring, 2 to 3 minutes until hot. Serve with rice. Preparation: 45 minutes. Serves 4 to 6.

Sally Moxley

Orange Chicken

2 to 3 whole chicken
  breasts, boned
3 tablespoons oil
1 tart apple, chopped
1 rib celery, chopped
1 onion, chopped
1 carrot, chopped
1 tablespoon flour
2 teaspoons curry
  powder
½ cup orange juice

¾ cup chicken broth
2 teaspoons grated orange
  rind
⅓ cup Major Grey's
  Chutney
1 bay leaf
1 orange, sectioned or ½
  can mandarin orange
  sections
Cooked rice
Salt and pepper to taste

Lightly brown chicken in oil. Remove from pan and set aside. In same pan, combine finely chopped apple, celery, onion, and carrot and cook for 4 minutes. Sprinkle with flour and curry powder. Stir in orange juice, chicken broth, orange rind, chutney, and bay leaf. Bring to boil, return chicken and simmer covered for 20 minutes. Garnish with orange sections and serve with rice. Preparation: 45 minutes. Serves 4 to 6.

Kay Lowe

Persian Chicken with Peaches

⅓ cup flour
1¼ teaspoons salt
1 teaspoon black pepper
1¼ teaspoons marjoram
2 tablespoons finely
  chopped parsley
4 whole chicken breasts,
  halved and boned

½ cup milk
2 tablespoons butter
4 tablespoons oil
¾ cup finely chopped
  onion
¼ cup lemon juice
1 cup peach syrup
8 canned peach halves

Mix flour, salt, pepper, marjoram, and parsley. Dip chicken breasts in milk, then roll in seasoned flour. Save flour mixture. In a large skillet, brown chicken in butter and oil. Arrange in a single layer in a 2-quart baking dish. Add onion to skillet and saute until soft. Sprinkle onion over chicken. Add remaining seasoned flour to skillet and cook over medium heat until brown. Add lemon juice and peach syrup and cook about 5 minutes until slightly thickened, stirring frequently. Arrange peach halves on top of the onions and chicken. Pour sauce over all and bake uncovered for 45 minutes at 350°. Preparation: 30 minutes. Serves 4.

Leila Marie Bristow

Teriyaki Marinade for Chicken

1 cup soy sauce	4 garlic cloves
1/3 cup oil	1/2 ounce fresh ginger
1/3 cup sherry	1 whole chicken, cut up
2 tablespoons sugar	or 4 chicken breasts

Combine first 6 ingredients. Marinate chicken in sauce 12 to 24 hours. Roast or grill chicken. Preparation: 5 minutes. Serves 4.

Nancy Vaughan

Szechuan Chicken with Cashews

2 whole chicken breasts, boned and skinned	1 small green onion, chopped
10 dried red peppers	1/2 cup cashews
2 teaspoons ginger, fresh chopped or dried ground	4 tablespoons peanut oil Cooked rice

Marinade:

2 teaspoons cornstarch	1 tablespoon rice wine
2 teaspoons Kikkoman soy sauce	1 egg white
	1/2 teaspoon salt

Glaze:

2 teaspoons cornstarch	1 teaspoon vinegar
2 teaspoons rice wine	2 teaspoons sugar
2 tablespoons soy sauce	

Cut chicken into bite-size pieces and soak in marinade at least 1/2 hour. Cut off the ends of the peppers and shake out the seeds. Mix glaze ingredients and set aside. Heat the peanut oil in a wok over medium heat. Cook the red peppers until they begin to char. Turn the heat to high until the peppers are black. Reduce heat to medium and add the chicken. Stir-fry until chicken is white. Add the ginger and onion and cook a few seconds. Add the cashews and glaze and heat through until thickened. Remove and serve over rice. Preparation: 35 minutes. Serves 2.

Red peppers release an oil when they are charred which may burn your nose and throat. Be sure kitchen is well ventilated while cooking them.

Mary Roach

227

Hot Pepper Chicken

2 tablespoons peanut oil
2 slices fresh ginger, minced
3 to 4 dried red chili peppers, finely diced
1½ pounds chicken breasts, skinned, boned and cut into ¾-inch pieces
½ teaspoon salt
1 green pepper, diced

½ cup bamboo shoots, diced
¼ cup chicken broth or water
1 tablespoon cornstarch, dissolved in a little cold water
1½ tablespoons soy sauce
Dash of rice wine or dry sherry

Heat oil in wok or large skillet over high heat. Add ginger, chili peppers and chicken and stir-fry for 2 minutes. Add dash of wine, salt, green pepper and bamboo shoots and saute briefly. Dissolve cornstarch in water and add to chicken broth and soy sauce: Stir-fry with chicken and vegetables until peppers are tender and liquid is absorbed. Serves 2 as main course or 4 when served as accompaniment.

Fran Armstrong

Empress Chicken

½ cup whole almonds
1 13¼-ounce can pineapple tidbits
½ cup dry sherry
¼ cup soy sauce
1 teaspoon garlic salt
½ teaspoon ginger (or 1 slice fresh ginger)
2 tablespoons cornstarch

4 tablespoons peanut oil, divided
2 cups celery, sliced
1 green pepper, chopped
2 cups mushrooms, sliced
4 raw chicken breast halves, boned and cubed
½ cup green onions, sliced

Roast almonds at 350° for about 10 minutes until light golden brown. Drain pineapple; reserve juice. Combine juice, sherry, soy sauce, spices and cornstarch. Set aside. Heat 2 tablespoons oil in skillet or wok and stir-fry celery and pepper 2 to 3 minutes. Remove celery and stir-fry mushrooms for 1 to 2 minutes. Remove. Heat 2 tablespoons oil until sputtering, add chicken and stir-fry until creamy white. (Chicken may be done in 2 batches to prevent watering.) Add vegetables to pan with sauce and cook until thickened. Fold in pineapple. Sprinkle with green onions and almonds and serve over rice. Serves 4 to 6.

Partially frozen chicken is easier to bone and cut.

Sally Moxley

Chinese Chicken Livers

¼ cup soy sauce
½ teaspoon ground ginger
1 clove garlic, crushed
¾ pound chicken livers
5 slices bacon
1 cup uncooked rice
½ cup chopped water
    chestnuts

2 chicken bouillon cubes
¼ cup firmly packed light
    brown sugar
½ cup chopped green
    onions with tops
Water

Combine soy sauce, ginger, and garlic in small bowl; add livers, stir to coat. Let marinate while preparing recipe. Cook bacon in large skillet; drain and crumble. Reserve bacon fat. Measure 1 tablespoon bacon fat into medium size saucepan. Saute rice and water chestnuts until rice becomes white and opaque. Stir chicken boullion cubes into amount of water called for on rice package. Stir boullion mixture into rice and cook according to package directions.

Sprinkle brown sugar onto square of wax paper. Drain livers, save marinade. Roll livers in sugar to coat. Heat 2 tablespoons bacon fat in large skillet and saute livers until done (5 minutes). Stir in marinade and any sugar remaining on wax paper. Heat until hot. Spoon rice onto platter. Spoon chicken liver mixture over rice. Garnish with green onions. Preparation: 30 minutes. Serves 4.

Susan Gunter

Woodchuck

¾ stick butter
6 tablespoons flour
2½ cups milk
¾ pound sharp cheese,
    grated

1 pound mushrooms,
    sauteed
2 cups cooked chicken,
    cubed
1 can fried noodles

Melt butter; add flour and milk to make white sauce. Add cheese; cook until melted. Add mushrooms, chicken, and ½ can noodles. Bake in buttered casserole at 350° for 25 minutes. Sprinkle top with remaining noodles; keep warm.

Great for buffets. Can be made ahead and frozen.

Margaret Bargatze

Mike's Smoked Goose

1 Canada Goose, dressed   Onion
Celery

Parboil goose with celery and onion in cavity for 15 minutes. Place, breast side down, on gas or charcoal grill; cover and roast 40 minutes. Turn and roast 15 minutes. Skin and slice. Preparation: 30 minutes. Serves 4.

Pat Morrison

The M & M Hunting Lodge Goose

2 frozen or fresh geese
4 tablespoons salt
2 tablespoons white vinegar
2 pounds mild, sweet Italian sausage
¼ pound margarine
1 large onion, chopped
2 cups water or chicken broth

1 pound Pepperidge Farm stuffing
4 stalks celery, diced
2 eggs
Salt and pepper to taste
Lemon
Butter

Soak birds for 2 hours in salt, white vinegar, and enough water to cover. Break sausage into small pieces and place with margarine and onion in frying pan. Cover and stir over medium heat until half cooked. Combine water or chicken broth with stuffing, celery, eggs, salt and pepper and mix well. Combine with sausage-onion mixture. Drain birds, clean thoroughly, and dry inside and out. Rub birds inside and out with lemon. Stuff birds, baste with butter, and bake, covered, at 350° for 3½ to 4 hours. Serves 6.

Before baking, fill roasting pan with 2 inches of water and keep filled entire cooking time to keep birds from drying out. Variation: Fill roasting pan ⅓ full with cranberry juice.

Lynn Congdon

Goose Unlimited Casserole

3 cups wild goose,
  cooked and diced
1½ cups onion, chopped
1½ cups celery, chopped
3 cups chicken broth or
  bouillon
1½ cups Longhorn cheese,
  cubed

1 can cream of
  mushroom soup
3 cups Ritz cracker
  crumbs, crushed
Salt and pepper to taste

Combine all ingredients in large bowl, reserving 1 cup cracker crumbs. Mix well. Place in 9 x 13-inch baking dish. Sprinkle remaining cracker crumbs on top. Bake at 350° for 45 minutes. May be frozen and baked later. Serves 6 to 8.

Lee Merrick

Breasts of Wild Duck in Gravy

12 wild duck breasts
3 tablespoons bacon fat
3 tablespoons oil
3 tablespoons flour
1½ cups chopped green
  pepper
1½ cups chopped celery
4 large onions, chopped
3 cloves garlic, pressed
1 cup sherry

3 bay leaves
½ teaspoon thyme
¼ cup minced fresh
  parsley
3 to 4 cups water
1 small bottle green
  olives, sliced
Salt and pepper to taste
Tabasco to taste
Cooked wild rice

Brown breasts in bacon fat; remove to large glass oblong baking dish. Make a dark roux with oil and flour. Add vegetables and wilt. Add other seasonings and stir in 3 to 4 cups of water. Pour over browned breasts. Bake at 350° for about 2 hours. Stir in the sliced olives during last 30 minutes. Check during last hour; add water if necessary. Serve with wild rice or long grain and wild rice combination. Preparation: 45 minutes. Serves 12.

Judy Brown

Grilled Dove Breasts

8 doves	Salt and pepper
4 slices bacon	Butter
Worcestershire sauce	Cooked rice

Breast doves. Sprinkle each breast with salt, pepper, and a small amount of Worcestershire sauce. Wrap ½ piece of bacon around each breast and secure with a toothpick. Cook on a hot grill for 5 minutes on each side, basting frequently with butter. Serve with rice. Preparation: 20 minutes. Serves 4.

Mims Powell

Potted Dove Breasts

12 dove breasts	1 tablespoon butter
¼ cup water	6 slices of bacon
1 cup catsup	Tabasco to taste
1 onion, sliced	Salt and pepper to taste
3 tablespoons Worcester-	Long grain and wild
shire sauce	rice, cooked (optional)

Steam dove breasts on top of stove in water for 20 minutes. Add catsup, onion, and seasonings. Lay bacon on top of breasts. Cook covered for 1 hour and 15 minutes or until very tender. Remove top and brown in oven. Serve over rice, if desired. Serves 6.

Quail may also be used.

Judy Brown

Dove Breasts in Wine

2 or 3 dove breasts per person   **White or red wine**

Heat electric skillet to 300°. Place doves in pan; pour enough wine to cover bottom of skillet. Cover and cook ½ hour. If wine is boiling too hard, reduce temperature to 200 or 250° and add more wine. After ½ hour remove top and let doves brown for a few minutes. This may be done the same way in a pan in the oven. Preparation: 15 minutes.

Martha Bugg

Quail

Quail   **Salt and pepper**
Flour   **Oil**

Shake quail in flour seasoned with salt and pepper. Brown quickly in hot shortening in iron skillet. If they are to be served right away, continue frying like chicken until done - about ½ hour. If they are to be served later, place in baking dish, cover with aluminum foil and bake at 300° for an hour. Preparation: 10 minutes.

Anne Booker

Quail and Rice

1½ cups long grain rice, uncooked
10 quail (Manchester Farms), split
1 small package Lipton onion soup mix
1 can cream of mushroom soup
4 cups water

Place rice in 9 x 13-inch Pyrex baking dish and arrange quail on top. Combine onion and cream of mushroom soups and mix well; spread over quail. Pour water over all, cover with foil, and bake at 350° for 2 hours. Serves 10.

Chicken may also be used.

Terry Tosh

Roast Wild Turkey

1 wild turkey, about 15
  pounds
1 cup onion, chopped
2 cups celery, chopped
1½ cups white wine,
  divided

1 muslin cloth, about 15
  square inches
Bacon fat
Salt and pepper to taste

Preheat oven to 350°. Wash and dry turkey; brush with bacon fat. Sprinkle with salt and pepper, inside and out. Combine onion, celery, and 1 cup wine. Place turkey in shallow pan and stuff with wine mixture. Dip cloth in bacon fat and cover turkey. Roast for 3 hours, basting with drippings in pan and remaining wine every 15 to 20 minutes. If turkey varies in size from recipe, allow 20 to 25 minutes per pound roasting time. Before serving, discard onion and celery stuffing. Serves 8 to 10.

Susan Jenkins

Corn Bread Stuffing

2 10-ounce corn bread
  mixes
1 cup milk
2 eggs
3 large stalks celery,
  chopped
1 large onion, chopped
1 tablespoon poultry
  seasoning

1 teaspoon salt
¼ teaspoon pepper
½ cup melted butter or
  margarine
1 pound lightly seasoned
  sausage
Hot water or turkey
  broth

Prepare corn bread as directed (18 to 20 minutes or until golden brown). Saute onion and celery until tender in butter or margarine. (You might want to start celery first since it usually takes longer to saute.) Cook sausage and drain. Crumble corn bread, add poultry seasoning, salt, and pepper. Wet with hot water or turkey broth until moist. Add celery, onion, and sausage. Mix well. Stuff 18 to 20-pound turkey.

Kathy Adair

Orange Sauce for Cornish Hens

¼ cup sugar
2 teaspoons cornstarch
1 cup fresh orange juice
¼ cup orange liqueur

1 to 2 teaspoons orange
   rind, grated
Dash salt

Combine sugar, cornstarch, and salt in saucepan. Stir in orange juice. While stirring, cook until sauce is thick and clear. Remove from heat. Stir in liqueur and orange rind. Serve warm. Yield: 1½ cups.

Great for basting, but save some to serve on the table!

Mary Garrison

Zesty Lemon Butter

½ cup butter or margarine
2 tablespoons fresh
   parsley, minced (or 1½
   tablespoons parsley
   flakes)
1 teaspoon salt

3 tablespoons lemon juice
1½ teaspoons mustard
1 teaspoon onion, minced
   Generous dash cayenne
   pepper

Melt butter in saucepan. Stirring constantly, add remaining ingredients. Yield: ¾ cup.

A zesty basting sauce for Cornish hens, chicken, steak, or fish.

Grace Deane

Sweet 'n Sour Barbecue Sauce

½ cup onion, chopped
1 stick butter
½ cup catsup
3 tablespoons brown
   sugar
3 tablespoons lemon juice

1 tablespoon Worcester-
   shire sauce
1 tablespoon A-1 steak
   sauce
½ teaspoon salt
¼ teaspoon Tabasco sauce

Saute onions in butter. Add remaining ingredients and bring to a boil. Use for chicken or spare ribs, either on the grill or in the oven. Yield: 1½ cups.

Beats bottled sauce by a mile!

Gerry Lewis

Barbecue Sauce for Chicken or Ribs

1 large onion, chopped	2 cups catsup
1 large garlic clove, chopped	4 tablespoons barbecue seasoning
¼ pound margarine	1 tablespoon salt
2 ounces Worcestershire sauce	2 tablespoons brown sugar
1 ounce soy sauce	2 cups vinegar
4 ounces Heinz or Blue Plate barbecue sauce	1 teaspoon Tabasco sauce
	2 cups water
	Juice of 2 lemons

Place onion, garlic, and margarine in large saucepan; cook for 15 minutes. Add remaining ingredients and stir thoroughly. Continue to stir while cooking on medium heat for 10 minutes. Turn to simmer and let cook for ½ hour. Makes enough for 5 to 7 chickens. Yield: 2 quarts.

Jane Johnson

Always wait to stuff a bird until just before roasting. After serving, store stuffing and bird leftovers separately.

When boning fowl, be careful not to pierce the skin except for the initial incision. An unpierced skin will act as protection, encasement and insulation during cooking.

After removing a chicken from the oven, allow it to rest about 10 minutes (20 minutes for a turkey) to make slicing easier.

For turkeys less than 12 pounds, allow ¾ to 1 pound per serving. Allow ½ to ¾ pound per serving for those weighing more than 12 pounds.

When roasting duck, prick the bird frequently, but lightly, all over to allow excess fat to escape.

If a duck is not stuffed, you may rub the cavity with lemon juice or place a cored and peeled apple, a carrot, an onion, celery ribs or a potato in the body cavity to attract off-flavors. Discard these vegetables before serving.

Wild birds are, without exception, leaner than domestic varieties and for this reason should be cooked for shorter periods.

A true partridge can be cooked by any recipe for chicken if larded, or, if barded, as for pheasant.

Seafood to Virginians means the bounty of the Bay—the Chesapeake Bay—the largest bay in the country and the generous provider of blue crabs, oysters, clams, scallops and finfish from trout to flounder.

This larder helped sustain the settlers in the uncertain years of the 1600's and seafood quickly became an important item in the colonists' diet. Moreover, the shells were used to build roads and, when ground up, to make mortar for buildings.

Fishing and boat-building are traditional industries of Tidewater Virginia. Even as the Bay fills up with day sailors and sport fishermen, watermen can be seen at daybreak motoring out of a creek to check their crab pots or "drudge for arsters."

Tiny Tangier Island has been the home of Virginia watermen so long that residents there still have a trace of their forefathers' English accent. Tangier might be best known for Hilda Crockett's Chesapeake House restaurant, where guests sit at long common tables and serve themselves from great platters of hot, home-cooked crab cakes, fried oysters, hush puppies and corn pudding.

Chesapeake House Crab Cakes

2 slices bread	1 tablespoon Worcester-
1 pound crabmeat	shire sauce
1 teaspoon Old Bay	1 egg, lightly beaten
seafood seasoning	1 teaspoon mustard
¼ teaspoon salt	Vegetable oil for frying
1 tablespoon mayonnaise	

Break bread in small pieces and moisten with water. Mix all ingredients and shape into cakes. Fry quickly until golden brown. Preparation: 15 minutes. Serves 4.

This is a simple main dish, especially when served with potato salad, applesauce, and pound cake.

Hilda Crockett's Chesapeake House
Tangier Island, Virginia

Sauteed Crabmeat Randolph

1 pound lump backfin
  crabmeat
8 ounces Virginia ham,
  sliced

4 large croutons
Butter
Dijonnaise Sauce

Saute crabmeat in butter. Place 2 ounces ham on each crouton. Place 4 ounces crabmeat on each serving of ham. Cover with Dijonnaise sauce. Place under broiler until slightly browned. Serves 4.

Dijonnaise Sauce:

1 pound unsalted butter
10 egg yolks

Dijon mustard
Salt and pepper

Clarify butter. Heat egg yolks in double boiler, stirring until thickened. Slowly add butter to egg sauce. Add mustard, salt, and pepper to taste. Yield: 3 cups.

"One of our most popular entrees."

The Williamsburg Inn
Williamsburg, Virginia

Crab Imperial

1 pound crabmeat
½ teaspoon salt
½ teaspoon pepper
½ cup mayonnaise

1 tablespoon capers
½ cup dry bread crumbs
Paprika
Butter

Combine crabmeat, salt, pepper, mayonnaise and capers; stir and place mixture in baking shells. Top mixture with bread crumbs; sprinkle with paprika and dot each with butter. Bake at 350° for 25 minutes. Preparation: 10 minutes. Serves 6.

May be prepared ahead and frozen.

Georgia Luck

Mrs. Lee's Crab and Sherry

2 cups crabmeat
2 hard-boiled eggs, chopped
1 teaspoon parsley, chopped
2 teaspoons lemon juice
1 teaspoon onion, grated
1 cup mayonnaise

½ teaspoon prepared mustard
3 tablespoons sherry
½ teaspoon Worcestershire sauce
½ cup buttered crumbs for topping

Mix together. Place in greased shells. Cover with crumbs and bake in 400° oven for 15 minutes. Serves 6.

Frances Harris

Cheddar and Crabmeat Casserole

8 slices of dry, stale bread, finely cubed, divided
1 pound crabmeat
½ cup mayonnaise
1 medium onion, finely diced
1 cup celery, finely chopped

4 eggs
2¾ cups milk
1 cup cream of mushroom soup, condensed
¾ pound sharp Cheddar cheese, grated
Salt and pepper

Place 4 of the 8 slices of diced bread in bottom of large oblong casserole dish. Mix crab, mayonnaise, onion, celery, and salt and pepper to taste in bowl and spread over bread cubes. Mix eggs and milk and pour over mixture. Refrigerate several hours or overnight.

Bake casserole at 325° for 15 minutes. Remove from oven and spread with other 4 slices of diced bread. Then stir in mushroom soup and top with grated cheese. Bake, covered with foil, for 45 minutes. Uncover and bake an additional 20 to 30 minutes. Preparation: 20 minutes. Serves 4 to 6.

Frances Kusterer

Deviled Crab

12 hard shelled crabs or 1
  13-ounce can crabmeat
  - 2⅔ cups
4 tablespoons butter or
  margarine
2 tablespoons flour
1 tablespoon parsley,
  minced
2 teaspoons lemon juice
1 teaspoon prepared
  mustard

½ teaspoon bottled
  horseradish
1 teaspoon salt
1 cup milk
2 shelled hard cooked
  eggs, minced
½ cup soft bread crumbs
2 tablespoons butter or
  margarine, melted

Use meat from 12 hard shelled crabs that have been boiled, or
1 13-ounce can crabmeat, flaked. Reserve 7 of upper shells from
crabs and wash well. Meanwhile, melt 4 tablespoons butter in
double boiler, stir in flour; add parsley, lemon juice, mustard,
horseradish, salt, and milk. Heat, stirring until thickened. Add
crabmeat and eggs. Fill crab shells with this mixture, sprinkle
with bread crumbs which have been combined with 2 tablespoons melted butter and bake in moderate oven at 400° for 10
minutes. Individual ramekins can be substituted for crab shells.
Serves 4 to 6.

Grace Deane

Hot or Cold Crabmeat

1 pound backfin
  crabmeat
3 tablespoons
  mayonnaise
1 teaspoon Durkee's
  Sauce

Salt and Lawry's
seasoning salt to taste
Juice of ½ lemon

Mix sauce ingredients until smooth. Carefully stir in crabmeat.
Serve chilled. To serve hot, put in greased small casserole, top
with cracker crumbs, dot with butter, and heat at 350° until bubbly. Preparation: 10 minutes. Serves 6.

Serve on toasted muffins with spinach salad for lunch.

Mrs. James H. Scott

Coquilles St. Jacques

½ pound mushrooms	4 tablespoons flour
4 tablespoons shallots, chopped	¼ cup Swiss cheese, grated
8 tablespoons butter, divided	Heavy cream
2 tablespoons lemon juice	Salt and pepper
2 pounds scallops in juice	Parmesan cheese
⅓ cup dry vermouth	Bread crumbs
	Additional butter, melted

Saute mushrooms and shallots in 4 tablespoons butter. Add lemon juice and stir well. Poach scallops in vermouth, drain and set aside. Save liquid. In saucepan, melt 4 tablespoons butter and gradually stir in flour, making a roux. Add scallop liquid, stirring constantly. Pour in enough heavy cream to make thick, creamy sauce. Add Swiss cheese, scallops, and mushrooms. Add salt and pepper to taste. Spoon into 6 baking shells or casserole and sprinkle with Parmesan cheese and bread crumbs. Dot with melted butter. Bake at 350° for 25 minutes. Serves 6.

Sue Thompson

Fresh Sea Scallops

14 ounces fresh sea scallops	1 carrot
1⅓ cups whipping cream	2 celery ribs
⅓ cup fresh grapefruit juice	1 medium onion
4 tablespoons Grey Poupon mustard	1 bay leaf
	2 quarts water
	1 fresh lime
	Salt and pepper to taste

Make court bouillon from carrot, celery, onion, bay leaf, and water. Place scallops in a single layer in 2 small shallow casserole dishes. Do not overcrowd! Steam scallops over court bouillon in a 2-quart steamer for about 5 minutes or until just done. Remove from steamer and keep warm. Pour liquid which has come out of scallops into a 10-inch skillet; add cream and cook over high heat until reduction begins. Add grapefruit juice and continue cooking rapidly. When sauce thickens, add Grey Poupon mustard. Pour any additional liquid that has come out of scallops into sauce. Add salt and pepper to taste. Pour sauce over warm scallops. Garnish with three thin slices of fresh lime. Serves 2.

Can be doubled.

C & O Restaurant
Charlottesville, Va.

241

Sauteed Scallops, Mediterranean Style

¾ pound fresh sea
scallops
½ cup quartered
mushrooms
½ stick butter
2 tablespoons olive oil
½ teaspoon salt
1 pinch pepper
¼ cup flour

1 tablespoon shallots,
minced
1 teaspoon fresh garlic
½ cup cooked tomatoes,
diced
1 tablespoon lemon juice
½ teaspoon parsley,
chopped
Salt and pepper to taste

Cut any large scallops in half, horizontally. Rinse scallops under cold water and drain well in colander. Clean and quarter mushrooms. Heat 1 tablespoon butter and 1 tablespoon oil in large skillet over high heat. Saute mushrooms for 3 to 4 minutes and season with salt and pepper. Transfer mushrooms into small bowl and reserve. Wipe pan clean.

Season scallops with salt and pepper and dredge in flour. Remove excess flour by shaking scallops back and forth in strainer. Heat remaining butter and oil over high heat. When butter begins to brown, add scallops in a single layer. Brown scallops on one side for 2 minutes, turn with tongs and brown on other side, also for 2 minutes.

Scatter shallots over scallops and toss once or twice. Add garlic, tomatoes, lemon juice, and mushrooms. (Drain mushrooms if any juice has accumulated in bowl.) Toss several times until all are evenly distributed. Transfer scallops to warm plates and sprinkle with chopped parsley. Serve with lemon wedges and tomatoes provencale.

Do not crowd pan when you saute. Items should be in 1 layer so they will brown and not stew. When flouring small items such as scallops, drop dusted pieces into a sieve or wire screen and just shake. All excess flour falls off and you have a light coating.

L'Auberge Chez Francois
Great Falls, Virginia

Stuffed Chincoteague Oysters Yorktown

3 dozen oysters in shell, cleaned
½ cup parsley
¼ cup shallots
6 garlic cloves
6 ounces white wine
1 pound butter
1 teaspoon thyme
1 teaspoon salt
1 teaspoon ground pepper
36 slices red pepper
2½ cups Hollandaise sauce
1 cup Parmesan cheese, grated

Combine parsley, shallots, garlic, wine, butter, thyme, salt, and pepper in food processor and blend to a paste. Stuff oysters with paste; top with slice of red pepper and 1 tablespoon of Hollandaise sauce. Sprinkle grated cheese on top. Bake in oven at 480° for 8 to 10 minutes. Serve hot. Serves 6.

La Petite France
Richmond, Virginia

Wild Rice and Oyster Casserole

2 cups wild or Uncle Ben's mixed rice
2 cans consomme
2 cups water (approximately)
¼ pound butter, softened
2 quarts oysters
1 can cream of mushroom soup
1 cup light cream
1½ teaspoons onion powder
¾ teaspoon thyme
1½ tablespoons curry powder, dissolved in a little hot water
½ cup fresh parsley, minced
Salt and pepper to taste
Hot sauce

Prepare rice using consomme plus enough water to equal required cooking liquid. Add butter and toss to coat rice. Place half of rice in large baking dish. Cover with oysters seasoned with salt, pepper, and hot sauce. Top with remaining rice. Heat soup and add cream, onion powder, thyme, and curry powder. Pour over rice and oyster mixture. Bake at 325° for 45 minutes. Garnish with parsley. Serves 10 to 12.

Rice and sauce can be prepared ahead.

Torrey Shuford

243

Scalloped Oysters

1 12-ounce jar fresh
oysters
6 tablespoons oyster
liquid, reserved
6 tablespoons light cream

½ cup dry bread crumbs
1 cup saltine cracker
crumbs
1 stick butter, melted
Salt and pepper to taste

Drain oysters; reserve liquid. Mix cream with equal amount of oyster liquid. Mix bread crumbs, cracker crumbs, and melted butter. Grease a 9-inch pie pan. Cover bottom with half of crumb mixture. Place oysters on top. Sprinkle with salt and pepper. Pour cream mixture over oysters. Top with remaining crumbs. Bake at 400° for 20 minutes. Serves 3.

Can be doubled or tripled. Use 1 recipe per pan.

Kay Williams

Asparagus and Shrimp

2 10½-ounce cans cut
asparagus spears
¼ cup green onion,
chopped
4 tablespoons butter
4 tablespoons flour
½ teaspoon salt
2 cups half-and-half

1 cup Cheddar cheese,
grated
¾ cup Parmesan cheese,
grated and divided
1 tablespoon lemon juice
1½ pounds cooked shrimp
Pepper to taste

Grease a 1½-quart oblong casserole dish. Drain asparagus and layer in bottom of dish. In a separate pan, melt butter and saute onions until soft. Add flour, salt, and pepper and blend well. Slowly stir in half-and-half and cook, stirring, until sauce is thick. Add Cheddar cheese and ¼ cup of the Parmesan cheese and stir until melted. Add lemon juice and shrimp. Pour mixture over asparagus. Sprinkle with remaining ½ cup Parmesan cheese. Bake at 400° for 15 to 20 minutes. Serve over hot buttered rice. Serves 4.

Ann Chaffins

Jumbo Shrimp a la Provencale

20 large shrimp
2 sticks of butter, softened
1 tablespoon lemon juice
½ tablespoon garlic powder
1/8 cup parsley, chopped

1/8 cup chives, chopped
1 ounce Worcestershire sauce
1 ounce white wine
Dash white pepper
Dash hot sauce
Dash oregano

Split shrimp up to the tail and partially loosen from shell. Mix remaining ingredients well. Place ¼ of butter mixture in each of 4 individual casserole dishes. Place five shrimp in each dish, tails pointing up. Bake at 400° for 10 to 15 minutes. Serves 4.

The Hotel Roanoke
Roanoke, Virginia

Pepper Shrimp

½ cup butter
2 tablespoons soy sauce
4 tablespoons Worcestershire sauce
4 dozen large shrimp, heads removed

3 tablespoons black pepper, freshly ground
Juice of 2 lemons

Preheat oven to 350°. Combine butter, soy sauce, Worcestershire sauce, and lemon juice in saucepan. Heat until butter is melted. Pour over shrimp placed one layer deep in a 9 x 13-inch Pyrex baking dish. Sprinkle pepper over shrimp and cover with foil. Bake for 20 minutes; baste. Bake uncovered for 10 minutes or until shrimp are cooked. Preparation: 10 minutes. Serves 8.

Serve with a simple green salad, French rolls, and lots of napkins.

Jana Thomas

Hot and Spicy Baked Shrimp

½ teaspoon cayenne	½ teaspoon salt
1 tablespoon thyme	3 tablespoons olive oil
½ teaspoon celery salt	1 teaspoon rosemary,
1 tablespoon fresh	crushed
parsley, chopped	2 sticks butter
⅔ cup Worcestershire	3 to 4 pounds raw,
sauce	unpeeled shrimp
½ teaspoon black pepper	

Cook all ingredients, except shrimp, for 3 to 5 minutes. Marinate shrimp for 4 hours in this mixture. Bake at 350° for 20 to 30 minutes, or until shrimp are pink and firm. Serves 6 to 8.

Serve shrimp in bowls with sauce for dipping.

Kay Williams

Marinated Shrimp

1 stick butter or	2 teaspoons garlic puree
margarine	(through press)
⅓ cup Worcestershire	1 teaspoon thyme
sauce	2 teaspoons rosemary
1 teaspoon salt	½ teaspoon celery salt
1 teaspoon black pepper	1 teaspoon olive oil
1 teaspoon cayenne	50 to 60 headless shrimp,
pepper	medium size, washed

Use 1½-quart Pyrex dish. Melt 1 stick butter or margarine in dish in oven and add all other ingredients except shrimp to melted butter, stirring often. Cook slowly 10 to 15 minutes (taste for pepper seasoning and add if desired) but do not bring to rapid boil. Allow to cool slightly; add shrimp. Marinate 2 to 3 hours or refrigerate overnight. Preheat oven to 400°. Cook shrimp with marinade in oven for approximately 18 to 20 minutes, stirring several times. Cooking depends on size of shrimp. The shrimp are hard to peel if overcooked. Serve with lots of napkins. Serves 8.

Grace Deane

Florida's Spiced Shrimp

6 pounds raw shrimp
9 cups water
1 tablespoon caraway
  seed
1 tablespoon whole black
  pepper
1 tablespoon pickling
  spice

1 teaspoon cayenne
  pepper
1 bay leaf
1 teaspoon dry mustard
4 teaspoons salt
Leaves of one bunch
  celery

Shell and devein shrimp, if desired. Boil all ingredients except shrimp in a large kettle for 20 minutes. Add shrimp and, if necessary, extra water to cover shrimp. Bring water back to a simmer and cook until shrimp are pink and firm. Cooking time will vary with size of shrimp and their initial temperature, usually 5 to 10 minutes. Do not overcook. Dip in sauce.

Sauce:

½ pound butter
1 tablespoon tarragon
  vinegar
1 tablespoon Worcester-
  shire sauce

2 tablespoons soy sauce
1 teaspoon salt
7 to 8 dashes Tabasco
  sauce
Juice of 2 large lemons

Melt butter and add all ingredients. Heat until hot; do not boil. Serves 6 to 8.

Double the sauce recipe for generous servings.

Nel Laughon

Here are two ways to butterfly shrimp: (1) Before cooking, peel the shrimp down to the tail, leaving the tail on. Devein. Holding so the underside is up, slice down its length, almost to the vein. Spread and flatten to form the butterfly shape. (2) Before cooking, run a toothpick or small skewer the length of the inner curve to keep the shrimp from curling. After cooking, peel and devein. Cut along the inner curve about ¾ of the way through.

Seafood

Scampi

1 pound raw shrimp,
  peeled
½ cup butter
2 teaspoons Worcester-
  shire sauce
¼ cup sherry
1 clove garlic, minced

2 tablespoons lemon juice
1 tablespoon sugar
¼ cup fresh parsley,
  minced
Rice
Parmesan cheese

Melt butter over low heat. Add Worcestershire sauce, sherry, garlic, lemon juice, and sugar. Mix well. Arrange shrimp in single layer in baking dish and pour sauce over. Broil on low heat for 8 minutes. Remove and let stand 15 minutes. Sprinkle parsley over shrimp. Broil on high heat for 3 minutes. Spoon over cooked rice and sprinkle with Parmesan cheese. Preparation: 30 minutes. Serves 4.

Pooh Steele

Szechuan Shrimp

½ cup catsup
1 tablespoon soy sauce
1 tablespoon sesame oil
  (a must)
1 tablespoon Worcester-
  shire sauce
3 tablespoons brown
  sugar
3 tablespoons sherry
½ teaspoon chili paste
  with garlic or ¼ tea-
  spoon Tabasco sauce
3 tablespoons peanut oil

4 dried red peppers
  (optional)
4 cloves garlic, minced
1 tablespoon ginger root,
  minced
½ cup scallions, minced
  (white part)
1½ pounds medium raw
  shrimp, shelled
3 tablespoons water, cold
1 tablespoon cornstarch
¼ cup scallions, chopped
  (green part)
Rice

Combine catsup, soy sauce, sesame oil, Worcestershire sauce, brown sugar, sherry, and chili paste (or Tabasco). Set aside. Heat peanut oil in wok to 375°. Stir-fry red peppers 30 seconds. Add garlic, ginger root, scallions (white part); stir-fry 1 minute. Add shrimp; stir-fry until pink. Add sauce to shrimp and stir until hot. Mix water and cornstarch, add to shrimp mixture, and stir until thickened. Remove red peppers. Serve over rice and top with chopped scallions (green part). Preparation: 30 minutes. Serves 6.

Very spicy dish, definitely for Szechuan lovers.

Michele Seass

Markey's Shrimp and Olives

1 pound medium uncooked shrimp or ½ pound cooked shrimp
4 tablespoons butter
4½ tablespoons flour
2 cups half-and-half (if using uncooked shrimp, substitute ½ cup cooking stock)
¼ teaspoon garlic salt
1 teaspoon dry mustard
2 dashes Worcestershire sauce
1 egg yolk, lightly beaten
¼ cup sherry
1 cup black olives, sliced
2 ounces slivered almonds
Salt and pepper to taste

If using uncooked shrimp, shell, devein, and cook in:
1 cup water
1/8 cup vinegar
1 onion, sliced
3 cloves
½ bay leaf

Bring preceding 5 ingredients to boil, add raw shrimp, and simmer for 5 minutes. Do not overcook shrimp. Reserve ½ cup cooking stock.

Over medium heat, prepare a medium-thick white sauce by melting butter, blending in flour, and then slowly adding half-and-half. Add garlic salt, mustard, and Worcestershire sauce and stir until thickened. Remove from heat and pour a little white sauce into beaten egg yolk and mix well. Combine egg yolk mixture with remaining white sauce and stir in sherry. Add shrimp and olives to sauce. Season with salt and pepper. Just before serving, sprinkle with almonds. Serves 4.

Recipe may be halved or doubled. If prepared ahead and refrigerated, make sauce extra thick.

Louisa Sirles

Easy Crab and Shrimp Bake

½ small onion, chopped
2 tablespoons butter
1 6-ounce package frozen crabmeat and shrimp, thawed

⅔ cup Pepperidge Farm stuffing
¼ cup cooking sherry
1 egg, well beaten
Dash of Tabasco sauce

Melt butter and saute onions. Add crabmeat, shrimp, and stuffing; stir until well mixed. Add sherry, Tabasco sauce, and egg; mix well. Bake at 350° for 15 minutes. Serves 2.

Use a Corning Ware dish or other pan that can go on the range and in the oven. Combination crab and shrimp may be hard to find. Make your own combination using fresh, frozen, or canned seafood. This recipe doubles easily.

Jane Johnson

Kitty's Shrimp Casserole

2 tablespoons margarine
1 green pepper, chopped
½ cup onion, chopped
1 tablespoon flour
1 cup canned tomatoes
½ cup water
½ teaspoon salt
¼ teaspoon cayenne pepper

¼ teaspoon thyme
1 tablespoon Worcestershire sauce
3 cups cooked rice
1 cup tomato juice
2 cups cooked shrimp
½ cup sharp cheese, grated

Saute onion and green pepper in margarine. Add flour, tomatoes, water, salt, cayenne pepper, thyme, and Worcestershire sauce and blend well. Cook until pepper is tender, stirring occasionally. Sauce should be thin. Add rice, tomato juice, and shrimp. Pour into greased baking dish and top with ½ cup of cheese. Bake 15 to 20 minutes at 350°. Preparation: 1 hour. Serves 12.

Betsy Bullock

Curried Shrimp

1 can cream of mushroom soup, undiluted	1/8 teaspoon black pepper
1 4-ounce can mushrooms, undrained	3/4 pound fresh cooked shrimp, peeled, or 2 or 3 cans drained and washed shrimp
1/2 teaspoon Worcestershire sauce	1/2 cup slivered almonds, toasted slightly in a little butter
1/4 teaspoon dry mustard	Rice
1/2 teaspoon curry powder	

Mix soup, undrained mushrooms, seasonings, and shrimp. Refrigerate up to 24 hours. To serve; heat in top of double boiler until piping hot. Add almonds and serve over hot white rice. Serves 4.

Serve with a fruit salad for an interesting balance.

Lindsay Manley

Shrimp and Rice Casserole

1 cup raw rice	1 teaspoon salt
1 1/2 pounds shrimp, cooked and cleaned	1/8 teaspoon mace
1 tablespoon lemon juice	1 cup condensed tomato soup
3 tablespoons salad oil	1/2 teaspoon pepper
1/4 cup diced green pepper	1/2 cup sliced almonds, lightly toasted
1/4 cup minced onion	Dash red pepper
2 tablespoons butter	Dash paprika
1 cup heavy cream	
3 tablespoons sherry	

Cook rice according to package directions. Cover shrimp with lemon juice and oil. Refrigerate until cold and crisp and stir often. Saute green pepper and onion in butter. Drain lightly and add with all remaining ingredients except for 1/4 cup almonds and paprika. Pour into 2-quart greased casserole. Sprinkle with reserved 1/4 cup almonds and paprika. Can be made a day ahead. Cover and bake at 350° for 30 minutes. Preparation: 25 minutes. Serves 8 to 10.

Susan Norton

Unusual Shrimp Creole

2 pounds shrimp, raw
1 quart water
1 bay leaf
1 cup carrots, diced
1 cup celery, diced
1 cup green beans
1 cup onions, chopped
1 cup green pepper, diced
1 stick butter
1 small can mushrooms, drained
1 can consomme

1 8-ounce can tomato sauce
1 6-ounce can tomato paste
½ cup sherry
1 cup sour cream (optional)
Salt
Vinegar
Paprika
Cayenne pepper
Wondra or instant-blending flour
Water
Cooked rice

Cook shrimp in water with bay leaf, a little vinegar, and salt. Drain shrimp. Saute vegetables in butter until crunchy. Add paprika and cayenne pepper to taste. Cook for 3 minutes. Add mushrooms, consomme, tomato sauce and tomato paste. In a cup, mix flour with a little water. Stirring frequently, add enough flour mixture to sauce to thicken to desired consistency. Mix in sherry and simmer 10 minutes. Add shrimp and sour cream and heat but do not boil. Serve over rice. Preparation: 45 minutes. Serves 8.

Gwen Weeks

Shrimp Creole

2 large onions, finely minced
4 stalks celery, finely minced
2 tablespoons butter or olive oil
1 tablespoon flour
1 cup water

1 16-ounce can tomatoes (or equivalent of fresh)
1 6-ounce can tomato paste
1 tablespoon chili powder
1 tablespoon vinegar
1 teaspoon salt
2 cups raw shrimp
1 teaspoon sugar

Saute onions and celery in butter or olive oil until golden brown. Sprinkle in flour. Blend. Add water, tomatoes, tomato paste, chili powder, vinegar, and salt. Simmer for 1 hour. Add shrimp and sugar. Cook until shrimp are done. Thicken more if desired. Serve over fluffy rice. Preparation: 30 minutes. Serves 4.

Adding raw shrimp is the secret of this recipe.

Dorothy Hart

Lobster Mousse

1 small fresh onion, minced	2 tablespoons gelatin
4 cups lobster meat, minced	½ cup lemon juice (fresh or bottled)
2 cups celery, minced	2 cups mayonnaise
1 cup heavy cream	Salt and pepper to taste

Combine onion, lobster, celery, salt, and pepper and set aside. Whip cream and set aside. Soften gelatin in ¾ cup cold water, heating in double boiler to dissolve completely. Remove from heat and add lemon juice and mayonnaise. Stir in lobster mixture until well blended. Fold in whipped cream until uniform. Place mixture in casserole dish or mold and chill well.

The Tides Inn
Irvington, Virginia

No Bones Shad

3 to 4 pounds shad, split and cleaned	2 strips bacon, cut in half
	4 slices lemon

Dry shad thoroughly after cleaning. Place on large sheet of foil with 2 pieces of bacon placed diagonally underneath and 2 pieces placed diagonally on top. Lay lemon slices down the top side. Cover with a second piece of foil and seal tightly on all sides. Place on broiler pan in center of oven. Bake at 500° for 1 hour; reduce heat to 250° and bake 5 hours. serves 4.

Guaranteed - no bones!

Grace Deane

Easy Fried Shad Roe

Shad roe	Waxed paper
Crisco shortening	

Wrap shad roe in waxed paper, folding paper in a traditional "drugstore wrap." Melt shortening in frying pan and add shad roe. Fry until brown and crisp, turning over by using folded-up ends of wax paper as handles.

Waxed paper prevents popping, and roe is kept intact.

Anne Booker

253

Fishing Bay Bluefish

1 stick of butter, melted	Juice of 1 lemon
Fresh fillets of bluefish	Seasoned salt

Mix together lemon juice and melted butter. Place bluefish fillets skin side down on charcoal grill. Brush lemon/butter on fillets and sprinkle with seasoned salt. Cover grill with aluminum foil or grill top and cook for 20 minutes.

Can add ⅓ cup Worcestershire sauce as a variation.

Frances Harris

Bluefish, Onions and Parmesan

3 small onions, sliced thinly into rings	½ cup Parmesan cheese, freshly grated
2 tablespoons butter, unsalted	½ cup fine bread crumbs
4 ½-pound bluefish fillets	Salt
½ cup mayonnaise, divided (homemade would be nice)	Pepper, freshly grated

Saute onions in butter until brown and tender. Oil broiler pan rack (or spread heavy-duty foil on rack and oil it). Arrange fillets skin side down and season with salt and pepper. Spread each fillet with 1 tablespoon of mayonnaise and broil 4 inches under preheated broiler for 3 minutes. Divide onions among fillets and spread remaining ¼ cup mayonnaise over them. Sprinkle with mixture of Parmesan cheese and bread crumbs. Broil 2 to 3 minutes, or until they flake when tested with fork and top is golden brown. Remove with large spatula. Serves 4.

Trudie Steel

Broiled Fillets with Parsley-Parmesan Butter

6 fish fillets, about ⅓
pound each
1 stick butter, softened
2 tablespoons parsley,
finely chopped
⅓ cup Parmesan cheese
2 tablespoons capers
(optional)

1 teaspoon French-style
mustard
Juice of ½ lemon
Few drops of
Worcestershire sauce
Parsley, fresh

Preheat broiler. Line broiler pan with aluminum foil and brush lightly with cooking oil. Place fillets in pan skin side down. With a fork, whip butter until quite soft. Add remaining ingredients and mix well. Spread on fillets and broil, 5 to 6 inches from heat for 6 to 7 minutes. Serve garnished with thin lemon slices each topped with a mound of finely chopped parsley. Preparation: 30 minutes. Serves 6.

Butter mixture also good on broccoli, green beans, cauliflower, and other vegetables.

Anne Grier

Rainbow Trout Baked in Wine

4 rainbow trout
¾ cup onion, chopped
½ cup parsley, chopped

6 tablespoons butter
1 cup dry white wine
Bread crumbs

Clean trout, leaving heads and tails intact. Saute onion and parsley in butter. Spread ⅓ of this mixture in bottom of a baking dish. Fill cavities of fish with ⅓ of mixture and place remainder on top. Pour wine over top of fish and cover. Bake at 350⁰ for 25 to 30 minutes. Uncover and sprinkle with bread crumbs. Serves 4.

Pooh Steele

Stuffed Farm-Raised Catfish Almondine

½ onion, chopped
8 fresh mushrooms, sliced
2 shallots, chopped

4 tablespoons butter
8 catfish fillets
5 ounces white wine
Salt and pepper

Crabmeat Stuffing:

1 green bell pepper, finely diced
1 pimento, finely diced
1 tablespoon English mustard

½ teaspoon salt
¼ teaspoon white pepper
1 egg
½ cup mayonnaise
2 pounds lump crabmeat

Mix together well: green bell pepper, pimento, mustard, salt, white pepper, egg, and mayonnaise. Add crabmeat and mix carefully so that the lumps are not broken.

Saute onions, mushrooms, and shallots in butter. Add catfish.

Pile each catfish with a mound of stuffing and arrange in shallow casserole. Pour wine into bottom of casserole and salt and pepper fish. Bake in 400° oven 15 to 20 minutes. Serves 8.

The Hotel Roanoke
Roanoke, Virginia

Mayonnaise aux Fruits de Mer

½ cup mayonnaise
2 tablespoons catsup
½ tablespoon lime juice

½ tablespoon horseradish
¼ tablespoon sherry

Mix well and refrigerate. Good with almost any seafood. Yield: ⅔ cup.

Dorothy Hart

Jana's Remoulade Sauce

1 cup mayonnaise
(homemade best)
1 tablespoon onion, minced
1 tablespoon parsley, minced
2 tablespoons Dijon mustard

1 tablespoon horseradish
1 teaspoon paprika
½ teaspoon salt
1 tablespoon vinegar
½ teaspoon Worcester-shire sauce
¼ cup salad oil
Dash Tabasco

Combine all ingredients except oil. Whisk in oil slowly. Refrigerate several hours or overnight. Yield: 1½ cups.

Serve with lump crab, cold boiled shrimp, fried oysters, or fish.

Jana Thomas

Spiced Mustard Sauce

1 cup sour cream
2 tablespoons Dijon mustard
1 tablespoon soy sauce
1 tablespoon Worcester-shire sauce

1 teaspoon onion, minced
1 garlic clove, minced
Salt to taste
Pepper to taste

Mix all ingredients and refrigerate. Let flavors blend together overnight or longer. Serve cold. Yield: 1¼ cups.

Sally Ayers

Shellfish

Before using oysters in any fried or creamed dish, dry them in an absorbent towel.

Allow 1 quart undrained, shucked oysters for 6 servings.

If buying clams in the shell, test to see that they are tightly closed or, if slightly open, that they close tightly upon being touched. Discard any that float or have broken shells.

To test scallops for freshness, see that they have a sweetish odor. If in bulk, they should be free of liquid.

For sauteing or broiling, allow ⅓ pound of sea scallops or ¼ pound of bay scallops per serving.

Cooked scallops may be used in any recipe for fish salads or creamed fish, or they may be skewered and grilled.

Crabs must be alive and lively when cooked. Scrub if slimy.

Fresh shrimp should be dry and firm.

One pound of shrimp in the shell ("green" shrimp) equals ½ pound of cooked, shelled shrimp equals 1 cup or 3 servings.

To prevent curling and toughening of shrimp, drain them at once after cooking.

Devein shrimp before or after cooking by running an ice pick or a small pointed knife down the back of the tails.

If using canned shrimp, rinse briefly in cold water to remove excess salt.

Allow ½ large lobster or 1 small lobster per serving. Buy active, live lobsters weighing from 1¼ to 2½ pounds. Lobsters weighing 3 pounds or more are apt to be coarse and tough. A 2½-pound lobster yields about 2 cups of cooked meat.

Store live lobsters in the refrigerator, not on ice.

Fish

If you are in doubt about the freshness of a fish, place it in cold water. A newly caught fish will float.

Allow per serving 1 pound whole small fish, ¾ pound if entrails, head, tail and fins are removed, ½ pound fish steaks, or ⅓ pound fish fillets.

If cooked fish is to be served cold, keep refrigerated until the last minute. If served buffet-style, place it over cracked ice.

To minimize fish tastes and odors, use lemon, wine, vinegar, ginger, spring onions or garlic in the marinating or cooking.

Use thawed fish immediately, and do not refreeze. It may be cooked in the same way as its fresh counterpart.

Desserts

Fruits from Virginia vineyards, orchards and berry bushes figure prominently in desserts of the Old Dominion. Apple pies, blueberry cobblers and homemade peach ice cream are favorite fare for cooks and guests alike.

One of the old standbys of Virginia cooks is chess pie, traditionally a lemon and sugar syrup baked in a light crust. A new version of this Old Dominion recipe is chocolate chess pie, which combines chess pie and another Southern favorite, pecan pie, in exquisite richness.

The Tides Inn and its sister, The Tides Lodge, straddle a picturesque creek off the great Rappahannock River, just a few miles from the Chesapeake Bay. Guests who dock at the waterfront resort for a week or just for dinner can enjoy an elegant meal of regional dishes and top it off with a fine dessert such as chocolate chess pie.

The Tides Lodge Chocolate Chess Pie

4 heaping tablespoons of cocoa
1½ cups sugar
2 eggs, beaten
½ cup pecans, chopped
¼ cup butter, melted
½ cup unsweetened evaporated milk
½ cup coconut
1 9-inch pie shell, unbaked
Vanilla ice cream, or whipped cream

Preheat oven to 400°. Mix all ingredients and pour into an unbaked pie shell. Bake for 30 minutes. Cool. Serve with a scoop of vanilla ice cream or whipped cream. Yield: 1 9-inch pie.

The Tides Lodge
Irvington, Virginia

Ice-Water Pastry

1¼ cups all-purpose flour	1/8 teaspoon salt
4 tablespoons shortening, chilled	3 tablespoons ice water
2 tablespoons butter, chilled and cut into ¼-inch pieces	

Combine flour, shortening, butter, and salt in large bowl. Working quickly, use fingers or pastry blender until mixture resembles flakes of coarse meal. Pour ice water over mixture, toss together, and form dough into a compact ball. Dust lightly with flour, wrap in waxed paper, and chill at least 30 minutes. Lightly butter a 9-inch pie plate. On floured surface roll dough to circle of 13 to 14-inch diameter, about 1/8-inch thick. Place rolling pin on pastry, lift up and roll pastry around pin. Unroll pastry over pie plate. Fit into pie plate, trimming edges and pressing pastry around rim. Fill with favorite filling and bake in preheated 400° oven for 10 minutes. To bake unfilled pie crust, prick pastry before baking to prevent buckling. (Unfilled crust may also be lined with foil or parchment and filled with dried beans or rice to retain shape.) Bake in preheated 400° oven for 10 minutes; reduce heat to 350° and continue baking 10 minutes or until lightly browned. Yield: 1 pie crust.

Sue Reynolds

Lemon Chess Pie

6 eggs, beaten	1 stick butter, melted
2 cups sugar	1 9-inch pie shell, unbaked
3 lemons, juice and grated rind	

Beat eggs, add sugar, lemon juice and rind, butter, and blend in blender. Pour into pie shell and bake at 350° for 35 minutes.

Beverley Shannon

Brown Sugar Pie

1 stick butter, softened
1 pound brown sugar
4 eggs, beaten
4 tablespoons milk
2 teaspoons light corn
  syrup

1 teaspoon vanilla
2 9-inch pie crusts,
  unbaked

Cream butter and sugar and add eggs, milk, corn syrup, and vanilla. Mix well, but do not beat at high speed. Pour into pie crusts and bake at 375⁰ for approximately 40 minutes or until brown. Serves 8.

Anne Booker

Toasted Coconut Pie

3 eggs, slightly beaten
1½ cups sugar
1 cup margarine or
  butter, melted
4 teaspoons lemon juice

1 teaspoon vanilla
1 small can flaked
  coconut
1 unbaked pie shell

Combine all ingredients and pour into pie shell. Bake at 350⁰ for 40 to 45 minutes.

Marti Thomas

Japanese Pie

1½ sticks margarine,
  softened
1¾ cups sugar
4 eggs, beaten lightly
2 tablespoons vinegar

1 cup pecan pieces
1 cup raisins
1 cup coconut
2 9-inch pie crusts,
  unbaked

Cream margarine and sugar and add eggs. Stir in vinegar. Add pecans, raisins, and coconut and pour into 2 pie crusts. Bake at 350⁰ for 30 to 40 minutes. Serves 8.

Variation: Add ½ cup chocolate chips and/or use rum-soaked raisins.

Louise Mondy

Maple Pecan Pie

3 eggs, beaten
1 cup Highland County
  maple syrup
1 cup brown sugar
1 tablespoon vanilla

2 tablespoons butter,
  melted
2 cups pecan pieces
1 9-inch unbaked pastry
  shell

Preheat oven to 325°. Beat first three ingredients and add next three. Pour into pastry shell and bake 45 to 50 minutes. Yield: 8 servings.

*Highland Inn
Monterey, Virginia*

Pecan Pie

½ cup sugar
1 cup light brown sugar
½ cup margarine or
  butter, melted
1 teaspoon vanilla

¼ teaspoon salt
2 eggs
1 cup pecan halves
1 pie crust, unbaked

Preheat oven to 350°. Combine sugars, margarine, vanilla, salt, and eggs and mix well. Add pecan halves and pour into pie crust. Bake 45 minutes. Serves 8.

Freezes well.

Clare Lancaster

Grasshopper Pie

24 chocolate wafers, crushed
¼ cup butter, melted
¼ cup milk
¼ cup Creme de Menthe (or a few drops each peppermint extract and green food coloring)

1 jar Kraft Marshmallow Creme
2 cups heavy cream, whipped

Combine crumbs and butter. Press into 9-inch pie pan. Gradually add milk and Creme de Menthe to marshmallow and mix well. Fold in whipped cream. Pour into shell and freeze at least 5 hours. Serves 6 to 8.

May be garnished with chocolate curls or shaved chocolate.

Kitty Bayliss

Angel Lime Pie

3 egg whites at room temperature
¼ teaspoon cream of tartar
1 cup sugar
3 egg yolks

½ cup sugar
1/8 teaspoon salt
1 teaspoon lime rind, grated
½ cup fresh lime juice
1 cup whipping cream

Beat egg whites until frothy and add cream of tartar. Gradually add 1 cup sugar, beating constantly, until very stiff. Spread evenly over bottom and sides of a greased 9-inch pie plate. Bake at 275° for 1 hour; cool.

Beat egg yolks slightly; beat in remaining ½ cup sugar, salt, lime rind, and lime juice. Cook over medium heat, stirring constantly, until thickened. Do not boil. Cool thoroughly. Beat whipping cream until stiff and fold into lime custard. Pour into shell and chill at least 8 hours or overnight. Serves 6 to 8.

Betty Williams

Pineapple Pie

1 large can crushed pineapple	½ cup sugar
2 tablespoons cornstarch	3 egg yolks, beaten
½ teaspoon salt	1 9-inch pie crust, baked
	Juice of ½ lemon

Bring pineapple to a boil in medium saucepan. Combine cornstarch, salt, and sugar and stir into hot pineapple. Reduce heat and cook 10 minutes, stirring occasionally. Add egg yolks and lemon juice slowly. Cover and cook 5 minutes. When cool, spoon into pie crust. Cover with whipped cream or meringue.

Meringue:

3 egg whites	6 tablespoons sugar

Beat egg whites slowly and increased speed. Add sugar, 1 tablespoon at a time, until fluffy and thickened. Spread on pie filling and bake at 300° until golden. Serves 8.

Sandy King

Apple Crumb Pie

4 or 5 apples, peeled, sliced, and sprinkled with brown sugar and cinnamon	1 cup flour
	½ cup brown sugar
	½ cup margarine

Put apples in greased pie pan. Make topping by mixing together flour, brown sugar, and margarine. Sprinkle topping over apples and bake for 30 minutes at 375°.

Emily McLeod

Honey Apple Pie

1 9-inch unbaked pie
  shell
½ cup sugar
3 tablespoons flour
¼ cup honey
⅓ cup heavy cream

5 tart apples, peeled,
  cored, and thinly sliced
½ teaspoon cinnamon
¼ teaspoon nutmeg
1 tablespoon butter

Sprinkle bottom of pastry shell with 1 tablespoon each of sugar and flour. Combine remaining sugar and flour; stir in honey and cream. Pour over apples, mixing gently until slices are coated. Spoon into pie shell. Sprinkle with cinnamon and nutmeg; dot with butter. Bake at 425° for 45 minutes or until apples are tender and golden brown. Serves 6 to 8.

Trudie Steel

Brown Sugar Apple Pie

7 tart apples
1 cup brown sugar, light
  or dark
2 tablespoons flour
1/8 teaspoon salt
1½ teaspoons ground
  cinnamon
½ teaspoon ground
  nutmeg

¼ teaspoon mace
1 tablespoon lemon peel,
  grated
2 tablespoons butter
Pastry for 9-inch pie
(top and bottom)

Pare, core, and thickly slice apples. Combine brown sugar, flour, salt, spices, and lemon peel. Mix with apple slices. Line 9-inch pie pan with pastry. Fill very full with apple slices; dot with butter. Cover with top crust. Seal edges of pastry and cut 3 slits to allow steam to escape. Bake at 450° for 10 minutes. Reduce heat to 350° and bake 40 minutes longer. Serve hot. Serves 6 to 8.

Trudie Steel

Peaches and Cream Tart

Pastry:

1 ¼ cups flour
¼ cup ground almonds
½ cup butter, softened

3 tablespoons confec-
tioners sugar
1 egg yolk

Process all ingredients in mixer until crumbly. Press dough into 8-inch tart shell. Chill at least 1 hour. Bake in preheated 425° oven for 15 minutes or until golden and crispy. Cool.

Filling:

8 ounces cream cheese
2 to 3 tablespoons orange
liqueur
2 tablespoons grated
orange peel

¼ cup sugar
5 to 6 fresh peaches,
sliced

Combine first 4 ingredients and mix well. Pour into baked shell and arrange peaches on top.

Glaze:

½ cup apricot preserves

2 tablespoons orange
liqueur

Combine and pour over peaches. Serves 6.

Jane Hall

Debbie's Fresh Peach Pie

¾ cup water
1 cup sugar
2 tablespoons cornstarch,
  rounded, mixed with a
  little water

1 teaspoon salt
1 cup crushed peaches
1 8-inch pie shell, baked
Whipped cream
Sliced peaches

Cook first 5 ingredients, stirring until thickened (be patient, it will boil). Cool. Fill shell with fresh sliced peaches, pour cooled sauce over top. Refrigerate. Serve topped with whipped cream. Serves 6 to 8.

For 10-inch pie, prepare recipe 1½ times. Nectarines can be substituted for peaches.

Trudie Steel

French Silk

1 cup brown sugar
1 cup flour
½ cup pecans
¼ cup butter
1 cup butter
1½ cups white sugar

3 ounces unsweetened
  chocolate, melted
2 teaspoons vanilla
4 eggs
Whipped cream

Mix first 4 ingredients and spread in buttered 9-inch pie pan. Bake 15 minutes at 450° - do not overcook. Remove and stir up, then pat down and chill. Cream 1 cup butter, white sugar, chocolate, and vanilla. Add eggs, one at a time, beating 5 minutes after each. Fill pan and chill several hours. Serve with a dollop of whipped cream. Serves 6 to 8.

Anne Booker

Martha's Pie

¼ cup margarine
1 cup sugar
3 eggs, beaten
¾ cup light corn syrup
¼ teaspoon salt
1 teaspoon vanilla

½ cup chocolate chips
½ cup pecans, chopped
2 tablespoons bourbon
1 8 or 9-inch unbaked
   pie crust

Cream margarine and add sugar gradually. Add beaten eggs, syrup, salt and vanilla. Add chocolate chips, pecans and bourbon. Stir well. Pour into crust. Bake at 375° for 40 to 50 minutes. Serve with whipped cream. Serves 6 to 8.

Martha Wheeler

Caribbean Fudge Pie

¼ cup butter
¾ cup brown sugar,
   packed
3 eggs
1 12-ounce package semi-
   sweet chocolate bits,
   melted
2 teaspoons instant coffee
2 tablespoons rum

¼ cup flour
1 cup walnuts, broken
1 9-inch pie crust,
   unbaked
½ cup walnut halves for
   decoration
   Whipped cream
   (optional)

Cream butter and sugar and beat in eggs one at a time. Add melted chocolate, coffee, and rum. Stir in flour and broken walnuts. Pour into pie crust and top with remaining walnut halves. Bake at 375° for 25 minutes. Cool. Top with whipped cream, if desired. Serves 8.

Nancy Morris

Chocolate Mousse Pie

Crust:

3 cups chocolate wafer
crumbs

½ cup unsalted butter,
melted

Combine ingredients and press on bottom and sides of 10-inch pan or 2 pie pans. Refrigerate 30 minutes. (2 ready-made chocolate graham cracker crusts could be used.)

Filling:

1 pound semi-sweet
chocolate

2 eggs

4 egg yolks

2 cups whipping cream

6 tablespoons powdered
sugar

4 egg whites, room
temperature

Soften chocolate in top of double boiler over warm water (simmering). Let cool to lukewarm. Add whole eggs and mix. Add yolks and mix well. In separate bowl whip cream with powdered sugar until peaks form. In separate bowl beat egg whites until stiff, not dry. Stir a little of the cream and egg whites into chocolate mixture to lighten. Fold in remaining cream and egg whites. Turn into crust and chill at least 6 hours.

Topping:

2 cups whipping cream

Sugar to taste

Whip remaining 2 cups cream with sugar to taste until quite stiff. Spread over pie.

Leaves:

8 ounces semi-sweet
chocolate

1 tablespoon shortening

Waxy leaves (Camellia,
etc.)

Melt chocolate and shortening in double boiler. Using a teaspoon, generously coat underside of leaves. Chill or freeze until firm. Separate chocolate from leaves, starting with stem, and arrange on top of pie. Serves 12.

Pie can be frozen - thaw overnight in refrigerator.

Elizabeth Robertson

Pies

Chocolate Ripple Pie

Crust:

½ cup butter
2 tablespoons sugar

1 cup flour

Combine ingredients and mix with mixer on lowest speed until a dough forms. Place ¼ to ⅓ cup of mixture in small pan to make crumbs. Press remaining mixture into 9-inch pie pan. Bake at 375° until golden: crumbs, 10 to 12 minutes; crust, 12 to 15 minutes.

Filling:

1 cup semi-sweet chocolate bits
¼ cup light corn syrup
½ cup water, divided
½ cup sugar

1 unbeaten egg white
1 teaspoon vanilla
1 teaspoon lemon juice
1 cup whipping cream

Melt semi-sweet chocolate bits with corn syrup and ¼ cup water over low heat. Mix well and cool. Combine sugar, ¼ cup water, unbeaten egg white, vanilla, and lemon juice. Beat with mixer at high speed until soft peaks form. Beat whipping cream until thick. Fold cream and ½ chocolate mixture into egg white mixture. Spoon ½ of filling into pie shell. Drizzle ½ remaining chocolate over filling. Repeat with remaining filling and chocolate. Cut with knife to give swirled appearance. Sprinkle with crumbs. Freeze 4 to 6 hours. Serves 6 to 8.

Ann Davis

Chocolate Sundae Pie

1 cup small marshmallows
1 small can evaporated milk
6 ounces chocolate chips (not "chocolate flavor")

¼ teaspoon salt
1½ pints ice cream (vanilla, coffee, or mint)
Vanilla wafers or brown edge wafers

Butter or oil a 9-inch pie pan. Line bottom and sides with wafers. Combine marshmallows, milk, chocolate chips, and salt. Heat over medium heat until well blended and slightly thickened. Cool slightly. Spoon half of ice cream into wafer-lined pan. Top with half the sauce. Repeat. Freeze well. Serves 8.

Gale Cooper

Christmas Wine Jelly

2 envelopes gelatin
1 cup cold juices from
  cherries and pineapple
1 cup hot juices from
  cherries and pineapple
1 cup dry sherry
1 cup sugar
1 20-ounce can crushed
  pineapple

1 20-ounce can Queen
  Anne cherries, pitted
1 20-ounce can slivered
  almonds
Juice of one lemon
Whipped cream

Dissolve gelatin in one cup of cold juices. Add one cup of hot juices and mix well. Mix the remainder of the ingredients and pour into a mold. Refrigerate until firm. Serve with sweetened whipped cream as topping.

My grandmother's favorite holiday treat! It would not be Christmas without it.

Cabell West

Pineapple Torte

1 small can crushed
  pineapple, drained and
  liquid reserved
¾ cup sugar
3 egg yolks, beaten
1 small can Pet milk,
  chilled

3 egg whites
4 tablespoons sugar
Dash of salt
Juice of ½ lemon
About 20 vanilla
  wafers, crushed

Add sugar, salt, egg yolks, and lemon juice to pineapple juice in saucepan. Stir and cook until the mixture coats a spoon. Add pineapple and cool.

Whip milk until like whipped cream, and beat egg whites, adding 4 tablespoons sugar slowly. Fold whipped milk into the egg whites. Fold in pineapple mixture.

Butter a 9 x 9-inch pan and cover with crushed vanilla wafers, reserving some crumbs for the top. Pour pineapple mixture over crumbs and sprinkle top with the remaining crumbs. Freeze. Serves 9.

Light summertime dessert.

Sandy King

Fruit Salad Dessert

1 bunch white seedless
  grapes
2 quarts fresh
  strawberries

16 ounces sour cream
⅔ cup brown sugar

Mix sour cream and brown sugar together. Pour over fruit and chill for 2 to 3 hours. Serves 8.

Bananas, peaches, or pineapple can be added. Delicious and easy!

Peggy O'Neal

Chocolate-Dipped Fruits

1 cup semi-sweet
  chocolate chips
A few slivers of
  paraffin

Fresh fruit: strawberries,
oranges, pears, apples,
grapes or whatever
suits your fancy

Melt chocolate chips and paraffin slowly. Stir until smooth. Wash fruit. Leave strawberries whole, including caps. Peel and section oranges. Cut pears and apples into wedges and brush with lemon juice to prevent discoloration. Dip all or part of the fruit into the melted chocolate. Place dipped fruit onto plate or onto waxed paper and allow chocolate to harden before serving.

If the chocolate is heated in the top of a double boiler, it won't harden as fast.

Martha Wheeler

Lemon Spongettes

2 tablespoons butter
1 cup sugar
4 tablespoons flour
1 lemon, grated rind and
  juice

3 eggs, separated
1¼ cups milk
  Pinch of salt

Cream butter, sugar, flour, lemon juice and rind. Mix together unbeaten egg yolks and milk and add to creamed mixture. Beat egg whites until stiff and fold into mixture. Pour into slightly greased custard cups. Place cups in pan of warm water and cook at 350° for about 45 minutes. Test for doneness. They will have sponge cake on bottom and custard on top. Invert and serve plain or topped with strawberries or raspberries. Serves 4.

Louise Mondy

Evans Farm Apple Crisp

8 medium apples, peeled,
 cored, and sliced
1 cup sugar
2 tablespoons flour
¾ teaspoon ground
 cinnamon
2 tablespoons butter
1 cup sugar

1 cup sifted flour
1 teaspoon baking
 powder
¼ teaspoon salt
1 egg
1 teaspoon ground
 cinnamon

Blend apples with cinnamon, sugar, and flour. Place in a buttered baking dish and dot with butter. In a separate bowl, place remaining ingredients and mix until crumbly. Sprinkle topping over apples and bake at 350° until bubbly and brown. Serve warm with whipped cream or vanilla ice cream or just plain.

Evans Farm Inn
McLean, Virginia

Very-Berry Cobbler

¼ cup sugar
1½ teaspoons cornstarch
1/8 teaspoon salt
1 10-ounce package
 frozen raspberries,
 thawed and undrained
1 teaspoon lemon juice
1 16-ounce can pitted tart
 cherries, drained

½ cup butter or
 margarine, softened
½ cup sugar
1 cup flour
¼ teaspoon salt
 Vanilla ice cream
 (optional)

Combine first three ingredients in saucepan. Stir in raspberries and lemon juice and bring to a boil. Cook 1 minute, stirring constantly. Stir drained cherries into raspberry mixture and spoon into a greased 1-quart baking dish. Cream butter and ½ cup sugar. Stir in flour and ¼ teaspoon salt, blending just until mixture is coarse meal. Sprinkle over berry mixture. Bake at 375° for 30 minutes. Serve with vanilla ice cream. Serves 6.

Sandy King

Mousse de Kiwi Napoleon

3 eggs
¾ cup sugar, divided
6 tablespoons Cointreau, Grand Marnier or Curaco, divided
2 cups whipping cream

3 drops vanilla
3 kiwi fruit, peeled, finely chopped or grated
1 kiwi fruit, peeled and sliced for garnish

Break eggs into medium bowl; add ½ cup sugar and 4 tablespoons liqueur. Set bowl into large bowl filled with hot water. Whisk mixture until thick. Remove from water and continue whisking until cool (3 to 5 minutes). Cool completely in refrigerator.

Whip cream in medium bowl until thickened. Add ¼ cup sugar and vanilla and continue beating until stiff. Gently fold in chopped kiwi and remaining liqueur. Swirl egg mixture carefully into cream. Spoon mousse into large cocktail glasses or tall parfait glasses. Top with sliced kiwi. Refrigerate until ready to serve. Serves 8 to 10.

A perfect summer dessert or after a heavy meal.

Gwen Weeks

Mandarin Orange Souffle Mold

2 3-ounce packages orange Jello
1 cup boiling water
1 cup orange juice
1 cup sour cream
1 pint orange sherbet

1 cup pineapple tidbits, well drained
2 cups mandarin oranges, well drained
1 cup coconut

Mix Jello with water until dissolved. Add orange juice. Chill until mixture begins to thicken. Stir in sour cream and sherbet. Beat until thick and foamy. Add pineapple and oranges. Pour into a 2-quart mold. When set, sprinkle with coconut. Serves 12.

Ginger Chalkley

Easy Baked Custard

4 eggs
⅓ cup sugar
1 teaspoon vanilla
1½ teaspoons almond
   extract

2½ cups half-and-half
½ teaspoon nutmeg
½ teaspoon cinnamon
Dash salt

Mix all ingredients in a blender and pour into Pyrex baking dish or 6 six-ounce custard cups. Place dish or custard cups in oblong baking pan filled with very hot water. Water should come to about ½ inch from top of cups or dish. Bake at 350° for about 45 minutes or until knife inserted into custard comes out clean. Remove cups or dish from pan of water and serve. Serves 6 to 8.

May be refrigerated and served cold.

Terry Tosh

Elegant Bread Custard

¾ cup butter, melted
12 slices French bread, cut
   ½-inch thick, crusts
   trimmed
5 whole eggs
4 egg yolks
1 cup sugar
1/8 teaspoon salt

1 quart milk
1 cup heavy cream
1 teaspoon vanilla
Pinch of nutmeg
Confectioners sugar
Puree of raspberries or
   strawberries (optional)

Preheat oven to 375°. Butter one side of each slice of bread and set aside. Beat together eggs, yolks, sugar, salt, and nutmeg in a large bowl until thoroughly combined. Set aside. Combine milk and cream in a saucepan and heat until scalded. Blend very gradually into egg mixture. Stir in vanilla and mix well. Arrange slices of bread, buttered side up, in a 2-quart baking dish or oven-proof bowl; strain custard mixture over bread. Pour boiling water into a roasting pan to a depth of about 1 inch. Set baking dish in pan, place in oven, and bake about 45 minutes or until a knife inserted in the center comes out clean. Remove custard from pan and sprinkle generously with confectioners sugar. Place pudding under broiler for a few minutes, watching carefully until bread is just glazed. Delicious served with puree of raspberries or strawberries. Serves 10 to 12.

Frances Shield

Mud Pie

3 or 4 dozen macaroons,
slightly crumbled
2 or 3 jiggers of bourbon
2 quarts of coffee ice
cream

1 pint of whipping
cream, whipped

Fudge sauce:

3 tablespoons butter
2 squares of bittersweet
chocolate
1 cup powdered sugar

3 tablespoons milk

Line the bottom of a 2½-quart serving bowl with macaroons.
Sprinkle with bourbon. Top with softened coffee ice cream. Put
in freezer.

To prepare sauce, melt butter and chocolate in double boiler. Add
sugar and mix well. Add milk gradually; beat until smooth. Bring
to a boil, stirring constantly until thick. Set aside. Ten minutes
before serving, remove dish from freezer, cover with whipped
cream and pour fudge sauce on top. Serves 10 to 12.

*Substitute sherry for bourbon, or liquor may be deleted. Add 1
cup of toasted slivered almonds to ice cream. Commercial
chocolate syrup may be used.*

Ann B. Haskell

Betsy's Pots de Creme

¾ cup light cream or
half-and-half
1 egg
1 6-ounce package
Nestle's semi-sweet
chocolate morsels

2 teaspoons sugar
2 teaspoons black coffee
2 teaspoons creme de
menthe
Pinch of salt
Whipped cream

Heat cream to scalding point; do not scorch. In blender, add egg, chocolate morsels, sugar, coffee, creme de menthe, and salt; cover with scalded cream. Blend for 1 minute. Pour into pots de creme and chill overnight in refrigerator. Serve with a dollop of whipped cream. Serves 6 to 8.

Jane Cowles

Chocolate Rousse

12 ounces semi-sweet
chocolate bits
6 tablespoons water
7 egg yolks

7 egg whites, stiffly
beaten
3 packages ladyfingers
2 pints whipping cream

In top of double boiler, melt chocolate bits. Add water and slightly beaten egg yolks. Cook until smooth and thick. When cool, fold in beaten egg whites. Line the sides and bottom of a 9 or 10-inch springform pan with halved ladyfingers. Fill with chocolate mixture and refrigerate for at least 12 hours. When ready to serve, unmold and serve with whipped cream. Garnish with chocolate shavings if desired. Serves 10 to 12.

Judy Brown

Chocolate Ring

4 eggs, separated
1 cup sugar
1½ envelopes unflavored
gelatin
⅓ cup cold water

4 ounces unsweetened
chocolate
½ cup boiling water
Dash of salt
Whipped cream

Beat egg yolks until light in color. Add sugar and salt and beat again. Soak gelatin in cold water. Melt chocolate squares in double boiler. Add melted chocolate slowly to egg mixture. Mix boiling water with gelatin and add slowly to chocolate mixture. Beat egg whites until stiff. Gently fold into chocolate mixture. Pour into ring mold and refrigerate. Serve with whipped cream in center of ring. Serves 6 to 8.

Nancy Leary

Chocolate Mousse

6 ounces semi-sweet
chocolate morsels
½ cup Kahlua
2 envelopes unflavored
gelatin
½ cup water
4 egg yolks
⅓ cup sugar

2 cups milk
4 egg whites, stiffly
beaten
2 cups heavy cream,
whipped
2 packages lady fingers,
split
18 whole chocolate chips

Place 6 ounces of chocolate chips in a bowl. Place bowl in another bowl of hot water. Stir until melted. Gradually stir Kahlua into chocolate. Set aside. In a saucepan, combine gelatin and water. Stir in egg yolks, sugar, and milk. Stir over low heat until mixture thickens slightly and coats a metal spoon. Stir in chocolate mixture. Chill until mixture mounds. Fold in egg whites. Remove 1 cup of the whipped cream and set aside for decorating top. Fold remaining cream into chocolate mixture. Chill until mixture mounds. Line the bottom and sides of an ungreased 9-inch springform pan with split lady fingers. Pour in chocolate mixture. Chill until firm. Remove sides of pan. Place reserved whipped cream in a pastry bag and pipe 18 rosettes around outer edges of cake. Press a chocolate chip into each rosette. Chill until ready to serve. Serves 12.

Can also be made with Amaretto and almonds instead of Kahlua and chocolate chips.

Cynthia Moore

Rum to Riches

1 quart coffee ice cream

3 to 4 ounces light or
dark rum

Combine ingredients in blender and blend until smooth. Pour into wine glasses and serve with a spoon. Preparation: 5 minutes. Serves 4.

A wonderful way to end a meal! Combines dessert and after-dinner drink.

Anne Grier

Penny's Dessert

1½ cups chocolate wafers, crushed
⅓ cup butter, melted
½ cup sugar
8 ounces cream cheese
1 teaspoon vanilla
2 eggs, separated

6 ounces chocolate chips, melted
1 cup whipping cream, whipped (or Cool Whip)
¾ cup pecans, chopped

Have ingredients at room temperature. Combine chocolate wafers and butter. Make a crust in a springform pan and bake at 325° for 10 minutes. In separate bowl, cream together ¼ cup sugar, cream cheese, and vanilla. Mix well. Stir in two well-beaten egg yolks and the melted chocolate chips. Beat two egg whites, gradually adding ¼ cup sugar. Fold into chocolate mixture. Whip cream until stiff and fold into mixture. Fold in pecans. Pour over chocolate crust and decorate with chocolate curls if desired. Refrigerate several hours before serving. Serves 10 to 12.

Anne Grier

My Aunt Margie's "Better Than Sex"

1 cup chopped pecans
1 cup flour
½ cup butter, softened
1 8-ounce package cream cheese, softened
1 12-ounce container Cool Whip
1 cup powdered sugar

1 small package instant vanilla pudding
1 small package instant chocolate pudding
3 cups milk
Chocolate bits or Hershey's chocolate slivers

Mix together pecans, flour, and butter. Pat crust on bottom of a 9 x 13-inch Pyrex dish. Bake 20 minutes at 350°. Cool completely. Beat together cream cheese, 1 cup Cool Whip, and sugar. Spread layer over crust. Mix together the puddings and milk until well-blended and spread over the cream cheese mixture. Layer remaining Cool Whip over pudding. Sprinkle with chocolate chips or chocolate slivers. Refrigerate overnight. Yield: 3 to 4 dozen squares.

Lynn Congdon

Frozen Rocky Road

¼ cup sugar
¾ cup milk
1 1-ounce square
   unsweetened chocolate,
   grated
1 teaspoon unflavored
   gelatin

1 tablespoon cold water
1 cup or more miniature
   marshmallows
½ cup walnuts, chopped
3 tablespoons Kahlua
1 cup whipping cream,
   whipped

Combine sugar, milk, and chocolate in saucepan. Bring to a boil, stirring constantly. Soften gelatin in cold water and stir into milk mixture. Remove from heat and cool slightly. Stir in marshmallows, nuts, Kahlua, and whipped cream. Pour into a 9 x 9-inch pan and freeze. Serves 9.

Sandy King

Toffee Delight

1 package ladyfingers
6 large Heath bars (or 1
   package bite-sized
   Heath bars)

1 large container Cool
   Whip
   Kahlua liqueur

Freeze Heath bars. Sprinkle flat sides of ladyfingers with Kahlua. Line springform pan with ladyfingers on sides and bottom of pan. Put 5 frozen Heath bars in blender or food processor until crushed (but not too fine). Stir into Cool Whip and pour into springform pan. Freeze. Unmold on pedestal plate and garnish with remaining crushed Heath bar. Serve frozen. Serves 10 to 12.

Very simple but quite elegant and delicious. Arrange ladyfingers in pan so they create a scalloped effect.

Gerry Lewis

Mocha Freeze Dessert

6 tablespoons butter,
melted

3 cups chocolate chip
cookies, crushed

1 generous quart coffee
ice cream, softened

1 3-ounce box instant
chocolate pudding

1 cup milk

Mix butter and cookies and press into greased 2½-quart mold or bowl. Freeze for several hours. Add milk and pudding to softened ice cream and beat for 1 minute until blended. Pour into frozen cookie mold and freeze. Unmold about 30 minutes before serving. Serves 12.

Super special served with hot fudge sauce. To make it extra good, use homemade cookies and the best ice cream you can buy.

Gerry Lewis

Raspberry-Pineapple Freeze

2 10-ounce packages
frozen raspberries

8 ounces crushed pine-
apple, partially drained

½ cup heavy cream

3 large scoops Cool Whip

1 tablespoon lemon juice

In medium-sized bowl, whip cream for 2 minutes. Add semi-thawed raspberries (reserve some for garnish, if desired), pineapple, and Cool Whip. Stir well until thoroughly mixed. Add lemon juice and mix well. Place in serving bowl and freeze. Serve partially thawed. Garnish with reserved raspberries. Can be made ahead. Serves 6.

Jane Johnson

Orange Ice

2 cups sugar

2 cups boiling water

3 cups orange juice

¼ cup lemon juice

Grated rind of 2
oranges

Whipped cream
(optional)

Make a sugar syrup by combining the sugar and water, boiling for 5 minutes. Cool. Chill in refrigerator. Mix orange juice, lemon juice, orange rind and chilled sugar syrup. Pour into serving bowl and freeze. Remove from freezer 5 minutes before serving and top with whipped cream. Serves 8 to 10.

Molly Hood

281

Desserts

Mile High Ice Cream Mold

1 stick butter	1 quart lime sherbet
18 ounces sweetened	1 quart pineapple sherbet
flaked coconut	1 quart orange sherbet

Melt butter in a large frying pan and stir coconut until lightly browned. Reserve ¾ cup coconut for topping. Soften each variety of sherbet. Pack lime layer in 2½-quart souffle, followed by a layer of coconut, then the pineapple layer, then coconut, and finally the orange layer. Freeze at least 24 hours. Unmold by running a knife dipped in hot water around edge of mold; then invert the mold onto a serving plate, applying a hot dish towel to bottom of mold. Do this 2 hours before serving. Top with remaining coconut for "frosting". Replace in freezer until served. Serves 10.

Experiment with different ice creams: e.g. coffee, vanilla, and chocolate, using ¼ cup Amaretto or Kahlua when softening, but not too much or dessert will never freeze solidly enough to unmold.

Catherine Whitham

Pauline's Snow Cream

½ cup brown sugar	1 teaspoon vanilla
½ cup milk	2 quarts clean snow
1 egg	

Mix all ingredients together and dig in!

Sally Flinn

Homemade Ice Cream

4 eggs	4 cups whipping cream
2¼ cups sugar	5 teaspoons vanilla
5 cups whole milk	½ teaspoon salt

In a large mixing bowl, beat eggs, gradually adding sugar until very stiff. Add remaining ingredients and pour into ice cream freezer. Process as directed in freezer instructions. Yield: Approximately 1 gallon.

Judy Brooks

Mother's Chocolate Sauce

3 squares unsweetened chocolate
¾ cup sugar
1¼ cups milk
2 tablespoons light Karo syrup

2 tablespoons butter
1 teaspoon vanilla
Pinch of salt

Melt chocolate slowly, stirring constantly. Then add other ingredients. After mixture boils for a minute, it is done. Yield: 1 cup.

Melinda Shepardson

Chocolate Ripple Whipped Cream Sauce

4 ounces semi-sweet baking chocolate
3 tablespoons milk
3 tablespoons white Creme de Menthe or white Creme de Cacao

1 cup whipping cream
1 teaspoon vanilla
1 tablespoon sugar

Place chocolate and milk in top of double boiler and melt over hot water. Blend in selected liqueur. Stir until smooth and let cool. Whip cream until stiff; add vanilla and sugar. Spoon over chocolate sauce and ripple lightly with fork. Turn into glass serving bowl. Yield: 2½ cups.

If you do not wish to to use a liqueur, substitute 3 tablespoons additional milk.

Connie Garrett

Chocolate Rum Sauce

1 cup cocoa	¾ teaspoon salt
2 cups sugar	6 tablespoons butter
2 cups light corn syrup	¼ cup rum
7/8 cup light cream	½ tablespoon vanilla

In a large saucepan, combine all ingredients except vanilla. Cook, stirring constantly, over medium heat until mixture comes to a boil. Boil 4 minutes, stirring frequently. Remove from heat, stir in vanilla, and pour into sterilized jars. Seal with sealing wax or screw-on tops. Yield: 5 cups.

A very light sauce.

Stephanie Ayers

Mother's Hot Sauce for Pound Cake

1 cup dark brown sugar	4 tablespoons heavy
½ cup butter	cream

Mix ingredients well in top of a double boiler. Cook 10 minutes, stirring constantly. Serve hot over pound cake. Yield: 1¼ cups.

Frances Barnes

Homemade Butterscotch Sauce

1 1-pound box light brown sugar	1 13-ounce can evaporated milk
1⅔ cups light Karo syrup	Pinch cream of tartar
1½ sticks butter	Dash vanilla

Boil brown sugar, Karo syrup, and butter in double boiler or heavy saucepan over medium heat, stirring constantly, until you can make a hard ball. Take off heat. Add remaining ingredients; beat well. Yield: 4 cups.

If you like butterscotch, you will love this. An old Virginia recipe.

Cabell West

Strawberry-Raspberry Sauce

1 10-ounce package frozen raspberries, thawed	2 tablespoons Kirsch or Framboise (optional) Sugar to taste
1 tablespoon lemon juice	
2 cups whole strawberries (or 1 10-ounce package frozen strawberries), thawed	

Puree raspberries in blender. Stir in lemon juice. Halve strawberries and sprinkle with liqueur (optional) and sugar. Let stand 10 minutes. Add strawberries to raspberry puree. Cover and chill until serving. Yield: 3 cups.

Connie Garrett

Reducing the amount of water called for in a packaged pie crust mix will produce a more tender and flaky pastry.

Roll pie crust between two sheets of waxed paper covered with flour. This makes it much easier to put the crust in the baking dish.

Pie meringue will not stick to the knife when you are cutting it if you mark meringue before baking. Mark sections in the meringue almost down to the filling.

To avoid spills in the oven when you are baking a custard pie, pour in the last cup of filling just before closing the door.

Lemons will keep for weeks covered with water and refrigerated.

When beating eggs with sugar, never add all the sugar at one time. Add sugar a little at a time.

Pepper strawberries before serving to bring out the flavor. Then add cream or whipped cream.

To whip heavy cream that won't whip, chill cream, beaters and bowl; set bowl in ice water; or add 3 to 4 drops of lemon juice.

Whipped cream will keep in the refrigerator for an hour or so if you pour it into a finely meshed strainer over a bowl.

Use kitchen shears dipped in hot water to cut marshmallows, dates, prunes, candied fruits and other sticky foods.

To measure sticky liquids such as honey or molasses, use container in which you measured oil or shortening.

To open a coconut, puncture and drain off the water. Bake at 350° for 45 minutes to an hour, until it begins to crack. Hit with a hammer when cool enough to handle.

To shred fresh coconut, peel off the skin and place small pieces of the flesh in blender with some coconut water.

To prevent formation of skin on sauce or pudding, cover with margarine, butter, cream or milk while cooling. Stir in when ready to serve. Or tightly cover dish or pan.

Our foremothers were as busy in the kitchen as our forefathers were in the state house, as this cake recipe from Martha Washington shows. This recipe comes to us from the Evans Farm Inn, which learned of the cake from Mrs. Helen Duprey Bullock, America's pre-eminent authority on colonial cooking.

Martha Washington's Great Cake

3¼ cups white raisins
3¼ cups currants
1⅓ cups citron
  1 cup candied lemon peel
1⅓ cups candied orange
    peel
  1 cup brandy
  1 pound butter, softened
  2 cups sugar
 10 eggs, separated

2 tablespoons lemon juice
5 cups flour
1 teaspoon mace
½ teaspoon nutmeg
⅓ cup sherry
½ cup candied red
    cherries
½ cup candied green
    cherries

Two nights before baking, place raisins, currants, citron and candied peels in bowl. Pour brandy over ingredients and cover tightly. (Do not soak the cherries!) The day of baking, cream butter and 1 cup sugar until light and fluffy. With electric beater, beat egg yolks until light. Slowly add remaining 1 cup sugar to yolks; beat until thick and creamy. Beat in lemon juice with a whisk. Fold yolk mixture into butter and sugar. Sift together flour, mace and nutmeg. Add 3½ cups of dry ingredients to batter alternately with sherry. To remaining dry ingredients, add brandy, soaked fruits, and red and green cherries, reserving a few for decoration. Mix floured fruit into batter. Beat egg whites until stiff but not dry. Grease and flour three 9 x 5-inch loaf pans. Spoon batter into pans. Bake in preheated oven at 350° for 20 minutes, turn down heat to 325° and bake additional 30 to 40 minutes or until done. If cake is baked in large pan or mold, baking time will be about 1 hour and 40 minutes. Test for doneness by pressing finger on the surface; if it springs back, it's done. While cake is still warm and in pan, brush surface with brandy. Cool 15 minutes. Remove from pans. Dip fruits in brandy and arrange on top. When cake is cool, wrap in wax paper and foil and refrigerate. Cake should not be cut for at least one day, and it should be sliced very thin while cold. Yield: three 9 x 5-inch cakes.

Since no baking powder or soda is used, bake with large water-filled pan at bottom of oven to add moisture. Evans Farm Inn
Mclean, Virginia

Cakes

Best Cheese Cake Ever

14 Zwieback crackers,   ½ cup butter, melted
   finely crushed   ½ cup sugar

Mix above ingredients and line two 10-inch springform pans.

  3 pounds cream cheese,   2½ cups sugar
    softened   1½ cups whipping cream
  6 eggs   1 teaspoon vanilla
 ½ cup plus 2 tablespoons   Juice of 1 lemon
   flour

Combine and mix all ingredients. Pour into lined pans. Fill another pan with 1-inch water and place under cake pans and bake at 350° for 1 hour. Turn off heat. Leave in oven with door closed for an additional 30 to 40 minutes. Chill before unmolding. Preparation: 30 minutes. Yield: Two 10-inch cakes.

Janet Northen

Mini Cheese Cakes

20 vanilla wafers   1 tablespoon vanilla
20 paper cupcake liners   1 can of your favorite pie
 2 8-ounce packages   filling - blueberry,
   cream cheese   cherry, etc., or fresh
¾ cup sugar   fruit sprinkled with
 2 eggs   Kirsch (cherry brandy)
 1 tablespoon lemon juice

Put one wafer in each cupcake liner and place in muffin tins. Beat cream cheese, sugar, eggs, lemon juice, and vanilla until light and fluffy. Pour batter on top of wafer in cupcake liner and fill to approximately ¾ full. Bake at 375° for 30 minutes. Cool in oven with door open until set. Chill, remove paper liners, and top with chilled pie filling or fresh fruit. Preparation: 30 minutes. Serves 12 to 15.

May be made the day before and garnished with pie filling before serving. Perfect for those who find a slice of cheesecake too filling.

Frances Kusterer

Woodland Nut Cake

2½ cups cake flour
1¾ cups sugar
2 teaspoons baking powder
1½ teaspoons salt
1 cup Crisco (no substitute)
¾ cup milk

3 eggs, whole
1 egg yolk
1 teaspoon orange extract
1 teaspoon almond extract
1 cup nuts, finely chopped

Sift all dry ingredients together twice and place in large mixing bowl. Make a center hole in dry mixture, drop in shortening, milk, and 1 egg. Beat for 2 minutes. Add remaining eggs, flavorings, and nuts. Beat well. Put into well-greased tube pan. Bake 1 hour at 350°.

Frosting:

3 teaspoons butter
¼ teaspoon almond extract
4 tablespoons hot milk
2 pounds (1 box) confectioners sugar

1 teaspoon vanilla
1 tablespoon orange rind, grated

Mix together, beat well, and frost.

A family favorite, this cake is different tasting, lasts a long time, and remains moist.

Margie Ayres

Rum Fruit Cake

1 cup sugar	1½ cups vegetable oil
1 cup brown sugar	2 cups raw apples, chopped
1 teaspoon vanilla	2 cups bananas, chopped
3 eggs, beaten	½ cup dates, chopped
3 cups flour	1 cup pecans, chopped
½ teaspoon salt	½ cup white rum, divided
2 teaspoons baking soda	⅓ cup apple juice
1 teaspoon cinnamon	2 cups confectioners sugar
½ teaspoon nutmeg	
½ teaspoon cloves	

Combine sugars and vanilla. Beat in eggs, one at a time. Combine in separate bowl flour, salt, soda, and spices. Add to sugar mixture alternating with oil. Add apples, bananas, dates, and pecans by folding in with wooden spoon. Add ¼ cup rum. Pour into greased and floured tube pan. Bake at 350° for 1 hour. Remove from oven and immediately pour apple juice and ¼ cup rum over cake and sprinkle with confectioners sugar. Allow to set for 5 minutes; then remove cake from pan.

Best to let stand overnight in covered container; will keep forever.

Gwen Weeks

Sherry Cake

6 egg yolks, beaten	1 teaspoon vanilla
2 cups sugar	2 teaspoons baking powder
1½ boxes Zweiback, crushed	1 cup sherry
1 cup pecans, broken	1 pint whipping cream
6 egg whites, stiffly beaten	

Line 2 aluminum cake pans with waxed paper. Beat egg yolks and gradually add sugar, beating until smooth and creamy. Add crushed Zweiback and pecans. (This mixture will be stiff.) Fold in stiffly beaten egg whites. Stir in vanilla and baking powder. Bake at 350° for 20 to 30 minutes. Remove cake and cool. Pour ½ cup sherry over each layer and let soak for 2 hours. Frost with whipped cream. Yield: 1 cake.

Peg Freeman

Black Forest Cake

¾ pound cake flour
12 ounces sugar
4 ounces shortening
1 teaspoon salt
1 teaspoon baking
   powder

1 teaspoon soda
2 ounces cocoa
7 ounces buttermilk
6 ounces egg yolk
½ pint buttermilk
1 teaspoon vanilla

Combine flour, sugar, shortening, salt, baking powder, soda, and cocoa and mix well. Add 7 ounces buttermilk and egg yolks and mix. Add remaining buttermilk and vanilla and mix. Pour into two 9-inch cake pans and bake at 375° for 25 minutes. After cooling, cut each layer twice, making 3 layers for each cake.

Filling:

1½ cups chocolate icing
1 can cherry pie filling
1 pint whipping cream,
   whipped

Kirschwasser

On the bottom layer, put three concentric rings of chocolate icing; in between each ring, put cherry pie filling; sprinkle with Kirschwasser. On the second layer, sprinkle with liquor and spread on some whipping cream. On the third layer, sprinkle with liquor and frost with whipping cream. Yield: 2 cakes.

The Hotel Roanoke
Roanoke, Virginia

Coconut-Sour Cream Layer Cake

1 regular box yellow
butter-flavored cake mix
2 cups sugar
1 16-ounce carton com-
mercial sour cream

1 12-ounce package frozen
coconut, thawed
1½ cups frozen whipped
topping, thawed

Prepare cake mix according to package directions, making two 8-inch layers; when completely cool, split both layers.

Combine sugar, sour cream, and coconut, blending well. Chill. Reserve 1 cup sour cream mixture for frosting. Spread remainder between layers of cake.

Combine reserved sour cream mixture with whipped topping; blend until smooth. Spread on top and sides of cake. Seal cake in airtight container and refrigerate for 3 days before serving. Preparation: 20 minutes. Yield: one 8-inch layer cake.

Nel Laughon

Best Yet Chocolate Cake

1 stick butter or
margarine
4 tablespoons cocoa
1 cup vegetable oil
1 cup water

2 cups flour
2 cups sugar
2 eggs
1 teaspoon baking soda
½ cup buttermilk

In a saucepan over medium heat, melt butter and add cocoa, vegetable oil and water. Mix well. Combine flour and sugar in large bowl and pour in the heated mixture. Add eggs and mix well. Dissolve baking soda in buttermilk and add to batter. Pour mixture into a 10 x 13-inch Pyrex baking dish and bake at 350° for 30 to 35 minutes or until set.

Icing:

1 stick butter, melted
4 tablespoons cocoa
3 tablespoons milk

1 tablespoon vanilla
1 box powdered sugar

Combine all ingredients, adding enough milk to make creamy spreading consistency. Spread on hot cake. Let cool and refrigerate. Serve cold. Serves 12 to 15.

Becky Symons

Jimmie's Chocolate Pound Cake

2 sticks margarine
½ cup Crisco shortening
3 cups sugar
5 eggs
3 cups flour

½ cup cocoa
½ teaspoon baking
  powder
1 cup milk
2 teaspoons vanilla

Cream margarine, shortening and sugar. Beat in eggs one at a time. Combine flour, cocoa and baking powder and sift 3 times. Add milk to shortening mixture and combine with dry ingredients. Stir in vanilla. Bake at 325° in ungreased tube or bundt pan for 1½ hours. Yield: 1 tube or bundt cake.

Delicious served with vanilla ice cream and topped with chocolate syrup or iced with chocolate frosting. Freezes well.

Beverly Bates

Martha's Pound Cake

3 sticks butter
1 pound confectioners
  sugar
6 eggs

2 cups plus 2 tablespoons
  cake flour
2 teaspoons lemon extract
1 teaspoon vanilla

Mix butter and sugar together well. Add eggs one at a time, beating 1 minute for each egg. Add flour and mix. Add lemon and vanilla. Use tube or bundt pan, greased. Bake at 350° for 1 hour. Preparation: 15 minutes. Serves 12.

Make day before so flavors will blend. Serve at room temperature.

Annette Chapman

Black Bottoms

1 8-ounce package cream cheese	1 cup sugar
	¼ cup cocoa
1 egg	1 teaspoon baking soda
½ cup sugar	1/8 teaspoon salt
1/8 teaspoon salt	1 cup water
1 6-ounce package chocolate chips	⅓ cup vegetable oil
	1 tablespoon vinegar
1½ cups flour	1 teaspoon vanilla

Combine cream cheese, egg, ½ cup sugar and 1/8 teaspoon salt and mix well. Stir in chocolate chips; set aside. Sift together flour, 1 cup sugar, cocoa, baking soda and 1/8 teaspoon salt. Add water, oil, vinegar and vanilla to flour mixture and mix until well blended. Drop chocolate mixture by tablespoon into cupcake papers; add ½ tablespoon cream cheese mixture on top. Bake at 350⁰ for 15 to 20 minutes. Do not overcook. Yield: 24 large cupcakes or 48 small.

Larkin Bynum

Brownie Cupcakes

4 squares unsweetened chocolate	4 eggs
	1 teaspoon vanilla
2 sticks margarine	1¾ cups sugar
1 cup pecans, chopped	1 cup flour

Melt chocolate and margarine over hot water. Stir in nuts when melted. Cream eggs, vanilla, and sugar until fluffy. Add flour. Mix well and combine with chocolate mixture. Pour into tins lined with cupcake papers. Bake at 325⁰ for 15 to 17 minutes. Yield: 2 dozen regular cupcakes; 4 to 5 dozen mini-cupcakes.

Rosemary Davenport

Whiskey Cake

1 box white cake mix
1 3-ounce package instant
  vanilla pudding
1 ounce whiskey
4 eggs

1 cup milk
½ cup oil
1 cup walnuts, finely
  chopped
2 tablespoons flour

Combine cake and pudding mix with whiskey and eggs; beat well. Beat in milk and oil. Toss nuts with flour and fold into cake mixture. Pour into a greased and floured 10-inch tube pan and bake at 325° 55 to 60 minutes until cake is tested done. Leave cake in pan while you make glaze.

Glaze:

¼ pound butter
¾ cup sugar

½ cup whiskey
Powdered sugar

Heat together butter, sugar, and whiskey until mixture is bubbly and butter is melted. Pour mixture over cake while still warm in pan. Then let cake cool in pan for 2 hours. Remove from pan. Place cake on dish and wrap in foil. Refrigerate for at least 24 hours so that whiskey can soak into cake. When ready to serve, sprinkle with powdered sugar. Preparation: 30 minutes. Serves 12.

This cake can be made about a week ahead, wrapped, and refrigerated.

Robin Traywick Williams

Chocolate Heavenly Hash Cake

2 sticks butter or
   margarine
2 cups sugar
4 eggs

1½ cups flour
4 tablespoons cocoa
1 teaspoon vanilla
1 cup pecans, chopped

Icing:

1½ cups miniature
   marshmallows
1 stick butter or
   margarine
4 tablespoons cocoa

4 tablespoons milk
1 teaspoon vanilla
1 box powdered sugar,
   sifted
1 cup pecans, chopped

Preheat oven to 350º. Cream butter or margarine, sugar, eggs, flour, cocoa, vanilla, and pecans. Spray 13 x 9-inch pan with Pam. Pour cake batter into pan and bake for 30 minutes. Test for doneness with toothpick. Do not remove from pan. Sprinkle marshmallows over hot cake and return to oven until just melted.

Melt in saucepan margarine, cocoa, milk, and vanilla. Remove from stove. Add powdered sugar and beat until smooth. Pour icing over hot cake and sprinkle with chopped pecans or add pecans to chocolate icing before spreading on cake. Cool completely before cutting. Preparation: 30 minutes. Serves 10.

Karen Feigley

Strawberry Angel Cake

1 angel food cake
2 cups whipping cream
1 pint fresh strawberries,
  sliced

2 10-ounce packages
  frozen strawberries,
  thawed
Sugar

Slice cake into 2 layers. Beat cream and sweeten to taste with sugar. Fold fresh sliced and frozen (thawed) strawberries into whipped cream. Spread some of mixture between cake layers and frost cake with the remaining. Keep refrigerated. Best if served within two hours of preparation. Serves 1 to 12.

If time is short, may substitute two 8-ounce cartons frozen whipped topping for whipping cream (thaw first). Also, reserve a few strawberry slices for garnish, if desired.

Kathy Adair

Carrot Cake

4 large eggs
1 cup brown sugar
1 cup white sugar
1¼ cups salad oil
2 cups sifted flour
2 teaspoons baking
  powder

2 teaspoons baking soda
3 to 4 teaspoons
  cinnamon
3 cups carrots, finely
  grated
½ to 1 cup pecans,
  chopped

Beat eggs; add sugars, oil and dry ingredients. Beat well. Add carrots; stir in nuts. Grease three 9-inch round cake pans; cut wax paper circles to line bottoms of pans. Pour batter into pans. Bake at 325° for 45 minutes or until done. Cool in pans for 10 minutes. Spread icing over warm layers.

Icing:

1 8-ounce package cream
  cheese, softened
1 stick butter, softened

1 teaspoon vanilla
1 box confectioners sugar

Cream ingredients together and frost cake. Keep cake refrigerated. Preparation: 45 minutes. Serves 12.

Betsy Worthington

Raw Apple Cake

½ teaspoon cinnamon
½ cup brown sugar, light or dark
1½ cups sugar
¾ cup shortening
2 eggs
1 teaspoon baking soda
2½ cups flour
¾ teaspoon cinnamon
¾ teaspoon salt
¾ cup warm coffee
3 to 4 apples (3 cups diced)
½ cup walnuts, chopped

Combine ½ teaspoon cinnamon and brown sugar for topping and set aside. Cream sugar and shortening. Add eggs and beat. Gradually add dry ingredients to creamed mixture, alternating with coffee. Fold in apples and nuts. Pour into greased and floured tube pan, a 13 x 9-inch pan, or 2 loaf pans. Sprinkle topping on top. Bake at 350° for 45 minutes. Preparation: 30 minutes. Serves 12.

Great as a coffee cake too!

Beth Witt

Blueberry Cake

2 cups sugar
1 cup butter, softened
3 eggs
3 cups flour
¼ teaspoon mace
1½ teaspoons baking powder
1/8 teaspoon salt
½ cup milk
2 cups blueberries, washed and picked over
2 teaspoons flour
2 teaspoons sugar

Cream together 2 cups sugar and butter until light and fluffy. Add eggs, one at a time, beating well after each addition. Combine flour, mace, baking powder and salt and add to creamed mixture alternately with milk, beating well after each addition. Sprinkle blueberries with 2 teaspoons flour and 2 teaspoons sugar. Fold berries into batter. Pour batter into greased and floured bundt or tube pan. Bake at 325° for 1 hour and 10 minutes or until knife inserted comes out clean. Yield: 1 bundt cake. Serves 12 to 15.

Cindy Vogel

Jam Cake

1¼ cups sugar	1 cup buttermilk
½ pound butter, softened	1 teaspoon baking
4 eggs	powder
2 cups flour, sifted	1 teaspoon baking soda
1 teaspoon cinnamon	1 18-ounce jar
½ teaspoon cloves	strawberry preserves
½ teaspoon nutmeg	1 cup pecans, chopped

Cream sugar and butter. Add 4 eggs, one at a time. Beat thoroughly. Sift together flour, cinnamon, cloves, and nutmeg. Add alternately to batter with buttermilk, baking powder, baking soda, strawberry preserves, and pecans. Pour into bundt pan. Bake at 325° for 1 hour or until done.

Frosting:

3 cups sugar	1 stick butter, softened
1 cup milk	Cream, if necessary
1 teaspoon vanilla	

Brown 1 cup sugar slowly in heavy saucepan. While this is browning, beat together 2 cups sugar and 1 cup milk. After sugar has browned, add milk mixture and cook until mixture forms a soft ball in water. Add 1 teaspoon vanilla and 1 stick butter. Beat until ready to spread on cake. If it gets too hard, add cream to soften.

"This is my mother's recipe; very old-fashioned. The frosting is like making candy, but if you take the time and effort to do it, it's delicious!"

Nancy Gottwald

Pineapple Cake

1 box Duncan Hines
   yellow cake mix
1 small can mandarin
   oranges, undrained
½ cup oil
4 eggs
1 20-ounce can crushed
   pineapple, drained

1 small package instant
   vanilla pudding mix
1 12-ounce container
   Extra Creamy Cool
   Whip

In a large bowl, blend together cake mix, oranges, oil, and eggs. Beat for 2 minutes. Pour into three 9-inch layer pans that have been greased and floured. Bake at 375° for 15 to 20 minutes. Let cake cool.

Combine crushed pineapple with pudding mix and let sit 10 minutes. Then fold in Cool Whip. Chill overnight. Spread over cake. Preparation: 15 minutes. Serves 12.

Ginger Chalkley

Prune Cake

1 level teaspoon baking
   soda
1 cup buttermilk
2 cups sugar
1 cup Crisco oil
3 eggs
2 cups flour
1 teaspoon baking
   powder

1 teaspoon salt
½ teaspoon ground cloves
½ teaspoon nutmeg
½ teaspoon cinnamon
½ teaspoon allspice
1 cup pitted prunes
   (cooked, mashed)
¼ cup prune juice
1 teaspoon vanilla

Dissolve baking soda in buttermilk and set aside. In a large bowl, combine sugar and oil; stir well. Add eggs, one at a time. In a separate bowl, sift together flour, baking powder, salt, and other spices. Add ½ of dry ingredients to cream mixture, then add soda and buttermilk. Add remaining dry ingredients and beat well. Fold in prunes, juice, and vanilla. Grease and flour a tube pan or bundt pan. Pour in batter. Bake at 325° for 40 minutes. Freezes well. Preparation: 20 minutes. Serves 15.

Annette Chapman

Sugar Cookies

3 cups flour
1 teaspoon soda
2 teaspoons cream of
  tartar
1 cup butter, softened

2 eggs
1 cup sugar
1 teaspoon vanilla
Colored sugar or
sprinkles

Sift flour, soda, and tartar. Cut in butter with two knives or pastry blender until mixture is like peas. Beat eggs, sugar, and vanilla; add to flour mixture. Refrigerate 15 minutes or until firm. Roll out thinly on floured board and cut with cookie cutter. Decorate with colored sugar or sprinkles. Bake at 400° for 4 to 5 minutes. Yield: 6 dozen.

Jeanne Davies

French Cookies

3 sticks butter, softened
1 cup sugar
3 egg yolks
4 cups flour, sifted
1 10-ounce jar currant
  jelly

Additional flour (if
needed to make dough
stiff)

Combine all ingredients except jelly. Flour hands and roll dough into ½-inch balls. Dent each ball with finger and drop small amount of currant jelly into each indentation. Bake at 325° for 30 minutes or only until bottom turns brown. Yield: 4 dozen.

Good Christmas cookie. Freezes very well. Put waxed paper between layers so jelly doesn't stick.

Jane Marmion

Russian Tea Cakes

½ cup butter, softened
2 tablespoons sugar
1 teaspoon vanilla
1 cup cake flour, sifted
    before measuring

1 cup pecans, finely
    ground
Powdered sugar

Cream butter and sugar; add vanilla. Stir flour and pecans into first mixture. Roll into small balls. Place on greased baking sheet. Bake at 300⁰ for about 45 minutes. Roll hot puffs in powdered sugar. Repeat when cool. Yield: 3 dozen.

Frances Shield

Double-Daters

¾ cup sugar
8 ounces dates, chopped
½ cup butter, melted
1½ cups Rice Krispies

1 cup pecans, chopped
1 teaspoon vanilla
¼ teaspoon salt
Sifted powdered sugar

In saucepan, cook the first 3 ingredients over low heat for 8 minutes. Remove from heat. Add Rice Krispies, pecans, vanilla and salt. Mix thoroughly. Drop by teaspoonsful on waxed paper and roll into logs. Then roll in powdered sugar.

Place on cookie sheet and freeze if desired. They keep well if stored in tin or Ziploc bags in freezer until ready to use.

Ruthie Roberts

Cattle Range Cookies

1 cup margarine, softened
1 cup brown sugar
1 cup granulated sugar
2 eggs
1 teaspoon baking soda
1 teaspoon salt
1 teaspoon baking powder
1 teaspoon vanilla
2 cups flour
2 cups oatmeal
2 cups Rice Krispies cereal
1 cup coconut
½ cup chopped pecans

Mix ingredients together in listed order. Drop by teaspoonsful on greased cookie sheet. Bake 10 minutes at 325º. Don't overcook. Yield: 5 to 6 dozen.

Kay Whitworth

Fabulous Lace Cookies

½ stick butter, softened
2 cups brown sugar
2 eggs, well beaten
1 teaspoon vanilla
1 teaspoon baking powder
½ cup flour, sifted
½ pound pecans, coarsely ground

Cream butter and sugar; add eggs and beat well; add vanilla. Add baking powder to flour and mix with nuts. Combine the two mixtures and chill until firm.

Drop half-teaspoonsful three inches apart on greased and floured cookie sheet. Bake in 400º oven for 6 to 8 minutes. Watch carefully. Remove from oven and let cool. Remove from pan. Yield: 3 dozen.

Lindsey O'Brien Clark

Winter's Best Ginger Snaps

¾ cup butter or margarine	2 teaspoons baking
¾ cup shortening	powder
2 cups sugar	2 teaspoons cinnamon
2 eggs	2 teaspoons cloves
½ cup dark molasses	2 teaspoons ginger
4 cups flour, sifted	½ cup sugar

Preheat oven to 375º. Mix ingredients in order listed in food processor (if small food processor make ½ recipe). Without processor, cream butter and shortening until smooth. Gradually work in 2 cups of sugar and continue creaming until mixture is light. Beat in eggs and molasses. Sift all dry ingredients together and work into butter/sugar mixture. Roll dough into small balls, roll in remaining sugar, and place on cookie sheet about 3 inches apart. Bake 10 minutes (less if chewy cookies desired). Yield: 8 dozen.

Fast and easy using food processor.

Jane Helfrich

Mom's Paper-Thin Cookies

1 cup sugar	½ teaspoon (scant) salt
¾ cup (1½ sticks) butter	1 egg, beaten (use only 2
or margarine	tablespoons)
2 cups flour	1 teaspoon vanilla
½ teaspoon baking soda	Powdered sugar
½ teaspoon cream of	
tartar	

Cream sugar and butter. Sift flour, soda, cream of tartar, and salt together. Set aside. Add 2 tablespoons beaten egg and vanilla to creamed mixture. Gradually add dry ingredients. Roll dough into small balls about the size of a marble by rolling between both hands.

Place on aluminum cookie sheet 2 inches apart so balls can be flattened. Dip fingers into powdered sugar and press each ball until very flat, thin, and round. Cook at 350º until golden brown, approximately 8 to 10 minutes. They will cook very quickly and must be watched. Almost immediately, lift each cookie with a spatula onto rack to cool. They come up beautifully, but do not wait as they may break. Yield: About 150.

Stacy Fonville

Ellie's Grandma's Zucchini Cookies

¾ cup butter or margarine, softened
1½ cups sugar
1 egg
1 teaspoon vanilla
1½ cups zucchini, grated
2½ cups flour
2 teaspoons baking powder
1 teaspoon cinnamon
½ teaspoon salt
½ cup almonds, coarsely chopped
1 6-ounce package chocolate chips
Powdered sugar

Cream butter and sugar. Beat in egg and vanilla; stir in zucchini. Stir in flour, baking powder, cinnamon and salt. Add almonds and chocolate chips. Drop by heaping teaspoons onto greased cookie sheet. Bake at 350° for 15 minutes or until lightly browned. Cool on wire rack. Sift powdered sugar over cookies. Yield: 4 to 5 dozen.

Judy Brown

Pretzel Cookies

1 cup sour cream
1 cup sugar
2 eggs, well beaten
1 teaspoon vanilla
3½ to 4 cups flour
1 teaspoon soda
Pinch of salt

Combine ingredients in the order listed. Chill dough overnight or at least 2 hours. With your hand, roll into approximately 8-inch strips. Twist strips into large pretzels. Bake in a 400° oven for 10 minutes. Do not brown.

Janet Smith

Almond Chocolate Chip Cookies

1 stick butter
1 cup light brown sugar
1 egg
2 teaspoons vanilla
2 teaspoons cinnamon
½ teaspoon nutmeg

1 cup self-rising flour
1 6-ounce package semi-
sweet chocolate morsels
1 2½-ounce package
sliced almonds

Preheat oven to 350°. Cream butter, sugar, and egg. Add vanilla, cinnamon, and nutmeg. Add flour, chocolate chips, and almonds. Drop by teaspoonsful on a cookie sheet. Bake about 10 minutes or until edges are lightly browned. Let cool 5 minutes and place on brown paper bag to finish cooling. Yield: About 3 dozen.

Very rich!

Ginny Tompkins

Sesame Seed Cookies

½ cup sesame seeds
1 stick butter, softened
¾ cup light brown sugar,
firmly packed

1 egg, beaten
¾ cup flour
½ teaspoon vanilla

Toast sesame seeds for 10 minutes at 350°, stirring occasionally, until they are golden. Cream butter and sugar. Add egg; beat in flour gradually. Add seeds and vanilla. Butter baking sheet and drop mixture by teaspoon 3 inches apart. Bake at 350° for about 8 minutes, or until they spread (lacy, brown edges). Yield: 4 dozen.

Cindy Vogel

Connie's Almond Crescents

1 cup shortening, softened
(can use ½ butter)
⅓ cup sugar
⅔ cup ground blanched
almonds

1⅔ cups flour
1 cup confectioners sugar
1 teaspoon cinnamon

Cream shortening and sugar; mix in almonds. Sift flour and gradually add to creamed mixture. Chill dough. Roll with hands until pencil thin; cut into 2½ inch lengths. Form into crescents on ungreased baking sheets. Bake at 350° for 14 to 16 minutes, just until lightly brown. Mix confectioners sugar and cinnamon together and after cookies cool on pan, dip in sugar mixture. Yield: About 5 dozen.

Delicious if baked properly...don't overbake! Cookies break easily if removed from pan too soon. Good Christmas cookie.

Charmian Matheson

Summit Lemon Squares

Pastry:

2 sticks butter, softened
2 cups flour

½ cup powdered sugar

Mix butter, flour and sugar until well blended and press into a 9 x 13-inch Pyrex baking dish. Bake at 325° for 15 minutes.

Filling:

4 eggs, beaten
2 cups sugar
6 tablespoons lemon juice
1 tablespoon flour

½ teaspoon baking
powder
Powdered sugar

Combine all ingredients and mix well. Pour on top of pastry. Bake at 325° for 40 to 50 minutes or until golden. Sprinkle with powdered sugar. Cut into squares. Yield: 24 squares.

Becky Symons

Sunshine Lemon Squares

1½ cups flour, sifted
1 teaspoon baking
  powder
½ teaspoon salt
1 14 or 15-ounce can
  sweetened condensed
  milk
½ cup fresh lemon juice

10⅔ tablespoons butter, softened
1 cup dark brown sugar,
  firmly packed
1 cup old-fashioned or
  quick oatmeal
  Finely grated rind of 1
  lemon

Preheat oven to 350°. Grease 13 x 9-inch pan. Sift together flour, baking powder, and salt. Set aside. Pour condensed milk into medium-sized bowl. Add grated lemon rind and lemon juice, stirring to keep mixture smooth. Set mixture aside.

In a large bowl, cream butter and sugar, beating well. On low speed of mixer (or with a fork), gradually add dry ingredients, beating only until well mixed. Mix in oatmeal. (Mixture will be crumbly and won't hold together. If too soft, freeze briefly.)

Sprinkle about half (2 generous cups) of oatmeal mixture evenly over bottom of pan. Pat crumbs to make a smooth, compact layer. Drizzle or spoon lemon mixture evenly over crumb layer and spread it to make a smooth layer. Sprinkle remaining crumbly oatmeal mixture evenly over lemon layer. Pat the crumbs gently with fingers to smooth them - it's okay if a bit of the lemon layer shows through in small spots.

Bake at 350° for 30 to 35 minutes until cake is lightly colored. Cool cake completely in pan; refrigerate about 1 hour. Cut into small squares and remove from pan with a wide metal spatula. Refrigerate until serving. Yield: 24 to 32 squares.

Sue Reynolds

Dad's Favorite Coffee Pecan Chews

¾ cup flour	1 cup sugar
1 tablespoon instant coffee	½ cup butter, melted
½ teaspoon salt	1 teaspoon vanilla
2 eggs	½ cup pecans, chopped

Sift together flour, instant coffee, and salt. Set aside. Beat eggs until foamy. Gradually add sugar and continue beating until thick. Stir in melted butter and vanilla. Add dry ingredients and mix until well blended. Stir in nuts. Pour into greased 8-inch square pan. Bake at 350° 30 to 35 minutes or until done. When cooled completely, drizzle with Confectioners Sugar Icing.

Confectioners Sugar Icing:

1 cup confectioners sugar, sifted	½ teaspoon vanilla
1 to 2 tablespoons warm water, milk, or cream (use amount desired for thickness)	

Mix together; consistency should be fairly thin.

Lynne Kreger

Mother's Scotch Shortbread

2 cups flour	½ cup sugar
1 cup butter, softened	

Mix ingredients with hands or in food processor. Roll out and cut with a small or medium-sized cookie cutter. Bake at 325° until just browned around the edges. Don't overcook or they will be bitter. Yield: 3 to 3½ dozen.

Cindy Vogel

Deluxe Brownies

1 cup margarine
3 squares unsweetened
  chocolate
4 eggs, beaten
2 cups sugar
1½ cups all-purpose flour
1 teaspoon baking
  powder

1 cup chopped pecans
2 teaspoons vanilla
4 cups miniature
  marshmallows
Deluxe Icing

Melt margarine and chocolate in top of double boiler. Set aside. Combine eggs and sugar, beating well; add flour and baking powder, mixing well. Add chocolate mixture, pecans, and vanilla. After mixing well, pour into 2 greased 9 x 13 x 2-inch pans and bake at 325° for 30 minutes. Remove brownies from oven and cover with marshmallows. (Brownies may need to go back in oven long enough for marshmallows to melt.) Frost with Deluxe Icing.

Deluxe Icing:

1 cup sugar
¾ cup evaporated milk
½ cup margarine
2 squares unsweetened
  chocolate

1 16-ounce box confec-
  tioners sugar
1 teaspoon vanilla

Combine sugar, milk, margarine, and chocolate; cook over medium heat until soft ball stage (236°). Add powdered sugar and vanilla and beat well. Spread icing over marshmallows. Cool brownies and cut into squares. Yield: About 6 dozen brownies.

Begin to prepare icing a few minutes before brownies are done so both will be hot at same time.

Ann Gray Wood

Chocolate Caramel Brownies

1 14-ounce bag caramels
⅔ cup evaporated milk, divided
1 18½-ounce package German chocolate cake mix

¾ cup butter or margarine, softened
1 cup chopped pecans
1 6-ounce package semi-sweet chocolate morsels

Unwrap caramels and combine with ⅓ cup evaporated milk in top of double boiler. Cook and stir until caramels are completely melted. Remove from heat.

Combine cake mix with remaining ⅓ cup milk and butter. Mix with electric mixer until dough holds together; stir in nuts. Press half of cake mixture into greased 13 x 9 x 2-inch baking pan. Bake at 350° for 6 minutes.

Sprinkle chocolate morsels over baked crust. Pour caramel mixture over chocolate morsels, spreading evenly. Crumble remaining cake mixture over caramel mixture. Return pan to oven and bake for 15 minutes. After removing from oven, refrigerate for 1 hour. Cut into squares. Yield: Approximately 5 dozen.

Jeanie Vertner

Easy Brownies

1 stick butter
2 1-ounce squares unsweetened chocolate
1 cup sugar
½ cup flour
1 teaspoon baking powder

1 teaspoon vanilla
2 eggs, beaten thoroughly
½ package Brickle Bits (chopped Heath Bars)

Melt butter and chocolate in heavy saucepan, stirring constantly. Remove from heat and add sugar, flour, baking powder and vanilla. Beat in eggs and Brickle Bits. Bake in 8-inch pan at 325° for 40 minutes. Cool and cut into squares. Yield: 12 to 16 squares.

Double and bake in 9-inch by 12-inch pan at 325° for 40 minutes.

Staige Nolley

Cookies

Grandmother's Golden Squares

1 8-ounce package
  chocolate chips
15 graham crackers,
  crushed
½ cup chopped pecans

1 can Eagle Brand
  sweetened condensed
  milk
1 teaspoon vanilla

Mix all ingredients together and press into a greased 8-inch square pan. Bake at 350° for 30 minutes. Let cool and cut into squares.

To keep squares from sticking to pan, cut 8-inch square piece of waxed paper to line bottom of pan. After squares have baked, flip onto cooling rack and tear waxed paper off in strips.

Robin Ware

Butterscotch Brownies

¾ cup margarine
2 cups light brown sugar
1 cup granulated sugar
3 eggs
1 teaspoon vanilla

2½ cups flour
2½ teaspoons baking
  powder
½ teaspoon salt
1 cup pecans, chopped

Combine margarine and both sugars in saucepan over low heat. Stir until margarine is melted and mixed well with sugar. Remove from heat and beat in eggs one at a time. Add vanilla. Combine dry ingredients and add to sugar mixture. Stir in pecans. Bake in a 2 or 2½-quart greased flat Pyrex pan at 325° for 30 to 35 minutes. Check for doneness. Cool and cut into squares. Yield: 3 to 4 dozen.

Anonymous

Chocolate Mint Brownies

1 cup sugar	2 cups confectioners
1 stick butter, softened	sugar
4 eggs	1 stick butter, softened
1 cup flour	4 tablespoons green
½ teaspoon salt	Creme de Menthe
1 16-ounce can Hershey's	1 6-ounce package semi-
syrup	sweet chocolate chips
1 teaspoon vanilla	6 tablespoons butter

Cream sugar with 1 stick butter. Add eggs, flour, salt, Hershey's syrup, and vanilla. Pour into greased and floured 9 x 13-inch pan. Bake 30 minutes at 350°. Cool completely.

Mix confectioners sugar, 1 stick of butter, and Creme de Menthe together. Stir until smooth. Spread on cooled cake and let set in refrigerator.

In double boiler or microwave, melt chocolate chips and 6 tablespoons butter. Stir until smooth. Cool slightly and spread on cake. Let set in refrigerator. Cut in small squares to serve. Yield: 3 to 4 dozen.

Kitty Bayliss

Broadwater Club Sorry Squares

1 pound brown sugar	1 cup chopped pecans
3 eggs	1 3½ ounce can coconut,
2 cups Bisquick	optional

Cream together sugar and eggs; add other ingredients and mix well. Spread mixture in greased 12 x 14-inch pan. Bake in preheated oven at 325° for 30 minutes. Let cool in pan then cut into squares. Yield: 2½ dozen.

Annette Chapman

Church Window Candies

1 12-ounce package
   chocolate chips
1 stick margarine

1 package Kraft colored
   marshmallows

Melt chocolate chips and margarine in top of double boiler. When completely melted, remove from heat and beat until cool. Add marshmallows in a folding motion. Drop on sheets of waxed paper and form into logs (should make 2 to 3 logs). Refrigerate until chilled. Slice before serving. Yield: 50 ½-inch slices.

Wonderful for Easter and Christmas!

Jane Ruth

Chocolate Almond Brittle

1 pound butter
2 cups sugar
8 ounces blanched whole
   almonds

1 8-ounce Hershey
   chocolate bar

Melt butter over medium heat in saucepan. Add sugar and stir until color of peanut butter (it will become bubbly). Remove from heat and stir in almonds. Pour onto buttered cookie sheet and quickly spread until mixture is ¼ to ½-inch thick. Break chocolate bar on top. Yield: 48 pieces.

Gretchen Gieg

Pecan Nougat

1 cup pecan pieces
½ cup sugar
½ teaspoon vanilla

½ teaspoon salt
1 egg white, unbeaten

Combine pecans, sugar, vanilla, and salt and stir well. Add egg white and stir gently with fork. Drop by teaspoonsful on lightly greased cookie sheet and, working quickly, shape each into a ball. Bake at 275° for 30 minutes. Cool before removing from cookie sheet. Yield: 3 dozen.

Marti Thomas

"Never Fail" Fudge

4½ cups sugar
1 13-ounce can
   evaporated milk
3 6-ounce bags chocolate
   chips

½ pound butter (softened)
3 tablespoons vanilla
Nuts (optional)

Boil sugar and milk for 6 minutes, stirring constantly to keep from sticking. Remove from heat and stir in chocolate chips and butter. Add vanilla and nuts. Pour into a greased 9 x 13-inch dish and let set in refrigerator for 6 hours. Cut into small squares. Yield: Approximately 4 pounds.

Will keep in refrigerator for months, tightly covered.

Lynn Congdon

Double Delicious Fudge

2½ cups sugar
1 cup evaporated milk
¼ cup margarine or butter
¼ teaspoon salt
1½ cups miniature
   marshmallows

1 cup chopped pecans
1 teaspoon vanilla
1 cup semi-sweet
   chocolate morsels
1 cup milk chocolate
   morsels

Bring first 4 ingredients to a rolling boil over medium heat, stirring constantly. Boil 6 minutes, stirring occasionally. Remove from heat and stir in marshmallows, pecans, and vanilla. Stir until marshmallows are melted. Add semi-sweet chocolate morsels to 2 cups of mixture. Stir until morsels are melted and blended. Pour into a foil-lined 8-inch square pan. Add milk chocolate morsels to remaining mixture, stirring until melted and blended. Pour over semi-sweet mixture and chill until firm (about 4 to 6 hours). Cut into squares. Yield: Approximately 3 pounds.

Judy Brooks

Creamy Pralines

2 cups sugar
1 cup light brown sugar
½ cup milk
½ cup condensed milk

¼ cup unsalted butter
¼ teaspoon salt
3 cups pecan pieces

Butter sides of a heavy saucepan and combine sugars and milks with butter and salt. Slowly bring mixture to a rolling boil over medium heat. Add pecans and continue boiling until candy reaches soft ball stage (234°). Remove from heat and stir until candy becomes creamy. Spoon out on buttered waxed paper. Allow to cool. Yield: 6 dozen.

Corinne Davis

Instant Energy

⅓ cup honey
½ cup crunchy peanut
butter

½ cup non-fat dry milk

Mix honey and peanut butter in a bowl. Stir in non-fat dry milk, a little at a time, until thoroughly blended. Shape into narrow roll. Wrap in waxed paper and chill until firm. Cut into 1-inch pieces and wrap in cellophane. Yield: approximately ½ pound.

May shape into balls and roll in chopped peanuts, wheat germ, granola, or cereal. Chilling unnecessary. This is delicious and can be spooned from the mixing bowl onto a plate for an "at home" snack or sent wrapped for school lunches.

Sally Flinn

For perfectly round refrigerator cookies, pack the dough in a washed, frozen juice carton. Cover and freeze or refrigerate. When ready to use, run hot water on the sides, push dough out and slice.

A few drops of lemon juice make icing really white.

To remove layer cake from pans without a knife, place the cake pans on wet cloths for a few minutes when they are removed from the oven.

Before icing a cake, dust a little cornstarch or flour on top to prevent icing from running off.

Table of Measures

Pinch . . . . .less than ⅛ teaspoon
60 drops . . . . .1 teaspoon
3 teaspoons .1 tablespoon
4 tablespoons . . . . .¼ cup
5⅓ tablespoons . . . . .⅓ cup
2 tablespoons . . . . .1 fluid ounce
1 cup . . . . .8 fluid ounces
1 cup . . . . .½ pint
2 cups . . . . .1 pint
2 pints . . . . .1 quart
4 quarts . . . . .1 gallon
8 quarts . . . . .1 peck
4 pecks . . . . .1 bushl
16 ounces . . . . .1 pound

Can Sizes

No. 300. . . . . .14 to 16 ounces . . . . 1¾ cups
No. 303. . . . . .16 to 17 ounces . . . . .2 cups
No. 2½ . . . . .1 lb. 13 ounces. . . . . 3½ cups

Emergency Substitutions

Baking powder, 1 teaspoon = ¼ teaspoon soda plus ½ teaspoon cream of tartar
Chocolate, 1 ounce or square = 3 tablespoons cocoa plus 1½ teaspoons fat
Cornstarch, 1 tablespoon = 2 tablespoons flour (when used for thickening)
Cream, heavy, 1 cup = ¾ cup milk plus ⅓ cup fat
Cream, light, 1 cup = ⅞ cup milk plus 3 tablespoons fat
Flour, cake, 1 cup = ⅞ cup all purpose flour
Garlic, 1 clove = ⅛ teaspoon garlic powder
Herbs, fresh, 1 tablespoon = 1 teaspoon dried herbs
Milk, 1 cup = ½ cup evaporated milk plus ½ cup water
Milk, 1 cup = 4 tablespoons powdered milk plus 1 cup water
Milk, sour, 1 cup = 1 cup sweet milk plus 1 tablespoon lemon juice or vinegar (let stand 5 minutes)
Molasses, 1 cup = 1 cup honey
Mustard, dry, 1 teaspoon = 1 tablespoon prepared mustard
Sugar, 1 cup = 1 cup molasses or honey plus ¼ to ½ teaspoon soda (reduce liquid in recipe by ¼
     cup)
Sugar, 1 cup = 1⅓ cups brown sugar, lightly packed
Tomato juice, 1 cup = ½ cup tomato sauce plus ½ cup water

Table of Equivalents

Apricots, dried, 3 cups = 1 pound
Beans, dried, 1 cup = ½ pound
Bread, sandwich, 22 ounces = 30 slices
Bread, white or wheat, 16 ounces = 16 slices
Butter, 2 cups = 1 pound
Butter, 1 stick = ½ cup
Cheese, cream, 3 ounces = ⅓ cup
Cheese, freshly grated, 5 cups = 1 pound
Chocolate, 1 square = 1 ounce
Chocolate, 1 square = 5 tablespoons grated
Cocoa, 4 cups = 1 pound
Coconut, 5 cups = 1 pound
Cottage cheese, 2 cups = 1 pound
Dates pitted, 2 cups = 1 pound
Egg whites, 8 = 1 cup
Egg yolks, 16 = 1 cup
Eggs, whole, 5 = 1 cup
Flour, 4 cups = 1 pound
Lemon, 1 juiced = 2 to 3 tablespoons
Macaroni, raw, 3 cups = 1 pound
Macaroni, raw, 1 cup = 2 cups cooked
Marshmallows, 16 = ¼ pound
Noodles, raw, 1 cup = 1¼ cups cooked
Nut meats, chopped, 4 cups = 1 pound
Olives, mammoth, 1 quart = 65 to 75
Olives, small, 1 quart = 116 to 140
Orange, 1 juiced = 6 to 8 tablespoons
Oysters, 1 pint = 20 large or 30 small
Peanuts, chopped, 3 cups = 1 pound
Raisins, seedless, 3 cups = 1 pound
Rice, raw, 2⅓ cups = 1 pound
Rice, raw, 1 cup = 3 to 4 cups cooked
Sugar, brown, 2¼ cups firmly packed = 1 pound
Sugar, confectioners, 3⅓ cups = 1 pound
Sugar, granulated, 2 cups = 1 pound
Yeast, active dry, ¼-ounce package = 1 tablespoon

Index

Index

B

Index

Index

Index

Index

Index

Index

Index

Index

Index

Index

VIRGINIA SEASONS
The Junior League of Richmond
205 W. Franklin St.
Richmond, Virginia 23220
(804) 782-1022

Please send _____ copies of **Virginia Seasons** .... @ 16.95 each

Add postage and handling .... @3.00 _____
Add gift wrap* .... @1.00 each _____
Virginia residents add 4½% sales tax .... @.76 each _____
                                         Total _____

☐ Check or money order enclosed. Make checks payable to **Virginia Seasons**
Please charge to: ☐ Mastercard   ☐ Visa
Card Number: ☐☐☐☐ ☐☐☐☐ ☐☐☐☐ ☐☐☐☐

Expiration Date:_____Signature of card holder:_____

From: Ship to:
Name:_____   Name:_____
Address:_____   Address:_____
City:_____State:_____Zip:_____City:_____State:_____Zip:_____
*If gift, enclosure card to read_____

Prices for shipping will be higher outside of the continental United States.

- -

VIRGINIA SEASONS
The Junior League of Richmond
205 W. Franklin St.
Richmond, Virginia 23220
(804) 782-1022

Please send _____ copies of **Virginia Seasons** .... @ 16.95 each

Add postage and handling .... @3.00 _____
Add gift wrap* .... @1.00 each _____
Virginia residents add 4½% sales tax .... @.76 each _____
                                         Total _____

☐ Check or money order enclosed. Make checks payable to **Virginia Seasons**
Please charge to: ☐ Mastercard   ☐ Visa
Card Number: ☐☐☐☐ ☐☐☐☐ ☐☐☐☐ ☐☐☐☐

Expiration Date:_____Signature of card holder:_____

From: Ship to:
Name:_____   Name:_____
Address:_____   Address:_____
City:_____State:_____Zip:_____City:_____State:_____Zip:_____
*If gift, enclosure card to read_____

Prices for shipping will be higher outside of the continental United States.

Please gift-wrap **Virginia Seasons** and send to the following:

Name _____

Address _____

City _____ State _____ Zip _____

Gift card to read:

_____

Name _____

Address _____

City _____ State _____ Zip _____

Gift card to read:

_____

Please gift-wrap **Virginia Seasons** and send to the following:

Name _____

Address _____

City _____ State _____ Zip _____

Gift card to read:

_____

Name _____

Address _____

City _____ State _____ Zip _____

Gift card to read:

_____